PATH OF
LIGHTNING

ALSO BY BARBARA SCHMITZ

What Bob Says (2010)

How Much Our Dancing Has Improved (2005)

The Upside Down Heart (2002)

How to Get Out of the Body (1999)

The Lives of the Saints (1996)

Path of Lightning

A Seeker's Jagged Journey

by Barbara Schmitz

Pinyon Publishing
MONTROSE, CO

Cover Painting by Bob Johnson, Raghubar Dass

Photograph of Barbara Schmitz Copyright © 2012 Tiffany Tichota

Interior Photographs Copyright © 2012 by Bob Schmitz

Book and Cover Design by Susan E. Elliott

First Edition: October 2012

Pinyon Publishing
23847 V66 Trail, Montrose, CO 81403
www.pinyon-publishing.com

Library of Congress Control Number: 2012949133
ISBN: 978-1-936671-11-3

I WISH TO THANK

The Mabel Dodge Luhan House, Taos, for the two-week residency where I worked on an early version of the book

Suzanne and Karl Kehm and Kelly Madigan who critiqued the earliest version of *Path of Lightning* and Suzanne for spiritual support, brainstorming, final editing, and her endless faith in me and this work

Salima Carol Gaskin for line by line editing, suggestions, marketing ideas and much else

Lucy Adkins for reading and correcting; Mary Pipher also for reading for errors and passing the manuscript to her agent

Gretchen Ronnow and Karen Wingett for reading and editing

Northern Lights Writing Group and Lisa Sandlin for various kinds of help through the process

The Cabin Girls on the Platte for the ceremony we performed to release the book and always showing up to write and support each other

My dedicated, resourceful, hard-working, intelligent editors, Gary Entsminger and Susan Elliott, for their fabulous work and devotion to The Path

Husband Bob for everything he gives in constancy

My mother for gifting me with stubbornness

Contents

FOR SHAHABUDDIN

Dear Teacher, Guide, and Friend

MY GURU DOES NOT LIFT WEIGHTS

He does do yoga   occasionally
Mostly he exercises
by hoisting us up
gradually   a little at a time
so we may experience Heaven
Then squatting down
with our dense bodies
sets us back gently
on our Mother ground
Showing us how
to do our own exercises
How to lift our own hearts up
and practice   practice
so we can keep them elevated

PROLOGUE

$\mathcal{J}$ grew up in the fifties, when television began to intrude into American living rooms. Somehow I found books, although there weren't many in our house. My parents let me carry stacks of them home every week from the library. My dad read us the funny paper on Sunday. Near the big wooden radio, my two brothers and I piled into the old rocking chair with him, and we'd listen to Fibber McGee and Molly, all kinds of stuff falling out of their closet. Sky King and Penny soared into the horizon. My parents let me read, but my mom spent lots of time yelling at me to put down my book and come help her put green beans into the jars, help with dishes after supper, or dip the cinnamon twists in egg, then the cinnamon and sugar mixture before she'd tie them into knots in the Friday baking routine. I'd retreat back to my room each time as soon as I could get away. Back to the quiet, and back to my reading and daydreaming, escaping this little world of vegetables and dinner rolls in Plattsmouth, Nebraska. I'd sink back into my longing. That longing I now recognize had to do with a desire for God …

I was afraid to go to sleep at night because I didn't want to die in my sleep. I didn't know that Protestant prayer about "dying before I wake," but I wanted to be "awake" when I died. There must have been other kids with similar fears, but no one talked about it. I devoured all the stories in the little blue Bible history book we had in school and read my parent's copy of *Lives of the Saints* — one of the few books in the house. For some reason I was fascinated, not horrified, by the tortures done to the martyrs — absolutely amazed that these humans would endure their eyeballs being plucked out, fingernails torn off, because they loved God so much.

PATH OF LIGHTNING

When our neighbor had large cardboard boxes leftover from getting a new stove and refrigerator, I talked my neighbor's daughter—her name was Barbara too but not a Catholic like me—into making not a house but a convent out of them for us to play "nuns." Her parents were surprised. And underneath it all was always a longing, like a mild homesickness when you go to camp. I knew there was some beautiful place, home, somewhere that had gotten torn away, and I was always seeking to find it, dwell in it, safe, happy, protected again.

I used to press my nose against the living room window at twilight and promise myself I was going to see the sky turn dark. Looking toward my father's huge garden, my child eyes turned to the sky, I'd vow, "Tonight, I'm going to see the exact moment it turns dark. I'll stand here and not miss it!" But I didn't understand that, like many things in life, there might not be a precise line between afternoon and evening—now it's light, now it's dark. The evening, like spiritual realization, descended at its own gradual sweet pace; and no matter how hard and how many times I tried to detect it, that instant of turning dark eluded me. So too, my spiritual development has been a lengthy process barely discernible at times, not the lightning bolt revelation of God I imagined as a child and kept hoping for. All the spiritual teachers say "God realization" isn't how you expect it to be. You have to divest yourself of concepts. Probably I had too much mythology growing up Catholic—wanting too many visions and miraculous revelations.

The name my Sufi teacher gave me when I asked for one after my first trip to India was *Vajra*. It's Tibetan Buddhist and means "transformation by the lightning bolt!" We had been to Ladakh, India, high in the Himalayas beside Pakistan. Buddhism began here before it proceeded to Tibet. I felt deeply connected with the culture and religion while in the high Himalayas as if I had lived there before. Only recently did I discover that Saint Barbara is the patron saint of the lightning bolt, also of firemen, cannons, and mortars. When her pagan father beheaded her after cutting off her breasts, he was struck by lightning.

4

It seemed a delightful synchronicity that my parents and my Sufi teachers gave me a name that related to the power of lightning. I've never been afraid of storms or lightning. I've always been fascinated by its brilliant flashes illuminating the black sky.

Recently, lightning struck the walnut tree in our backyard, then jumped to the power line and followed that into the house. It blew out several phones, some stereo equipment, a computer and printer. I saw a fireball roll across the living room. My friend asked me later, "Were you scared?" I had to think. "Honestly," I said, "what came to mind was, 'My name is Vajra; it won't kill me.'"

My husband says our tree took the hit for us. The lightning didn't kill it either. It stripped away the bark from many of the branches and scattered pieces of tree around the backyard. But the sixty-foot tree is still standing, still reaching toward the heavens in benediction, blessing, and thanksgiving.

The pattern lightning makes is an appropriate image for my journey on the spiritual path. No straight going here—much zigzagging like the jagged edge of the lightning bolt—even with my teacher.

There is a saying among spiritual seekers: when the seeker is ready, the teacher will appear. I just hadn't been able to find the form or practice that began to quench my thirstiness for God. Catholicism had lovely rituals but left me dry as an adult. Like Goldilocks who kept on trying porridge, chairs, and beds until she finally got it right, my husband and I tried most every opportunity for spiritual growth that presented itself. We practiced Transcendental Meditation for several years in the seventies, had been introduced to Kundalini yoga, done "sitting" with the Buddhists at Naropa. Still nothing seemed to be a fit. We had been gravitating toward some Sufi activities.

At an early seminar with Shahabuddin David Less during a question and answer period, I raised my hand. When Shahabuddin called on me, I said, "I can't find a good spiritual teacher where I live." This was not surprising. Norfolk, Nebraska, offered the conventional Protestant pastors and a few priests and nuns. I was seeking someone more esoteric. Shahabuddin paused, doing what I've come to recognize as his traditional pause as he waits a few seconds for—wisdom? Inspiration? Divine intervention? He cracked a big grin and replied, "Get a bad one then" and went on to the next question. I sat stunned, as though the Zen master had whapped me with the Zen stick. Was he being flippant? From the times I had been around Shahabuddin, I'd known him to be a serious and deep teacher. I was sincerely searching and in need. Didn't he understand? I wanted to get on with it!

It honestly didn't occur to me that my teacher was sitting right in front of me. Or that other arrangements could be made. The teacher could live in another locality than the student—there were even commuter marriages nowadays. I simply felt confused and slightly hurt.

An arduous trip to India and a two-year series of intensive seminars with Shahabuddin all had to take place before I could clearly see that Shahabuddin was my guide, and the given wazifas (mantras) and breathing practices felt right. I began doing these practices every day. They made sense in my heart like returning home after a long trip.

A colleague recently asked me to speak to her multicultural class at the community college about being a member of the Sufi Order. I agreed because she is my friend, and I wanted to do something for the tiny Sufi Order (the saying goes, "to a small band of sowers is given a handful of seed") to make people more aware of its presence and teachings.

I puzzled for a long time about how to make such a presentation to a class of students who would have had no exposure to esoteric religions. I finally settled on speaking about my own search and then segueing into Sufism and Murshid (Sufi Master) Hazrat Inayat Khan, the founder of the Sufi Order of the West. About three-fourths of the way through my talk, a student raised her hand and asked, "How did you, coming from a small Midwest town, get involved in *this*? My father's a minister, and he's never heard of it." I laughed and answered, "That's a good story" and then realized that it was. Around this time I had noticed also that my life, spiritual practices, and writing all appeared to be merging. I had found myself writing bits and pieces about Shahabuddin and my experiences with him more regularly in my journal. Just that morning I had written about traveling with him in Turkey. Now my writing practice seemed to be becoming one of my spiritual practices. I decided I would write about this search for the Divine I had been undertaking since I was a young child.

I am in my sixties. I have done yoga off and on for thirty years and been an English teacher for over thirty years. To my surprise and disappointment sometimes my students weren't very interested in reading. Every year I had to try to demonstrate what was wonderful about literature—it could broaden their lives, mirror the human experience, illustrate what it was like to be an individual soul struggling on the planet. Most of them didn't want to read anything sad—certainly not anything tragic. They wanted stories to have happy endings. No discussion of shadow qualities here, but I trudged on, connecting with some, illuminating a few with the magic of literature and writing.

I'm the mom of an only son who's grown, married, and an elementary school teacher. I'm a published poet. "Took her a long time on her arduous path," friend and writer Natalie Goldberg writes about me in her book *Thunder and Lightning*. My early poems were abstract not grounded. I resisted writing about my ordinary life in Norfolk, Nebraska. Like most beginning writers, I didn't think my own everyday life was anything anyone else would be interested in, so my poems were not "present" for a long time.

I studied writing during the summers at Naropa Institute in Boulder, Colorado with Allen Ginsberg, who was invited there by the Tibetan Lama Chögyam Trungpa, who founded a school of Tibetan meditation studies in the Rockies in the seventies. I was thirty and decided if I was ever going to learn to write, it was time. I ended up being Ginsberg's apprentice one summer; he told me to take myself seriously as a writer. I did, but it took twenty years and slow progress—a publication here and there—for me to perfect my poetry—to finally have a book published.

I continued to teach at our local community college, mostly composition courses, although I also helped establish the creative writing courses, added a Visiting Writers series, and developed a comparative mythology course where we studied Carl Jung, Joseph Campbell, and archetypes, dreams, and religions. Also on my "arduous path" I found the Sufis and my teacher, Shahabuddin.

Many of my generation were spiritual pilgrims. Countless "flower children" journeyed to India seeking gurus, the most famous being Richard Alpert, who became our beloved Ram Dass. Natalie Goldberg said the ingesting of psychedelics opened the way for the expansion of consciousness and awareness of the deeply spiritual, making our generation ready for the flood of spiritual teachers who arrived in the West in the seventies.

What follows is an account of my voyage from attending Catholic school to typing Ginsberg's journals and climbing the flatirons high on acid, back to teaching English and family life in ordinary Nebraska, trying to levitate with a psychic from Columbia, to eventual Sufi initiation and traveling on Shahabuddin's intense pilgrimages to esoteric sacred places — all the while having heart-opening experiences, struggles, Sufi practices, seeking and finding and not finding mystical moments. Along the course of my path and the writing, I also hit some bumpy traveling even *after* meeting up with my guide.

I recount my journey that my fellow travelers may find something of benefit here to assist them along their own paths.

PART ONE

Homesick for Heaven

y parents didn't marry until their mid-thirties; my mother was thirty-eight when I was born. We didn't have much money. My father was foreman for the city water department. He had dreams of being an engineer, but it was the 1930s and college was out of the question for him. He was lucky to finish high school. He had to ride his horse from his family's farm to the school in Weeping Water, Nebraska. The other kids laughed, called him a hayseed. He never went back to a high school reunion, not even his fiftieth.

He claimed he could throw a baseball a city block. I don't know if he could or not. He played ball on the town teams during his young adult years; would occasionally mention a possible career in the minor leagues.

My mom was a "town" girl. She worked in private homes after high school as domestic help. She had gone off to Omaha at one point, gotten lost and scared late at night on the bus in the big city, and beat a hasty retreat for home, Plattsmouth, Nebraska, where she stayed her whole life; first in her parents' house and then in the home she went to as a bride.

During the Depression my father busted rock in the limestone quarry in Louisville (about forty miles from Plattsmouth). He'd laugh at Tennessee Ernie's "Sixteen Tons" song and say, "I broke forty ton a day." You had to keep a steady rhythm. Some guys would get up and swing the hammer like mad when the boss was coming around, and then they'd be pooped and have to sit down. He gave his paycheck to his parents so they could keep the family farm.

He and my mother were engaged for five years but didn't have the money to get married. When the date was set my father took my mother to see the farm. She shook her head. She didn't want to be a farmer's wife. By that time she was keeping books for the Plattsmouth Water Department. She got him a job there instead. My uncle and aunt—my father's brother and my mother's sister who had a double wedding with them and went to the Ozarks on the honeymoon too—got the farm. (They became very successful dairy farmers.)

My father stayed with the Water Department for forty-five years, often getting passed over for boss, which he thought he deserved. I'm sure he did. My theory is he was such a hard worker and knew so much about the technical end, they wanted to keep him where he was most valuable to them.

After the marriage, my mother never worked outside the home, but oh, boy, did she work. The city lot next to our house was our garden. We grew peas, beans, cabbage, carrots, turnips, beets, rhubarb, kohlrabi, corn, potatoes, tomatoes, and cucumbers. There were cherry trees, apricots, peaches, and pears. All summers involved planting, picking, canning, and freezing. My mother baked all of our bread, rolls, pies, cakes, and cookies; made all of our food. She cleaned, sewed, mended my father's socks and work clothes; washed with a wringer wash machine and tubs in a little adjacent building we called "the wash house." My father remodeled our 100-year-old house; my mother helped.

The men in the family helped build onto the church, digging out the basement, adding more rooms. The women did bake sales, rummage sales, church dinners. Our family holiday dinners were for extended family, about thirty people with long tables stretched across our living/dining room, combined when my dad knocked out walls remodeling the old house. My father was a volunteer fireman—I wonder if he had some kind of intuition about St. Barbara protecting firemen. He took care of the pump trucks. Every Sunday after church he went to service them. Often he had to unload a railroad car full of lime for the water purification plant. He went to work at 5:00 AM.

Even with their sparse resources my parents felt it important to send us to Catholic school where my brothers and I were saddled with nightly homework, carting home heavy books in brown grocery paper bags. Much of the homework required parental assistance as did many of the assigned projects. I remember having to make a grotto during the month of May, Mary's month. My father didn't help me make just any ordinary grotto. We (he) made a wire frame, covered it with cement, painted the outside white with gold glitter, the inside gold, attached it to wood painted green (grass), glued on a tiny ceramic flower vase, and added painted wooden stairs for my grandma's Czechoslovakian statue of Mary. My grotto won first prize.

We dressed our dolls as our patron saints. My bride doll had to be transformed into St. Barbara, virgin martyr, with red velvet robe, white gown, crown, prayer book. What were these nuns thinking? A fifth-grader couldn't sew! Didn't our parents already have enough work? But our parents didn't complain; they pitched in! Lent was one of the Church seasons of special devotions: stations of the Cross were enacted every Friday, and a week's worth of special services occurred during the week before Easter. Somewhere in there was Forty Hours, several nights of special prayer. Benediction (lots of incense) filled Sunday afternoon. In the spring the church and school conducted the annual May Procession. The grade school children and their parents spent hours wrapping wire arches with lilacs and tulips. All the school children and one special first-grade girl dressed as a tiny bride "processed" beneath these arches held up by the "big" girls' aching arms on the first Sunday of May to crown a statue of Mary at the exact moment we all sang "Oh, Mary we crown thee with blossoms today / Queen of the Angels / Queen of May." Our family attended all of these services. Clean and dressed up. My brothers were altar boys, often serving the masses and special events.

When I grew up there were two Catholic churches in Plattsmouth: Holy Rosary, where the Czechoslovakian immigrants attended, and St. John's, attended by the more affluent and professional families. At our humble church, Holy Rosary, the priest still heard confession in Czech for the old folks. The mass was still celebrated in Latin. When I was in high school, the church prayers were switched to English, and a priest could no longer be found who understood Czech. My grandfather was outraged and rather bewildered about all the changes happening in "his" beloved church.

Shortly after that, with the shortage of priests and monies, the two parishes had to merge, and the little white wooden church

with the beautiful porcelain life-sized statues of Mary giving
the rosary to Saint Someone didn't exist anymore. The statues
were removed. The building was sold, and some Protestant
denomination used it for worship.

FORTY HOURS

Late at night,
past my bedtime,
still a small child,

once a year,
the priests from neighboring towns
marched in our Forty Hours Service.

The Host in its gold monstrance,
transparent glass where it could be viewed
exposed on the church altar,
for forty hours straight. Parishioners
had to sign up for an hour
to stay in the presence of "The Lord"
through the odd hours of the night,
keeping him company, praying.

Special devotions
three nights in a row.
Incense, chants, bells.

My favorite part—
The Closing.
Deep male voices
Reciting: Santa Lucia,
Ora Pro Nobis.
Santa Barbara
Ora Pro Nobis
Santa Raphael,
Ora Pro Nobis.
On and on.

My eyes drifting
under drooping lids,
down through the saints,

angels, Mary,
urging them all —
Ora Pro Nobis —
to pray for us —
Intercedant Pro Nobis —
to intercede for us.

The priests in their black cassocks
white surplices.
Trooping around the church.

And Jesus,
his white round bread self,
sniffing the sweet smells
wafting through the hard wooden pews,

watching us kneel, about to keel over
from exhaustion and ecstasy,

witnessing all this,
from his golden container,
there on the altar,
high above us all.

(from *How Much Our Dancing Has Improved*)

On George Harrison's devotional album, his song "My Sweet Lord" verbalizes exactly the longing I felt throughout my childhood and much of my early adult life, seeking a deep connection with God. Harrison sings, "I really want to see you, Lord, but it takes so long, my Lord … / I really want to know you / I really want to go with you / … but it takes so long, my Lord" until he eventually reaches "It won't take long, my Lord." But I don't recall hearing *those* words in the seventies, only the ones about how long it takes and my heart responding, YES! YES!

My search for God started as early as I can remember — long before the preparations for my first communion. When we were receiving instructions for this significant event in our Catholic faith, a nun at our parochial school told us a marvelous story about a saint, a little girl, who prayed to die when she received

Jesus as the Host upon her tongue the first time. And it happened. Our teacher told us how wonderful dying at that moment was, because she had gone to confession and received the Sacrament of Communion, the Holy Eucharist! Her soul was totally pure, so when she died she went straight to Heaven to be in God's arms for all eternity. When Sister Ursula was telling us this story she held her own hands, and her face shone; it was one of the few times I had ever seen her smile. I decided I would pray to die at the communion rail too. I had been lonesome for God since I was born. Something about being in my family made me feel homesick and alone.

And the story of eternity! The nuns loved to tell that one. Sister said to imagine a ball of the hardest steel the size of the earth, and every million years a hummingbird comes and flicks its tail on the ball; however long it would take to wear away the ball of steel is one instant of eternity. I used to sit outside on the front cement porch on hot summer nights, watching the traffic go by on Highway 75, and think about eternity and think about eternity until my head and neck would start to list like a banner in a breeze, and I'd feel sick to my stomach as though I'd just gotten off a long ferris wheel ride. As I think about it now, I might have been about to leave my body. I don't think the nuns knew it, but they were giving the Catholic school kids Zen-like riddles to think about.

Besides wanting to die at the communion rail and go straight to God, I remember disagreeing with some of the dogma that was being forced on me, a seven-year-old child. How could someone go to Hell for all eternity for eating meat on Friday? How could a little baby who died without baptism be denied Heaven forever? Should I bring up my misgivings, or should I even receive communion since I didn't believe all that stuff? But I had never heard of a child in Catholic school refusing to go through the ceremony, and my mom had already bought my white dress (it had a yoke with pretty white scallops). We borrowed my veil with lilies of the valley over the ears from my older cousin. My grandparents were invited to dinner.

I never thought how badly my family would feel if I did die at my communion ceremony and went on praying hard to be taken up into Heaven. But I remember how disappointed I was to get up still alive with the wafer on my tongue, ever so careful not to touch it with my teeth, trying as always to do as I was told, to do everything right— surely if I followed all the rules I would get to Heaven—and be guided by the two older girls dressed as angels back to my place in the pew. I had to work to hold back the tears.

Confirmation, Age 10

I was still alive! But wait, I remembered. This was Christ, Jesus, God, on my tongue. Here in my body. Inside me. This must be wonderful. I tried to check around inside. This was supposed to be a very important experience. But I didn't feel different. If God were inside me, wouldn't I feel something?

In a photograph of my first communion class standing outside the church doors afterward, the other kids are looking straight ahead and smiling. I'm looking into the distance, still looking for God, wondering if He's going to show up.

The rest of the day was disappointing, too. After dinner I walked into the bathroom, not knowing my grandpa was in there on the toilet with his pants down. My grandpa was embarrassed. I was shocked. And then after that nothing. Nothing had happened. I didn't go to Heaven. I didn't taste God. It had turned into an ordinary boring Sunday with a big dinner, and I had to go to school the next day.

I had rosaries that glowed in the dark. We all did in the fifties. The nuns and my mother said if we fell asleep before we finished praying them, the angels would finish them for us.

The nuns told us that the sun shone every Saturday because it was the Blessed Virgin's day. I tried to remember to check. When I paid attention, it seemed like the sun did come out even when the day was mostly cloudy.

The nuns told us that at midnight on Christmas Eve the cows in the fields knelt. I always wanted to drive out to the country to see that for myself.

When we were cleaning the house on Good Friday at three o'clock, supposedly the time Christ died on the cross, my mother and I knelt in the living room beside the Kirby vacuum cleaner and said an "Our Father" and a "Hail Mary."

My grandmother from Czechoslovakia said if we didn't move in church on Holy Saturday while the priest was reading the story of the Passion about Christ's arrest and torture and crucifixion — it was very long, maybe forty minutes — you could release a soul from the fire and suffering of Purgatory. I'd try with all my might not to move, but oh! my legs would be itching. I'd need so badly to scratch them! Just like when I was washing dishes at night after supper, my legs would itch like mad. (As I got older I discovered I was afflicted with dry skin, especially my legs.) I do believe I made it through the Passion reading a few times, not knowing then what good practice it was for sitting still in meditation which would come much later in my life.

All of these stories from the nuns and my family combined with the pageantry and special devotions made Catholicism rich and appealing and helped prepare me for the spiritual path that was coming. I did not find anything equivalent at first to replace the Catholic iconography when I decided I would no longer attend church as a young adult.

I tried to thank my mother for the excellent foundation, but she was too hurt and angry with my leaving the faith in which I was raised to listen.

The nuns were not the best part. They believed in corporal punishment and whacked the kids with rulers. Not me. I became scared and quiet. I was already trying to do everything right to get to Heaven. My middle brother, the defiant one, got whacked plenty. Me, they mostly humiliated. Mary Ellen Richter snatched the valentine I made for Tom Brink off my desk. I wasn't planning to give it to him; I was way too shy. She marched it and herself right up to Sister's desk. We had "combination" classrooms. Sister stopped whatever it was she was teaching to the other class (we were supposed to be *working* on our own), got a wicked grin on her face, and announced loudly, "Listen up, all you, Toms. You've got a girlfriend back there." "Back there" was next to the steam heat radiator with the bell cap that danced and spewed hot steam on my arm, burning me. Sister would not let me move my desk away from the radiator. She read the valentine at full volume while my face and arm burned. Then she told us all to get back to work. I could never make out what made these nuns so mean. I was doing my work and trying to do what was right.

I had to play baseball at recess although nobody wanted me on their team. My father never played catch with me like he did with my brothers. I was afraid of getting hurt when the ball came at me, and I ran the other way, making no attempt to catch it. I was always left standing unpicked, and Sister made some grumbling team choose me even though I'd say, "That's okay, I don't want to play anyway." Maybe if I had volunteered to dust the altar and pews they would have let me off.

When I examined my conscience before going to Confession, I rarely found *sins,* so I usually said the same things: "I forgot my prayers. I fought with my brothers. I didn't help my mother." I didn't know what some of the "sin" words (*adultery, covet*) in my prayer book meant.

I'd go into the little dark booth; and when the priest slid open the little silhouetted window I'd mumble, "Bless me, Father, for I have sinned" and rattle off the same list. Then I'd repeat, "three Our Fathers, three Hail Marys" to myself as I went out so I wouldn't forget how many prayers I was supposed to say for my penance. I'd rush through those and wait in my pew to get outside. Confession didn't mean much. It was just something that was supposed to be good for me.

One day at recess, old and wrinkled Sister Gertrude called some of the sixth-grade girls over to a corner of the playground, drew us into a circle and told us that we would go to Hell if we held hands with a boy. I went home that night, wanting to discuss it with my mother, but I didn't know how. Instead, I fretted alone in my room. I had seen my parents and other relatives hold hands; they were good people. They couldn't be going to Hell. It didn't make sense. But Sister Gertrude was a nun. She was not supposed to tell lies! My mind was ready to explode and fly off into space. Here were more *rules* that didn't make sense and didn't have anything to do with people being good and kind.

I loved the quiet devotions of the Catholic Church as much or more than mass. I loved the light through the stained glass in the daytime. I loved the smell of incense during services; the sound the bells made when the altar boys rang them. I went to mass in the summertime in the mornings. My father dropped me off in his Water Company pickup on the way to work. When mass was over I walked home. One old lady, Sister Janette, and I shared the large cool church on a summer morning, the sun just beginning to penetrate the dark interior. I carried my large missal with attached multicolored ribbons to mark the moveable prayers—some of the mass prayers changed depending on the church season: Advent, Lent, so many Sundays after Easter.

In sixth and seventh grades I began to think seriously about entering the convent. Surely if I lived a life as a Catholic nun, I would go straight to Heaven when I died. I still didn't want to take any chances on missing out on God for all eternity! This idea was also encouraged by Sister since I was the only child attending mass in the summer. Of my own free will. Not forced by my parents or teachers. She approached me one soft morning as I left church. I was holding onto the metal railing that ran along the many cement steps leading to the main doors of St. John's.

"Good morning, Barbara."

"Good morning, Sister," I answered in my usual dutiful tone.

PART ONE: HOMESICK FOR HEAVEN

She paused, clearing her throat. "Barbara, have you thought about entering the convent?"

I looked up. How did she know I had been thinking about it? Was this the call from God the nuns said we would receive if we had a vocation? They said we would *know*. That we would receive a *call* from God. I had my doubts. God hadn't shown himself in my life yet, no matter how much I prayed and wished and desired. But … could this be it?

I looked down. "Yes, Sister," I said softly. Too softly, I thought. "I have, Sister," I added.

"All right," she said. "You continue to pray about it."

Then she turned and walked away. That was all. But wait! I wanted to say. I let go of the iron rail. I wanted to reach out for her veil before she got away. Her stony face. She hadn't even smiled. She never smiled. She never touched my hand. *How will I know?* I wanted to ask, as I wanted to ask my mother about sex. The sex she never told me about. *How am I supposed to know?* But she was gone, around the corner back toward the convent.

DECIDING

I was all set—
Sister Janette quizzing me
on the concrete steps
with iron bar railing
after daily summer Mass,
"Yes," I'd thought about it.
I didn't tell her most of me
was already packed
had decided
had a pact in my mind
        my heart
        with God

I'd go live with him
        in a cell,
pray from morning to night,
do everything right.
Then I'd get the prize,
squeeze into those narrow gates—

a camel passing
through the needle's eye.

But a little butterfly thought
fluttered just at the edge
            of my decision.
Maybe ... just maybe ...
I should first try high school,
see what boys were like.

I didn't go to the convent.

(from *How Much Our Dancing Has Improved*)

I had no boyfriends in high school until my senior year. Mostly dances were misery for me waiting against the wall, unchosen, like for recess sports teams. I was tall, skinny, wore turquoise horn-rimmed glasses, and had funny tight home permanents my mother had the neighbor give me free. Toward the end of my junior year, I decided to stop wearing glasses, and once I almost got into a car with a guy I didn't know thinking he was someone else. But I was much happier with my appearance even if it required squinting and pretending to see.

These were the days of bouffant hairdos. I bought glamour magazines and pored over them, studying makeup tips and hair styles. I had a friend "tease" my hair into a bouffant, using a entire can of spray. By my senior year I was starting to look about like everyone else—except taller by a head.

Danny's father was in the Air Force, and he had lived all over the U.S. by the time his family was sent to Offutt Air Force Base, which was close to my hometown of Plattsmouth. His perception of beauty apparently was different from the boys I grew up with. His brother was in my class; Danny was two grades below, a sophomore. I thought he had one of the most interesting faces I had ever seen—black hair and slanted lovely, blue eyes. His brother was dating a girl in our class and asked if I'd consider a date with his little brother. "Sure," I answered.

"You would!" He seemed surprised.

22

"Why not?" I said.

"Most girls wouldn't go out with a sophomore," he shot back.

"Oh," I answered, aware for the first time that I didn't think like most girls.

Danny and I dated a few times toward the end of my senior year. I liked him a lot. I felt the stirring of some sexual awakening. I loved the softness of his lips when we kissed. I couldn't believe that a boy found me attractive, but something in me knew he wasn't the one I would be with forever and ever. His father was transferred to Alaska in the summer. "Write to me?" he asked.

"I will," I promised. A song by the New Christy Minstrels "I will never love you … / but I'll stay with you one year … / and we'll sing in the sunshine" was popular. I said, "That's our song." *That* made Danny mad.

I wrote. He answered. He sent something made of Alaskan gold for Christmas, but it fell out of the envelope before it arrived. I was away at college and realized this was the time to let Danny go.

I knew I needed a life that wasn't dictated by a garden and fruit trees, where no one could go on vacation because the green beans had to be picked and canned. As high school was coming to an end I'd sit in the swings in the little park across the street from our house next to Highway 73-75. My mother could look out her kitchen window while she washed dishes and watch me, assuming I was daydreaming. But I was planning my getaway.

The kitchen radio played sixties rock and roll as the big, black-enamel kettle boiled the Kerr canning jars. Another kettle in the basement boiled the red beets, which we would skin and put into the jars. With my hands in the hot beet water, slipping off skins, hot water steaming my face, my nose itching, then my eyes, hands full of slimy grey beet skins and rough chopped-off beet tops, I'd whine, "How much more?" I wanted to be outside in the July sunshine, on the grass, with my library book. My exasperated mother promised, "One more kettle" then finished the job herself. It's not surprising she didn't teach me how to cook.

I liked radio songs and especially one about Running Bear and Little White Dove who were separated by their warring Indian tribes. They met in the middle of the swirling water and kissed "as their hands touched and their lips met / the raging river pulled them down / Now they'll always be together / in their happy hunting ground." And Clifton Clowers had a pretty young daughter, who lived on "Wolverton Mountain." He was "mighty handy / with a gun and a knife."

I was off in my head, pushing halved green beans into clean Ball canning jars or stacking apricots pitted side down in regimented rows. My brother, David, complained even more than I did. I forgot listening to the music sometimes.

My favorite was "Red Sails in the Sunset" … "far away places with strange sounding names" were "calling to me." I wanted to travel. To see some of those places. The plan was: I'd go to school, get a job, take off on my own somehow. Have a big life. No staying home with a garden for me! Although it wasn't a solidified thought, I had a feeling that when I got away I was going to meet somebody.

My mom sent me to the family doctor for my mouthful of canker sores the week before I went away to college. She thought it was from eating too many tomatoes. I didn't tell her that I thought it was because I was so scared about leaving home. Doctor Dietz, our kindly family physician, counted over forty-five sores before he stopped counting and treated them with silver nitrate. Nonetheless, I was determined that nothing was going to stop me from leaving home. I knew I had no future in a small town where boys raced their souped-up cars up and down Main Street and then around the A&W Root Beer stand. An education was going to be my ticket to somewhere, although I didn't yet know where.

I didn't fit in well in high school, but college was different. I lived in Berry Hall, the first coed dorm on the Wayne State campus. Half guys, half girls, with a shared lobby in-between. I was a Berry Basement Beauty. Because it was a basement floor, it was only a half floor and most of us were in-coming freshmen. We celebrated each other's birthdays, gathered in each other's rooms to yak, and grew to be good friends. I liked the campus with its old buildings and old oak trees changing colors in the fall, and I liked almost all of my classes. Some of the teachers were quirky and interesting. Dr. Stern's salmon-colored shoes squeaked as he opened every window on both sides of the room, and J. R. Johnson sang to us "Good Morning, Glory" and taught us history.

Most of the girls thought Linda was strange and declined to room with her, but we got along fine and stayed together all through college. She told me she used to drive her dad's car backward to take miles off the speedometer. She was a drinker. I had no experience with alcohol. She cheerfully called a hangover "walking under water" and drew a rectangular "frustration box" on the wall in the hallway, which we could go kick when school and assignments and everything else got to be too stressful.

The smell of mock orange blossoms wafted through the balmy April evening the last night of my freshman year. I had finished my last final that afternoon; my parents were coming the next day to take me home for the summer. As I stood at the top of the walk that led down to Berry Hall, my inside voice spoke fleetingly — *something is about to happen* — then quickly disappeared.

A short while later, my roommate Linda, two beautiful foreign exchange students from Sweden and Denmark, and I sat in my Berry basement room, wishing we had something to do. Suddenly an all-call came on the intercom, "Are there any girls who would like to go to a party?" and made us jump off my bed. "You go look at them," the women insisted, shoving me toward the door.

Time stood still for a few seconds when I walked through the swinging lobby door. There stood Bob, spotlighted, and had it been a movie, the music would have surged up. "Oh, my beloved, there you are," scrolled across my heart as if we had made a pact somewhere in time to meet again. (Bob says the air was full of blue sparkles for him.) The impression was so fleeting, and then everything went quickly on.

I had seen Bob around campus. Wild, blond curls. Lit-up blue eyes. Smiling, happy face. Short. Shorter than me. Not that height made any difference—as Danny's brother had made me aware—I didn't perceive such issues like most women. Bob was with another guy I didn't know and definitely was not attracted to. The guys explained they were going to a beer party out of town, in a meadow, and would like to take some girls.

Bob's backseat was loaded with vacuum cleaner parts and equipment. He sold Kirbys to put himself through college. I didn't ask questions but announced, "I'm getting in front" and let the rest of them squeeze into the back with the hoses and attachments.

To my dismay I got separated from everyone upon arrival and found myself stumbling around in a field full of dirt clods and corn stubble with a plastic cup of beer wondering what had become of my friends and especially Bob, but I soon heard a female voice calling my name. I followed the sound. Disappointed by my disappearance, Bob found his debate partner who knew me, and she began bellowing my name around the pasture until I appeared. "Here she is," she smiled and trotted off. So Bob and I spent the rest of the evening together.

Except it was the sixties, and I still had dorm "hours." I had to be back in the dormitory by 1:00 AM. Bob began to lament that our time together was so short since I was leaving for home when my parents arrived. I surprised myself, "I've seen girls climb out the basement windows all the time after they check in. I've never done it, but it'd be easy enough. My room's by the little tree. Just wait until about 1:15."

He grinned. I couldn't believe I was being was so bold. And I couldn't believe how many girls were going out the windows that night! What a huge exodus from Berry Basement!

We drove to the country and sat under the crisp spring stars. We wrapped our legs around each other and talked for three more hours. I didn't see anyone else climbing back in the window when I did. Bob said he'd write over the summer. I wrote first, and he answered. And when he saw me on campus in the fall, he asked me to go to the drive-in. I came back from that date and told Linda if I married anybody, I'd marry Bob.

PART ONE: HOMESICK FOR HEAVEN

Ellen Gilchrist has a story where women order male companions from a catalogue. Soon all the society women had to have one of their very own real-appearing manikins. Unlike the fictional mail order men who were good-looking but not able to carry on a conversation, Bob was everything I could wish for in a companion but didn't believe it was possible to have. He loved books, music, beauty — wasn't interested in sports and cars (the dinner table talk I grew up with).

Nebraska has particularly gorgeous autumns. One October afternoon Bob called to tell me the day was so beautiful he had cut his classes to stay home to enjoy the colors of the leaves. I was flabbergasted that anyone would do such a thing. I was such a goody two-shoes I would never dream of cutting a college class, and I couldn't imagine a guy who would sit there looking at leaves.

Not long after this he handed me Hemingway's *A Farewell to Arms.*

"What's this?"

"A love story. You need to read it!"

A man was giving me a love story to read! I shook my head.

Over Christmas vacation he asked me to come visit his home. He sat me next to him on a piano bench that his mother had covered with blue contact paper (before she died of cancer a year earlier) and began to play the most astonishing music I'd ever heard. I didn't grow up with much music in my house. My parents' idea of good music was Lawrence Welk on TV on Saturday night and polkas on the Bohemian radio station on Sunday. How could anyone create such complex, haunting magic!

"What's the name of this?" I whispered.

"Moonlight Sonata." He played on.

My heart opened. I was falling in love.

Our courtship was not all smooth going, however. Bob had grown up in what in those days was known as a "mixed marriage." His mother was Methodist; his father was Catholic. His mother had joined the Catholic church for his father and agreed to raise the children Catholic, but she didn't always go to mass. Bob said sometimes the nuns at school would have all the children, including him and his little sister, praying for his mother's soul.

Being a person of integrity, even as a child, Bob battled with the priest and the nuns. He could see his mother was not a bad person. He also recounted an incident when a missionary visited school and told the children it was not a sin for cannibals to eat people because they didn't know it was a sin. When Bob didn't confess missing mass in the confessional, the priest asked him why. Bob said it wasn't a sin because he didn't think it was a sin. The priest kicked him, a small school child, out of confession without absolving him of his sins.

By the time I met Bob, he was having little to do with the Catholic Church. He said any institution that cared more for rules than for the feelings of people wasn't for him. I was still heavily under the Church's and my parents' influence. Bob certainly made sense, but all my life I'd done what my parents told me to do and had tried so hard to be good. I still wanted, most of all, to go to Heaven.

Eventually there was sex. It felt so good to kiss and touch. As we continued to date for two years we began petting heavily and coming closer and closer to intercourse. I thought what we were doing was probably sinful from everything I'd been taught, but it felt wonderful, Bob was pushing, and I didn't think I was going to stop.

One weekend he came home with me. My mother had been so pleased to learn that he was Catholic, although I told her he didn't go to church regularly. Just to keep the peace, I guess, Bob went to communion at Sunday mass. Later as my mother worked at the kitchen sink peeling potatoes and filling the enamel kettle she remarked to me that it was wonderful that Bob had gone to communion. I was putting plates around the kitchen table and couldn't stop myself from blurting out, "He didn't go to confession!" Those were the rules! You must go to confession before you receive communion, especially if it's been some time since you've "received the sacraments."

My mother's mouth clamped shut. "I'll talk to him," she said.

Now I've done it, I thought.

On the way back to college, Bob asked me if I'd put my mother up to that.

"No," I moaned, "I only said you hadn't gone to confession."

"Same thing," he said.

A lump came to my chest and stayed there a long time. I couldn't swallow without pain. How could they both be right? I felt like blinded justice holding up the scales, both seemed equally balanced. I was caught in a painful dilemma of having to decide what I must do. At such a serious point in a relationship in the sixties, couples either made marriage plans or broke up.

I accepted an engagement ring; but when people asked about a date, I'd say we still had some things to work out. Even if I went to a summer trimester I had the equivalent of a year of college to finish. I had told my parents I wouldn't get married before I finished college when they let me go. The birth control pill had just come out, but the Church would never approve of that. We did not want to have kids right away! And what about Bob not going to church?

My cousin, who was in nurse's training in Omaha, told me about a priest we could talk to. She said he had told their class it was okay to use "the pill." When Bob and I went to see him, I also brought up the issue of Bob not attending mass. Without batting an eye this "free-thinking" priest said sometimes it was better not to go to mass than to stand there like a stump just because you're *supposed* to be there. Then he gave us the permission I needed. To his way of thinking, he said, birth control was a private matter for the husband and wife to decide. I almost asked him to repeat it or if he would put it in writing so I could show it to my mother because I didn't think she was going to believe this! The best approach, however, seemed to be to skedaddle out of there while we had what we wanted and not even mention it to my mother. After all, she obviously wasn't going to bring up sex with me.

My cousin told me later the bishop removed that priest from his position in the nursing school when his views became known and assigned him to a rural community. God Bless Him wherever he is! (I wonder if he is still a priest.)

The lump didn't dissolve from my chest immediately. Even though my mother was desiring for me to adhere to her version of the truth, Bob was not. He had found his own path through his family situation and confusing childhood and was comfortable with his belief system. He didn't feel a need to have me believe likewise, but it took me quite a while to sort through my own confusion. Then one day I noticed I could breathe freely. I went to mass by myself after we got married, and I didn't mind that Bob stayed home. Not even aware of looking, I was starting my search for a greater accommodation into which to fit my spiritual belief.

After a while, I stopped going to mass on Sunday, too. The ritual had begun to seem hollow and empty for me. Bob had turned his college study of psychology into a counseling career. I had taught junior high and was back in graduate school. I still said the prayers I learned in childhood; I felt like God was listening, somewhere, but I missed having a community, and I missed having a formal ritual. And I missed having someone lead me in spiritual activities. I wasn't sure how to fill those spaces since I didn't want to go to a church.

One night after we had made love and were holding each other, relishing the closeness, a solution came to me.

"I have it," I said.

"What?" asked Bob.

"You can be my religion," I said. "I love you. You love me. That's clear and true. I can follow that. It can lead me where I need to go."

"Hmm," Bob murmured.

I wasn't sure he was following this line of reasoning or if he was particularly interested. He didn't seem to have the deep longing for God that was always haunting me.

"You can be my patron saint."

He grinned now. I could tell this was becoming more intriguing.

"St. Robert!" I announced.

"Okay," he agreed, tentatively, "but what do I have to do?"

"Nothing," I said, wrapping my arms around him. "I just love you."

"Perfect," he answered.

I wasn't being flippant but lighthearted, and perhaps this was an early intuition that led me to reach out for the Sufi message. It is said that Sufism is the religion of the heart: "the more living the heart, the more sensitive it is; that which causes sensitiveness is the love-element in the heart, and love is God."

For my parents' sake we kept up a pretense about attending mass for two or three years. We knew my mother in particular would be horrified if she knew the truth. She would believe I would be going to hell for not attending mass, and even worse, that she also would be punished for her failure to keep me in the Church because that's what the Church taught, and she'd been taught not to question its authority.

During one Christmas visit, Bob and I had gone for a walk, smoked marijuana, looked down on my parents' house from the top of a high Plattsmouth hill we had climbed, and decided it was time. It was too hard keeping up the pretense.

We came back in the house and broke the news. I don't think it was really news; I think she must have known it like a wife knows in her heart about her husband's affair but won't let herself admit it. My mother wept and then threw up. Her eye started twitching and wouldn't stop for several days. She ordered us to get out! Since it was Christmas we were planning to go to Oklahoma to visit friends. So we packed and left. We stopped by my parent's house on the way back; I didn't believe she wanted us to go away forever; she was just angry. She let us in, but the reception was icy. My father was there, and I remember him sitting quietly in the kitchen. This was the beginning of many years of turmoil and conflict.

She immediately wrote a letter asking for my reasons for leaving the Church. I wrote back trying to explain that the form of the Catholic Church no longer seemed to fit me. I was wanting something more, something experiential. But she didn't want to listen and accused me of being lazy and not wanting to get up on Sunday to go to mass. On other occasions when I tried to share something I was interested in, like the Sufi practices I did on my prayer beads that Bob made with rubber washers he got from my dad, she turned her head away. Often she would lecture me about going to hell and insist I must go back to church.

MOTHER WALTZ, Section 3

"You're going to fry in Hell,
for missing Mass, my mother insists,
pointing toward the glowing burner
beneath her pan of frozen chili.
She nods her chin down. "Hell
is much hotter than this."

I feel bad, not for my sin
she imagines, but for her
searing her own heart for me.
How to remove the cataracts
of dogma from her eyes,
skim the froth of concept
from her boiling brain
how to help her see —
we're all together in the pot,
her, God, me,
stewing on her stove.

(From *How Much Our Dancing Has Improved*)

My mother, who remained a devout Catholic all her days, could not understand why the religion she raised me in wasn't good enough for me. In great sorrow she proclaimed that she believed the greatest gift she could give her child was her religion.

PART ONE: HOMESICK FOR HEAVEN

I answered that I had formed much of my character from that religion, but the Catholic Church was no longer appropriate for me. I no longer needed a dogma or an institution with such a stern list of rules to guide me. I needed something more, a different form. She didn't choose to understand until much later, until just before she died. And, it took me several more years of seeking to find a form that matched with what my heart was longing for all those years.

My grandmother's sister, Veronica, came from Czechoslovakia and went into the convent in Lisle, Illinois. It was a cloistered order of nuns, so even though she was my great aunt, I only saw her one time when she was allowed to leave the convent on an anniversary to visit her extended family in Plattsmouth.

I was about nine years old, and she was a great mystery to me, all robed in her nun's habit with white wimple and long black gown. I was most fascinated with the long rosary that hung at her side.

We gathered at the city park so she could meet everyone. I wondered how she could possibly keep all these people straight, cousins, children, and second cousins and their children, a huge tribe. Now, as an adult, I wonder if it were pleasant or painful — this *one* lifetime reunion. No possibility, really, to maintain relationships. I don't believe she was allowed regular mail. This special reunion probably only made her painfully aware of the life she had missed. Or maybe it made her thankful. Maybe it was all just too much, all the voices, faces, noise. Maybe it was sensory overload. Maybe she was longing for the quiet and tranquility of the convent. Perhaps this little foray out into the world reinforced her vocation and made her realize she had made the right choice, a life of contemplation, focused on the things that "thieves could not steal," removed from all the "getting and spending" of the world.

I watched her off and on from a distance while I played with my cousins. A brief smile flickered across her face a few times as she talked quietly with the adults. The day passed quickly.

Veronica went back to the convent. We never saw her again. I was a married woman when my mother told me she had died and was buried in Illinois in the convent graveyard.

The next time I went home, my mother handed me Sister Veronica's rosary. "Why me?" I asked, bewildered since my mother and I had argued about my not going to mass on Sundays. "I don't know," my mother said. "The aunts said you should have it. Don't you want it?"

"I'd love to have it," I said. "But out of all the cousins?"

My mother shrugged. Maybe she thought it would somehow bring me back to the Church. I'm sure she hadn't told her sisters that I left.

I closed my fingers around Veronica's rosary and brought it close to my heart.

PART TWO

Without a Map

JOHN NEIHARDT, POET LAUREATE AND MYSTIC

Seeing John Neihardt lounging under his fruit trees, the villagers of Bancroft thought he was lazy. They didn't understand that he was communing with nature and composing poetry. Gorgeous, mystical poetry.

> O to be breathing and hearing and feeling and seeing!
> O the ineffably glorious privilege of being!
> All the World's lovely girlhood, unfleshed and made spirit,
> Broods out in the sunlight this morning—I see it, I hear it!
>
> So read me no text, O my Brothers, and preach me no creeds;
> I am busy beholding the glory of God in His deeds!
> See! Everywhere buds coming out, blossoms flaming, bees
>   humming!
> Glad athletic growers up-reaching, things striving, becoming!
>
> (From "April Theology")

He didn't attend church either, at least not how most of his neighbors did. He was "experiencing" his God, not reading about Him in scripture or mouthing Him in dogma.

> What! House me my God? Take me in where no blossoms are
>   blowing?
> Roof me in from the blue, wall me in from the green and the wonder
>   of growing?
> ...
> Out here where the world-love is flowing, unfettered, unpriced,
> I feel all the depth of the man-soul and girl-heart of Christ!
> 'Mid this riot of pink and white flame in this miracle weather,
> Soul to soul, merged in one, God and I dream the vast dream
>   together.

PATH OF LIGHTNING

We are one in the doing of things that are done and to be;
I am part of my God as a raindrop is part of the sea!

(From "April Theology")

    I didn't fully understand the depth of Dr. Neihardt either, but in my initial encounter with him I was captured by the spirit of his twinkling energy. As I sat in the Wayne State auditorium where Wayne's most famous alumnus was about to give his evening lecture, I saw speech instructor Dr. Bob Johnson (now my close friend) proceed toward the stage with a bit of bouncing fluff beside him. As I was puzzling about this phenomenon, Dr. Bob turned at the podium revealing an extremely short Neihardt with a wild white mane! The Native Americans had named him Little Bull Buffalo because he was also extremely strong, able to lift his own weight above him with one arm. Later, Black Elk rechristened him *Flaming Rainbow, Word Sender*, the Sioux equivalent of poet.

    I remember thinking I wouldn't be particularly interested in Neihardt's work—it seemed to me it dealt with the old West and cowboys and Indians—although many of my English instructors seemed to be quite excited about him. Still, this writer had been appointed Poet Laureate of Nebraska for eternity by the legislature; and a handsome bust of him made by his wife Mona, who had studied with Rodin in Paris, resided in the dormitory named after him. He must be worth checking out.

    I was captivated that first evening with his stories of hoeing in his garden and suddenly finding himself on his back looking up at his spirea bush, seeing it grow "all at once"—shooting out incredible white light. And how, in a dream, he flew through the air (only it was hard and slick—something like ether), his arms before him in the sacred manner of Native Americans, before he had ever heard about that tradition.

    I didn't comprehend entirely the word "mysticism," yet, but Neihardt's words and manner awakened a fluttering in me that drew me to his being. He was the mystic blaze and my soul the proverbial moth being drawn to the light. When I found out that he was going to teach a summer-school class in Creative Writing in 1966, I hurried to sign up even though I was timid about writing and hadn't shown my work to anyone.

Then we heard Neihardt was in the hospital with pneumonia, so I feared I wasn't going to get to study with him after all. Another instructor started the class, having us write pieces in rhyme and meter. I turned in something for assignments but wasn't happy with anything I produced. Suddenly, it was announced that John Neihardt had recovered sufficiently to teach the last week of the class. And there he was. Spry and sparkly! Full of vitality! In his late eighties. *This guy's been sick?* I mused.

He got right to it. He explained that *The Cycle of the West* (over 500 pages) was in iambic pentameter. The meter had helped him; had given him a mold into which to pour all that historic information and research. So, he announced, we were going to write lines in iambic pentameter; and he began to walk up and down the rows of desks tapping out the meter with his cane. He'd stop at a student's shoulder. "Let's hear a line." He'd grin mischievously and then tap on and on for the whole torturous class period. I kept praying he'd not stop by my seat. He must have very kindly noticed those students who looked like they were about to throw up and did not prevail upon them to perform.

Fortunately for me, his mind took a different turn the next day when he began to recite from memory, as he loved to do. Most of the rest of the class time was filled with John Neihardt, Poet Laureate of Nebraska, reciting from memory *The Cycle of the West*. He focused mainly on the last section, "The Song of the Messiah," which deals with a most mystical and poetic description of the Ghost Dance Messiah, Wovoka's, vision. A small example:

> All the living things
> With roots and leaves, with fins of legs or wings,
> Were bowed, beholding; and a sudden change
> Came over them, for all that had been strange
> Between them vanished. Nothing was alone,
> But each one knew the other and was known,
> And saw the same; for it had come to pass
> The wolf and deer, the bison and the grass,

And horse and man had lost their little dreams
And wakened all together.
…
                   The shapes that went and came
Were ways in which the something like a flame
Lived young forever; and the flame he knew
Was Wakantanka; for the mountains too
Were holy with it, and the soft earth flowed,
Til it was only light that lived and flowed
To make the shapes of animal and man,
The rooted and the winged. Where one began
The one did not end, for they were one,
All coming from and going to a sun,
That drew him now.

(From *The Cycle of the West*)

I sat mesmerized by the recitation and the visions. A feeling of familiarity wrapped around me. I was where I belonged!

A few years later, when I began to teach American Literature at Northeast Community College, I knew I needed to add Native American literature, even though there was none in the *Norton Anthology*. *What's more American than Native American literature?* I thought. Besides poetry and chants from various tribes, I included *Black Elk Speaks* by Neihardt.

Neihardt's hometown, Bancroft, was only about an hour away from our college, so every fall the class took a field trip to the Neihardt Center to see John's study where he wrote and the Sioux Prayer Garden, constructed with hedges and flowers replicating the symbols from Black Elk's vision. Black Elk experienced his vision as a boy of nine years old and dictated it to Neihardt in his later years when Neihardt was looking for stories about the Ghost Dance. The story goes that Black Elk was standing outside his door waiting for Neihardt and told the poet he had been sent "to save his vision" for the world. Black Elk said, "[I] did not have to remember these things; they have remembered themselves all these years" (*Black Elk Speaks*).

PART TWO: WITHOUT A MAP

The vision is a very complex narrative filled with symbolic colors, directions, animals (particularly horses), and numbers, which Black Elk struggled to use in order to save his people and their way of life from annihilation. Black Elk related that in his vision he was standing

> on the highest mountain of them all, and round about beneath me was the whole hoop of the world. And while I stood there I saw more than I can tell and I understood more than I saw; for I was seeing in a sacred manner the shapes of all things in the spirit, and the shape of all shapes as they must live together like one being. And I saw that the sacred hoop of my people was one of many hoops that made one circle, wide as daylight and as starlight, and in the center grew one mighty flowering tree to shelter all the children of one mother and one father. And I saw that it was holy.

(From *Black Elk Speaks*)

Although Black Elk had not been able to use his vision to preserve his people's way of life, he seemed to sense he was widening "the Hoop of the World" to include many peoples by disclosing the dream to Neihardt. With the Prayer Garden at Bancroft, visitors are able to share in the vision's power. Different-colored flowers have been placed at the four quadrants to represent the colors of the four directions, and a flowering crab tree in the center of the Circle stands for the Tree of Life. Narrow concrete paths painted red (the good red road) and black (the black road of difficulty) intersect close to the center, dramatizing the struggle of Black Elk's people and making a cross, which Neihardt explained was older than traditional Christianity. These archetypal symbols touched my spirit like a puzzling dream.

My students could feel the life of the elements here and wanted to stay on a while after the tour of the Center was over. They seemed to be experiencing Black Elk's ultimate understanding that "all over the world the faces of living ones are alike" (*Black Elk's Prayer*).

In the postscript to *Black Elk Speaks* Neihardt relates that Black Elk wished "to stand up there [Harney Peak] before I die," so he and John Neihardt made the journey where Black Elk predicted that if he had any power left there should be "at least a little thunder and a little rain."

Neihardt goes on to report,

> It was a season of drouth, one of the worst in the memory of old men. The sky remained clear until the conclusion of the ceremony.
>
> …
>
> With tears running down his cheeks, the old man raised his voice to a thin wail, and chanted: "In sorrow I am sending a feeble voice … O make my people live!"
>
> For some minutes the old man stood silent, with face uplifted, weeping in the drizzling rain.
>
> In a little while the sky was clear again.

(From *Black Elk Speaks*)

And, as Neihardt told it, "it didn't rain again all summer."

One of my students became so enamored of Neihardt, who was then in his nineties, that he wondered if he could possibly meet him. I told him to call Neihardt's caretakers in Lincoln, who then invited him for a short visit. He was impressed by Neihardt's wit and charm. Neihardt's friends were helping him across the hall from his bedroom to his study where he still wrote every day, and he quipped to my student, "Certainly is invigorating to walk to work every morning!" In those days Neihardt said he was looking forward to death as "the last great adventure."

The last time I saw John Neihardt was at Dana College, and he was still reciting. In fact, he wouldn't stop. He went on and on. Which was fine with me. His voice was still strong and oratorical, and he picked fine parts of his works to perform; but the program organizers had other ideas and, after about an hour, wanted him to quit. They whispered in his ear, gestured toward his seat, nodded and moved; trying to direct him toward his chair, but he spoke on anyway. Finally, one of them took the microphone from his hand as he paused only a moment. Neihardt seemed surprised that the evening was already over.

The day Neihardt died in early November 1973, a few snowflakes fluttered down—early for snow in Nebraska. I felt Nature was marking his passage to the other side. (They say eagles circled his family home in Missouri.) Nature has a way of being tuned to the spirits tuned to her. When Carl Jung passed, a huge tree in his garden was split by lightning. Neihardt's dog followed him into eternity two days later.

One early Saturday morning after a week of discussing Black Elk in my literature class, I was lying on my waterbed, thinking intently about what it was I was supposed to be doing on the planet. A voice said very clearly, "The purpose of life is to grow." If anyone else had been in the room I was sure the witness would have heard the voice as well. It seemed to me to have been spoken aloud. It did not frighten me. At the time it seemed like a natural occurrence. I remember thinking, *Oh, so that's what it's all about*— not even thinking—*What? Who said that?*—and going about my business. Only later in the day did it sink in that perhaps I'd had an auditory vision, precipitated by the mysticism of Black Elk, the power of his vision, and being tuned into the spirituality of the native people. For the first time, I had had an actual spiritual "experience," but it took a while for it to seep into my being.

JUNG, CAMPBELL, AND DREAMS

The heart of literature tuned my heart to the compassionate heart of the universe. Reading had led me here. Teaching the understanding I gleaned from literature led me further down the path. Soon after I finished college, I interviewed for and expected to teach eleventh grade American Literature. But I found myself instead in Council Bluffs, Iowa at Bloomer Junior High (named for Amelia Bloomer who invented bloomers). Here the students were tough, tracked inner-city kids. I was supposed to teach the lowest track seventh and eighth graders for two hours—reading, spelling, grammar, and penmanship. I couldn't even make them stay in their seats! They had learning disabilities, emotional problems, problems galore. The principal, nicknamed Wild Bill, would occasionally rush in, grab a kid at random by the neck, push him up against the wall, and shout into his face, "Are you chewing gum?" That was the extent of Wild Bill's support.

Florescent lights stretched across the drywall that separated the two classrooms down the middle. When the teacher next door watched a film, our lights went off too. One student was such a walking volcano, I was told to "let him do whatever he wanted" and "not to touch him." One day I was two minutes tardy returning from lunch, and he had shoved another student through the drywall, leaving a gaping hole. By spring, one of my eighth-grade girls was pregnant. I felt sorry for these kids, even liked most of them; but I couldn't control or teach them.

Every year a new teacher fresh from college would be placed in this job, and every year she would resign. By Christmas time, the kids asked, "Why are those black Xs on the calendar?" I answered them truthfully. "I'm marking off the days until the end of the school year." I went back to graduate school.

There I was introduced to Carl Jung and archetypes by a fellow graduate student. I had chosen Edward Albee's plays for my master's thesis, drawn and puzzled by his strange portrayal of women, especially mothers. I began one thesis, wrote about eighty pages discussing Albee as a social critic, then looked up and thought, *This isn't it!* I turned to Jung as Bob and I moved to Southern California. He was going to graduate school; I was going to work. I read on and on. I couldn't get a job; my former principal was giving me bad references, and there was a hiring freeze. Bob went to work as a school counselor, and I read and wrote all day—doing a very extensive examination of the female characters in Albee's plays from a Jungian perspective. I explored the Oedipus complex, discussing Jung, Freud, and Adler, the matriarchy and patriarchy, the Great and Terrible Mothers. I immersed myself in Jung's theories of dreams, archetypes, mythology, and art. My new thesis was 145 pages long and led me to other mythological scholars such as Erich Neumann, Robert Graves, and Joseph Campbell. I was finishing my thesis when we decided to move back to Nebraska and I was hired to teach at the community college.

My first semester at Northeast I designed a comparative mythology course where I shared these exciting ideas about archetypes and dreams. Preparing the syllabus for my new class, I studied Jung's *Man and His Symbols.* Jung had never tried to write for the general population; but had a dream that he was speaking before masses of people and was being understood, so he prepared the first chapter of that book. The other chapters were written by colleagues. As I was reviewing the book before the class began one evening, I fell asleep on the couch and dreamed that I was painting a mosaic-like painting, but I couldn't finish it because when it was finished my work would be over and then it would be time for me to go. I realized the painting was my life, and I had many pieces to put into place.

Jung and his minister father apparently would argue about faith and belief. Jung's father would insist that he must "believe." Jung, however, insisted that this approach was backward. Jung said he must first have an *experience* of God, and then he could believe. In the few moments of film where Jung is captured, I always get goose bumps when the interviewer asks Jung, "And do you *now* believe in God?"

Jung answers, "Hard to say. I don't have to believe, I KNOW!"

When I learned of Jung's dream in which God drops His divine excrement on His church below, shattering it, the image connected deeply with my own desire for some living experience of God, and fewer rules and regulations. There was such freedom in Jung's personal approach to the Divine. Jung's exploration included living alone in his towers in Bollingen, carving images from his dreams and imagination into the stone of that tower, communing in silence with nature and with his wise old man [Self] in the image of a figure he called Philemon. He traveled to Africa, to the natives of North America, and to the patients of mental institutions studying over 67,000 dreams to support his theory of archetypes. In his autobiography *Memories, Dreams, and Reflections*, Jung relates being a three-year-old child sitting on a rock wondering if he is the child sitting on the rock or the rock being sat upon. He also describes a great mystical dream of a phallus upon a throne dreamed as a very young child.

As I studied Jungian archetypes more deeply, Jung's "psychology of type" unraveled mysteries of relationships for me. Learning about the characteristics of his four psychological types (Thinking, Feeling, Sensation, Intuition) and that each of these kinds of people has a unique perception of time enabled me to understand my husband's experience in the world. Once I learned that Bob was a Sensation type who really was unaware of the time of the day (or even the day of the week) and was so absorbed in a particular task or joy of the moment that he often was not where he was supposed to be, I ceased being irritated by that trait. He certainly wasn't worrying about going to bed so he could get up to do something in the morning (like me, a Thinking type). His behavior wasn't something he did on purpose, and he definitely did not do it to irritate me, who always knew the exact date, time, and where I was supposed to be and what I was supposed to be doing. Suddenly, this understanding that we each were having a totally different experience with time, eased many of our martial tensions.

Jungian psychology attempts to move the individual psyche toward wholeness by uniting the dominant and subordinate parts, the conscious and the unconscious, female (anima) and male (animus). All of this activity is continuously occurring in our dreams, Jung points out; this is why we should pay attention and not only to an isolated dream but also to dreams occurring over an extended period of time. In Jungian dream interpretation dreams are messages from the unconscious to the dreamer about what needs to be done to bring him or her to greater individuation (wholeness). And the dreamer is the best person to interpret the dream by free associating and looking carefully at what is going on in the dreamer's life.

Jung also gave me a very valuable way to think about and interpret literature since so much of great and contemporary literature is filled with archetypes—think of Romeo and Juliet, Hamlet, Lear, Oedipus. Speaking of literature in this way provided me with a key to begin a discussion with students to unlock literature's many delights and mysteries. I was surprised and delighted at a literature conference in the late eighties to be introduced to an attendee as "the Jungian." I hadn't until that moment considered myself that way, but maybe I was ... I had incorporated the teaching of this "practical" mystic into my teaching and my life.

Another piece that fit neatly into the mosaic was Joseph Campbell. Particularly helpful for me and my students was Campbell's *Hero with a Thousand Faces*. The ritual of the Hero's Quest enacted repeatedly in myths, stories, dreams, and individual lives was a rich source of insight. The journey could be viewed as a literal hero's quest or as transitional stages through an individual life: Departure (leaving home), Trials (obstacles in the world), Mystical marriage (or real marriage), Descent into the Underworld (death), Resurrection—return with the trophy—(eternal reward). The hero often has a guide on his or her journey that is represented by his opposite—akin to Jung's idea of the anima or animus (like Dante's Beatrice guiding the poet through the circles of Hell). The Hero's Quest is another version of a journey to wholeness—an attempt to journey into the unconscious, face fears there, and overcome them.

My students and I decided to enact a Hero's Quest rather than discuss it. After all it was spring; we all wanted to be outdoors. So we chose a local park with hills, crevices, even a cave where we could stash a monster (a student in a borrowed dragon suit). Each student chose a stage of the quest: leaving home, facing temptation, meeting the monster, merging with the god [self], or a character that was most appealing, and then worked on that portion of this self-discovery pilgrimage. They each personally invited a guest to experience the quest. The activity even attracted the local press. We rated two front-page photos and a cover story the first year.

Everyone was required to keep a dream journal, even the students who claimed never to remember dreams. By the end of the course they were able to recall at least a few. Almost every class period someone had a dream he or she wanted to discuss. Sometimes students reported dreaming about me. I tried to give them practices for continuing to recall their dreams. Some very helpful ones I've taken from Patricia Garfield's *Creative Dreaming*. To increase dream remembrance tell yourself you will dream and remember your dream. Drink half a glass of water before going to sleep; drink the other half on waking and recall your dream. One of the most important techniques for me is to remain in the same posture on awakening. The dream is broken once the dreamer's body shifts. Also, tell your dream to your companion on waking. The Maori natives practiced this daily. The more attention you pay to your dreams, the more your unconscious will reward you with more dreams and better dream recall. Once I assured my nondreamers that they did indeed dream every night (everyone dreams at least forty-five minutes); they began recalling dreams.

My most startling dream was of my father having a heart attack and no one would believe him when he told them. Shortly after the dream Bob and I were camping in the Black Hills and for no particular reason decided to come home a day early. When we got home my mother called to say my dad was in the hospital and the doctors hadn't determined what was wrong. We drove to Omaha, where he was hooked up to an EKG in the cardiac ward, but there was no heart trauma being recorded. He was being treated for indigestion, although he kept repeating he was in terrible pain. I was scheduled to give a poetry reading in Norfolk, so we reluctantly drove 120 miles home. When we entered the house the phone was ringing. Dad had been taken into heart surgery. Immediately I remembered my dream, chastising myself for not recalling it sooner.

Some who suggest using dreams for spiritual growth advise that the final stage of dream work is to act on the dream in some way to bring its energy into the dreamer's life so it doesn't slip back into the unconscious. The dream work could include journaling, art work, or perhaps following through on some message from a dream. If the dream had something to do with the dreamer building his or her courage perhaps performing a simple task that would require courage could be performed. The dreamer has to have a dialogue with the dream for growth to occur.

Remembering my dreams, writing them down, sketching images, performing some of the actions my dreams prescribed all became regular occurrences for me. (I remember sketching a chrysalis after I dreamed the word.) Dreams became a spiritual practice before I was aware of the concept of spiritual practices.

YOGANANDA

After my first year of teaching at Northeast, I discovered *Autobiography of a Yogi* by Paramahansa Yogananda. I grabbed the book and headed up to Skyview, the newly made lake in Norfolk, to sunbathe and read, my two favorite activities. Since my college days I had always allowed myself the luxury of sunbathing and often have been competitive about getting the best suntan. But truly I loved the experience of not having to do anything else, and I felt justified lying there letting the sun caress my body. It was the only time I didn't have to be busy "accomplishing" something. Try as I would I hadn't been able to shake my parents' work ethic. I needed to be productive. My mother always expressed displeasure that Bob and I didn't get additional jobs in the summer, when our teaching jobs were over for the school year. When I was working on my suntan, I was "doing something."

Yogananda's autobiography was like being in Catholic grade school again only much better! It was full of fabulous and fantastic tales of saints and teaching, feats and fakirs. I loved the story of the woman who prayed to be able to live without eating because her mother-in-law disapproved of her appetite. Supposedly, the prayer was so unique God granted it, and she lived (there is a photo of her in the book) for over sixty years in India on air and light!

Another amazing tale was told of Yogananda witnessing a woman in France bleeding with the stigmata and being connected with her telepathically while she experienced Christ carrying His cross. Yogananda recounted how his guru, Sri Yukteswar, touched him, sending him into a vividly described experience of cosmic consciousness, and later how his teacher returned from the dead to report on the astral plane and its activities. The book concludes with a statement from Forest Lawn Mortuary in California about Yogananda's body showing no signs of decay after twenty days, when it was finally buried. Here were strange and far-out, modern-day miracles, and I wanted some of them! Bob and I joined Yogananda's Self-Realization Fellowship and started receiving lessons from them in the mail.

The next summer, when we took a trip to southern California, we went to the Self-Realization Temple and sat in meditation. We had received instructions on their form of meditation, but we hadn't read them very carefully. We weren't practicing their lessons diligently—or, honestly, not at all. I studied how the other people in the Temple were sitting—leaning forward in their chairs, trying to keep their backs very straight (in lieu of sitting cross-legged on the floor, a concession to Westerners). Everyone's hands were on their thighs, palms turned upward. I tried to imitate this posture and call out with my heart, much like my first communion experience, for God to come. And, much like that earlier experience, nothing happened. Something worse than nothing. I felt a great despair settle on my soul as if there were no hope. No hope at all for salvation. A black curtain of despair seemed to fall around me as I meditated there with an aching back, an uplifted face, and a pleading heart.

The wife of Bob's good friend suggested a trip to the beach the next day, and I was eager to do something fun and forget about all this meditation stuff. We had just situated ourselves and all our beach paraphernalia on our towels when she and the "friend" she'd brought along produced Jehovah's Witnesses' pamphlets and began to proselytize. The friend announced that she had belonged to the Self-Realization Temple first but now had found *The Truth*. Bob said nothing. I listened for a minute or two before I began to sob. Finally I was able to say, "I thought you wanted to spend time at the beach with us, and you only invited us here to preach to us. I feel preyed upon."

To their credit they stopped their missionary work when I protested. After that, we only lay in the sun, but for me the trip to the beach was spoiled. Yogananda's book had filled me with desire and expectation again. I wanted some of those cosmic flashes. Why wasn't anything happening for me. Why was it "taking so long, My Lord?"

REGINA 11

One fall evening our friend Adam called. He was excited; "You *have* to meet this psychic woman from Columbia," he said. He had been so disoriented about being with her that he had trouble finding where he had parked his car. His enthusiasm convinced us to enroll in her Mental Relax class in the old hotel in downtown Norfolk.

Regina was married to a man who used to farm in rural Nebraska. One day he had hopped on his motorcycle and ridden from Alaska to the tip of South America, standing in for Yul Brynner in *Taras Bulba*, slaying a twenty-foot python, and meeting and marrying Regina along the way. He didn't know she was a psychic until their baby was gravely ill and Regina promised if the little girl lived she would teach her psychic skills to others. So she began teaching in Columbia and amassed huge followings. She said she'd discovered her powers when she was about to be confirmed and saw the Bishop's aura. She wished for the Bishop to reach down and pick her up, which he did. Then that afternoon, alone in her room after the family dinner, she found herself levitating, and a voice began instructing her in her psychic powers. She told us the voice was Pope John XXIII. She called herself Regina 11 because she was the eleventh person in the world to have these powers; one of the eleven was Jesus.

Regina was a small, dark, beautiful woman with long, thick hair and magnetic eyes that she highlighted with black eyeliner. She seemed to enjoy enhancing her witchy appearance. Although she could speak English, she preferred to have her husband,

Danny Liska, translate. She began the first night by teaching us how to see auras. She dimmed the lights, had us look behind her head and slightly above it a few inches. Then she instructed us to let our eyes go slightly out of focus and just look for a long time. She assisted us by pumping up her breath. In just a few minutes I saw a whitish light outlining her head and arms. When she moved away, the outline of her body stayed. Everyone else said they saw this also. I don't think anyone saw colors.

Regina next announced she was going to take away our negative energy and came to stand in front of each of us individually. She had us close our eyes. When she came to me, she took both of my hands and started to sway, and soon I was moving in oval-shaped circles with her, around and around for a minute or two. She went to each person in the dim ballroom performing this procedure. After my turn, I waited quietly as she proceeded down the rows until I heard a loud crash. Our friend, Don Merriman, had fainted. Don was the retired Dean of Students from Wayne State College, a former Golden Gloves boxer. He said he'd felt as if a big dynamo had switched on and that was the last thing he remembered before he hit the floor. Regina said his energy started to come out of his body and collided with her energy.

That night at home in bed, I looked over at Bob and was convinced he wasn't in his body. His body was there, but I was sure his spirit was elsewhere. In a few minutes I felt him re-enter. He opened his eyes.

"Where were you?" I asked.

"I was listening to Don Merriman and Bob Johnson talk about the hot water radiator in their car."

"How weird!" Exhausted by all this stuff, I went to sleep.

At class the next night, Bob asked Bob Johnson and Don what they had been talking about on their hour-long drive home to Wayne. They tried to recall. "Oh," they said, "just water in the car radiator."

That night Regina told us she had removed our negative energy and we could now send positive messages. We just had to think of the message we wanted to send, close our eyes, and off

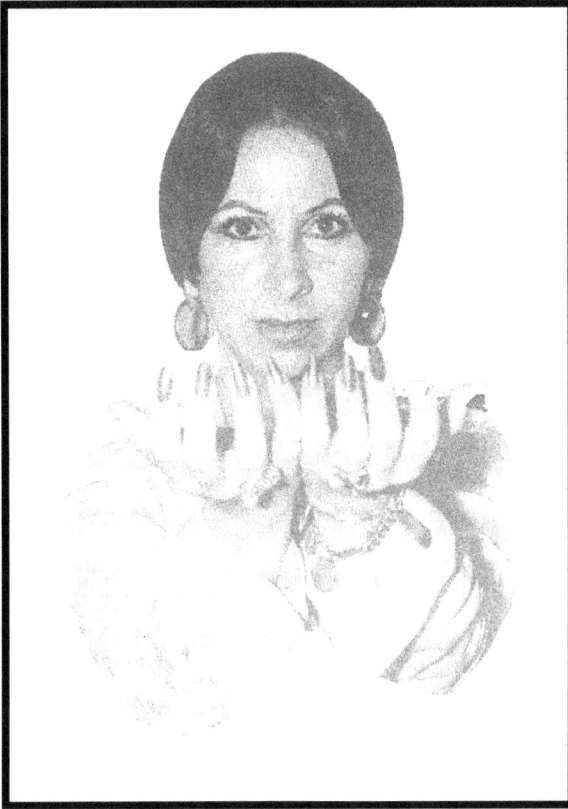

Regina 11

it would go. We were not to think of it again because that would cancel it out. Of course we couldn't wait to try this out. Bob had brought one of the other high school counselors home with him, and they were sitting outside in the car. He told his colleague he could send me a message to come to the door. I didn't have any reason to, but right then, I went to the back door, looked out, saw them in the car, and waved. The other counselor got spooked and said he had to go home.

Regina's next session was a very strange one. Bob thought he could smell death—he remembered the smell from when his mother died of cancer—and lots of ghoulish images came up in the course of the evening's work and lecture. Worn out and rather put off, we came home just wanting to go to sleep and put it all out of our minds for a while. We were just falling asleep when we both saw a ball of blue light whisk up the stairs and into our bedroom. Bob sat up immediately saying he thought if I held a piece of paper he could project the light through his head onto the paper like onto a movie screen. That sounded nuts to me, but this whole course had been "out there." I got a piece of typing paper; Bob's eyelids flickered, and I stared at the paper. There on the page appeared tiny images: a young girl, a skull, something I couldn't quite make out. Then the window shade flew up and the images, the blue light—all disappeared. The entire atmosphere changed.

"What was that?" I asked.

"Beats me," Bob said. "Let's go to sleep."

When we asked Regina about it the next night, she said that sometimes before people die they go around collecting their energy, and she was sorry. That didn't make much sense either until about two weeks later a schizophrenic friend of Bob's who used to pester us constantly on the phone until we told him he couldn't keep calling us committed suicide. Apparently, the visit from the blue light had something to do with him collecting the energy he had left with us; he needed that energy for his journey into eternity.

The last night of class Regina was supposed to levitate. She said she had her doubts whether she'd be able to do it in such a small class—she used the energy of the class to help raise herself up—and in South America she had hundreds of followers in her classes. She began by lying on a table in front of us with, as usual, dim lights. We watched her bounce strangely on her behind and maneuver her shoulders, which I am not sure would be possible to perform just by using gymnastics. Her body was almost entirely raised up with only one shoulder remaining on the table. She jackknifed so only a tiny part of her bottom was still anchored. She did seem to almost rise briefly, but I can't say I saw her levitate even though we wished her to and chanted "Arriba! Arriba!" Bob lay on the table and tried. I thought I saw a dark grey bar extend over the top of him, and he seemed to rise a bit; but he didn't levitate either.

I liked Regina's positive attitude. She told us we could only use these powers for good. If we tried to use them for bad things, they would turn back on us. She told us she was like our mother now, to call on her if we needed anything. She was funny and kind. When she came over for a party, suddenly all of our house lights went out. The circuit breaker was thrown in the fuse box. We looked at Regina. She giggled and said she was just thinking the fire would look nicer with the lights off.

However, there were also things I didn't like. I didn't like how she used events and sometimes people to her advantage. She claimed to have turned back a hurricane from the coast of Florida. She claimed that she projected her picture into the trunk of a tree when she was being held captive by terrorists in Bogotá (she was a hostage for almost two years)—it frightened them, and they set her free. Most of these claims, of course, could not be substantiated. When she later ran for public office in Colombia, she won by handing out hundreds of "magnetized" statues of herself in the nude.

Regina is a combination side-show performer, shaman, and someone with some legitimate powers. Being in her presence allowed us some entry into psychic realms. Bob says she shattered his purely scientific way of seeing the world by providing him with some unexplainable subjective experiences into human nature. He always calls Regina his favorite psychedelic. When he was in his counseling office, he could see images of people his counselees were talking about in balls above their heads so clearly he could describe their faces exactly. It appears that she opened our third eye. After we'd been with her, we'd often see a small oval of brilliant blue light ahead of us, as though it were being projected from that chakra. I felt that the experiences she gave us opened us for the teachers and events yet to come. And strange as it seemed, many of those teachings were coming to us right in our small Midwest town of Norfolk, Nebraska.

TRANSCENDENTAL MEDITATION

It was the Beatles' fault. Along with stories of them going to India to study meditation with a guru were pictures of them posing with a white-robed, silver-haired gorgeous being by the name of Maharishi Mahesh Yogi. Their music was changing. Some of the change seemed to come from experimentation with psychedelic drugs but, we thought, not only that. There was an expansive openness—a new sound with many levels of variation; something radiating from within encompassed what was going on within the outer layers. Mixed in with all the psychedelic images we could hear mantras and, of course, George Harrison's great longing, soaring guitar. We were intrigued by this new awareness in their work. They were practicing, they said, Transcendental Meditation.

It was 1971. A friend told us the TM instructors were coming to Norfolk and were looking for a house where they could initiate people into the technique. We had a big old house with lots of bedrooms and were very curious, so we offered ours. Bob was teaching psychology and had read about tests that had been done on meditators. Meditation had been proven beneficial for reducing blood pressure and stress levels. One of the other psychology instructors was also interested.

For the introductory lecture, the Transcendental Meditation teachers dressed like business people—the man wore a suit, the woman wore a skirt and heels. The talk was general, about how with the use of a mantra we would be going into a state of deep rest—dipping into consciousness for a few minutes every day and then out into activity until from continual "dippings" we would reach cosmic consciousness. They instructed us to not take recreational drugs for two weeks and to bring fruit, flowers, and a white handkerchief.

So in the empty upstairs room in our house before a picture of the Maharishi's guru, Guru Dev, the teacher took my fruit and flowers, covered the fruit with a handkerchief, and whispered a mantra she said was especially selected for me. She said it was a secret and never to tell anybody. (Bob and I never have, not even to each other.) Then we repeated the mantra out loud together a few times. The teacher left, leaving me to repeat my mantra silently. It was a most interesting experience. I felt flat—like a cartoon cat a steam roller had rolled over—all flattened out and at the same time extremely large. The experience was very physical as well as mental. The teacher returned after a while and said, "Jai Guru Dev," the signal to stop.

"How was that?" she asked. "Great!" I said. I hadn't ever felt like that before. I paid my money, $75, I think it was then. And after a little more instruction, that was it. The teacher asked if I noticed any thoughts. I nodded. Dealing with thoughts is the most important part of the TM instruction. The teacher instructs you to ever so gently move back to the mantra. This technique really is the basic practice of all meditation methods I've been exposed to: Insight Meditation, where the meditator notes his or her thoughts then moves gently back to the breath; and Buddhist Meditation, which I was instructed in by Allen Ginsberg at Naropa, observe what you are thinking and go back to the breath. Those moments during which you are *not* thinking are the moments of pure awareness. Always gently notice the straying, then move back to the mantra or breath.

The TM teachers seemed to have everything memorized. It was as if they were carefully programmed as to exactly what they were supposed to say. We got to ask questions in following lectures. When I said it seemed like maybe I was going to sleep, the teachers advised me to go to bed earlier. I didn't feel that they'd really answered my question, but I was so excited by the experience I gladly proceeded.

In follow-up lectures during the week the teachers stressed that by alternating the deep rest of meditation with the activity of work, TM would advance our enlightenment. They loved the metaphor of rest and activity and also of dyeing a cloth: dipping it in dye, drying it in the sun, dipping and drying until all the dye was in the cloth itself. Repeating the process was like Being and Self, stressing the concept of moving back and forth, into deep Being and out into activity. I think they even used "swinging on birches" from Frost's "Birches" poem to emphasize the "in and out" to make sure we got the idea.

So, they repeated, that was the technique, just repeating our mantra for twenty minutes in the morning and twenty minutes in the late afternoon or evening. We did it, my husband and I, faithfully for three or four years. Every day.

It wasn't hard to be faithful to the TM practice; it was pleasant and interesting. And because it was only twenty minutes it wasn't demanding. It was true, as the teachers had told us, if for some reason we had to miss the daily routine, the whole day seemed out of kilter. By doing the twenty-minute meditation, we entered deep relaxation and a witnessing awareness. We were able to bring enough of these effects back with us to alter our moods, perceptions, and how we proceeded through our days. I remember our sitting side by side in living room chairs silently repeating our mantras during those years. This daily routine seasoned us so that when meditation was offered at Naropa and during Sufi practices, we were ready.

Later I heard wild stories about Maharishi University in Iowa, where people were learning to fly. I thought the stories were funny. Maybe people were levitating, but psychic tricks didn't have much pull for me. TM had been good for me. It had helped me move along my path.

NAROPA, GINSBERG, TRUNGPA

I would write observations and bits of poems once in a while on scraps of paper and leave them lying around the house. Often I couldn't find them again when I went to look for them. I had been teaching English at the community college for a few years— composition, comparative mythology, American literature. I had aspirations of writing, just like I had always dreamed that someday I would travel; but my thirtieth birthday was approaching, and I hadn't truly approached writing seriously. This was before the days of Writers-in-the-Schools. I didn't grow up knowing you could "write" for a career. I didn't know any writers. There weren't any creative writers on the faculty at Wayne State College when I got my degree in English Education there. I think the University of Iowa was one of the few writing programs in existence in those early days. There was no such thing as a low-residency writing program where you could keep your present occupation and study writing at the same time.

Our friend Adam, who had introduced us to Regina, was attending the first summer of Naropa Institute in Boulder, Colorado and invited us to visit. He had gone to sample some of its esoteric offerings. Naropa's first summer was more like a carnival, with Ram Dass and many spiritual teachers from different venues. Adam was taking a workshop with Stanislav Grof in psychedelic perceptions and one with Larry Rosenberg on Insight Meditation. We had planned to sleep on the floor of his room, but his situation had changed by the time we arrived; he had found a companion. We tried to sleep in our van on the street, which worked for one night. However, the next morning when I was in the park doing yoga, the Boulder police disturbed my husband's blissful morning slumber to inform him he couldn't sleep in his van on Boulder streets and asked whether there was anyone else in there with him. They got a big kick out of being told his wife was in the park doing yoga. We found a room at a youth hostel and stayed long enough to know we wanted to enroll ourselves the next summer.

So the next summer off I went to Naropa to study writing. Bob signed up for psychology classes. The classes at Naropa were okay. The Beats in general weren't great teachers. Most of them had never taught before. Gregory Corso winged it and spent most of his time drinking and pulling shenanigans. He liked to be the "bad boy." Bill Burroughs was kind of nuts and boring, and he babbled on. Allen Ginsberg and Anne Waldman worked hard at trying to teach writing. I probably learned the most from them; they prepared, gave assignments, expected students to hand in work. Many of the younger students had read the Beats but not much literature before them. Allen decided everyone was ignorant of the classics, so he dutifully backed up and started through classical literature, which I had already studied, being an English major.

Still, I liked just being in his presence. He was a great man, a good human being. He was the one who took care of all the rest of the wacky Beats, the one who made some money and held the whole show together.

Ginsberg had met Chögyam Trungpa when they both were trying to get a taxicab in New York, and Trungpa became Allen's meditation teacher. Trungpa had fled Tibet when the Chinese Communists took over his country. He had gone to Oxford, gotten a Ph.D. in psychology, and founded a meditation center in Vermont. The story I heard about his founding the Naropa Institute in Boulder was that the Rocky Mountains reminded him of Tibet. Soon after meeting Ginsberg, Trungpa added the Poetics Program to the Naropa curriculum, explaining that if meditators were going to talk or write about the enlightened state of mind, they were going to have to use the poetic language of metaphor because there would be no way to write about it in ordinary language.

Naropa offered an opportunity to mingle with writers and aspiring writers from around the country and the world, and all who came to Naropa understood it was a Buddhist college with Buddhist meditation and classes at the core. Gregory Corso would often rant and rave about the Buddhists and how they didn't see what he saw, but he continued to teach there. There were even courses in "Buddhist" psychology.

A film crew from Italy came one summer to do a follow-up movie on the Beats (*Where are they now?*) and followed them to classes, readings, and other Naropa events and gatherings, filming for several weeks. And there were several readings every week. Getting to hear the sounds of poetry out of the mouths of poets gave me the experience of understanding it in a whole new way—from the inside out. I even stopped listening to content and just let myself be bathed in sound. I took my first baby steps forward as a poet with the writing assignments for Anne and Allen.

Allen was sincere about meditation. He taught it in every class. He'd often stop in the middle of a lecture and suggest we meditate for a short time. He'd loosen his belt, get in an upright

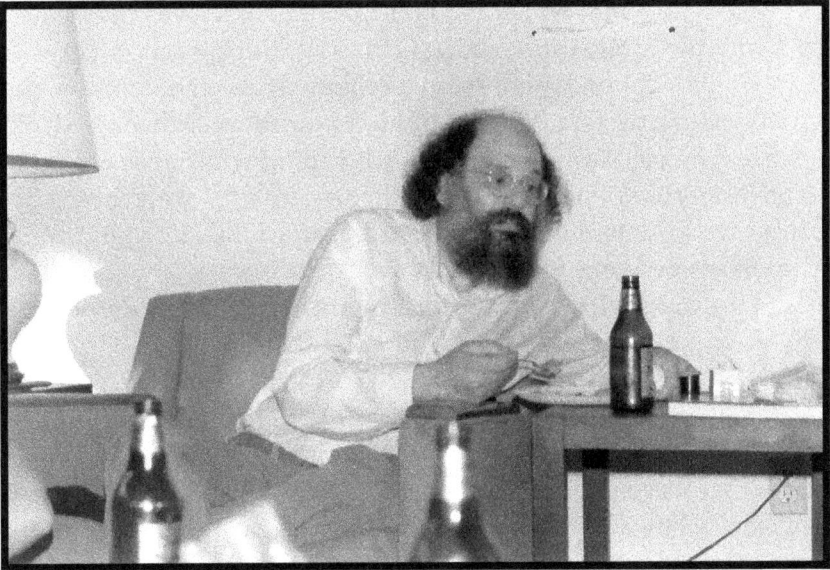

Allen Ginsberg at Naropa Potluck

position, put his hands on his knees, encourage the students to do likewise, and instruct us to pay attention to our outgoing breath. He'd usually only maintain the meditative stance for three or four minutes but long enough to give everyone a little dip into this state of consciousness. For one class he did require us to sit at least for two hours. We went to the gym at Sacred Heart which Naropa rented on weekends for meditation purposes. That was the most I ever "sat" at one time while attending Naropa. (It didn't occur to me at the time that I was back at Catholic school!)

Ginsberg had suggested we meditate and take our notebooks. If some images came we could write them down, then go back to the meditation process. Ginsberg taught, and I have learned, the process of following the mind in the process of writing, which is really a meditation process. Traditional Insight Meditation notes what the mind is experiencing and moves on. In this particular two-hour sitting I vividly remember feeling like I was beginning to peel my skin away, starting with my hand, up my arm, and so on with my body. It wasn't particularly scary or painful, more like I was just removing layers, getting down to the real stuff.

The whole atmosphere of Naropa, of course, was permeated by Trungpa, a most interesting and powerful presence. He was surrounded by bodyguards in Western suits called the Vajra guard. (Curious that Vajra would become my Sufi name.) He gave an open lecture every Wednesday night which was available to anyone—Naropa students whether or not they were taking his course or any meditation course and also to the local public. He always arrived late for his lectures, sometimes as much as two hours. I thought it was rude. The meditators and inside Naropa crowd expected it and took it in stride. Everyone congregated outside the Sacred Heart School auditorium. The sun went down; the Rocky Mountain night air grew chilly; someone juggled. There usually seemed to be some dancers, animated conversations, a party-like atmosphere. The limo pulled up, four tough burly men got out, followed by a small Tibetan man who walked with a limp and had a maimed arm. Trungpa had been in a serious car accident in England. The story goes that he had been in a severe depression, had come to a fork in a road, and had driven straight ahead, crashing into a joke shop, maiming himself for life.

One summer, the day before we were to leave Naropa, I decided to take the tab of acid my friend had sent with me to take sometime in the mountains. Bob and some of our friends had peyote, so we decided to go up into the Flatirons above Boulder. For some reason, I decided to climb the mountain barefoot thinking that the LSD would tune me in and I wouldn't hurt my feet. I don't know why I thought of it, but it turned out to be true. I was not aware that there were cacti with long spines growing out of the side of the mountain that could be very painful to bare feet; but every time before I nearly stepped on a cactus I would see white light shooting out of the side of the mountain, and I was able to avoid the spines.

I had taken the acid a little while before we began our drive, and as we started to ascend, all the mountain aspens and spruce began to swim across the windshield of our blue van in a passing river. I was totally taken with their natural beauty, how amazingly gorgeous they were and transient. Everything was passing. This moment, the trees, our lives, even the mountain would all crumble away—none of it would last. I began to cry silently. "Are you all right?" my friend Kathy asked, noticing my tears.

I nodded. "It's just so beautiful."

She nodded, even though I don't think she understood, and I couldn't explain right then.

My friends spent most of the rest of the afternoon trying to tell me they weren't high. Peyote is a subtle high, not nearly as dramatic as acid. I felt they were in the same space as I was. I just couldn't convince them of it as we spent the afternoon in the sunlit trees and mountain stream.

Later that afternoon we must have spent an hour arguing over where to get something to eat, finally settling on some bean burritos from Taco John's that we ate in the van. The creamy cheesy beans and chewy tortillas, eaten while laughing with my friends, has to have been one of the most delicious and memorable meals of my life.

Finally we ended up in the Naropa parking lot preparing to go to Trungpa's lecture, and Allen Ginsberg appeared from out of nowhere. He walked over to me, picked up my foot (I was still barefoot) and immediately began massaging it. "What 'cha been doin'?" he asked with his lop-sided grin. He'd had a stroke and part of his mouth didn't go up when he smiled.

"I've been up in the mountains. Took acid."

He took the other foot and rubbed it. "Ah!" he said and grinned bigger. "Take acid and meditate. You'll go into the Great Void!"

"I'm going home to Nebraska tomorrow, Allen. It *is* the Great Void!"

He laughed, put my foot down, kissed me on the cheek, and ambled off into the evening.

The third summer I decided I would apply to be Allen Ginsberg's apprentice. To apply for apprenticeship you had to write a letter stating what you could do for Allen; and if he chose you, you worked closely with him doing him some service, and he talked to you about your writing. I knew most of his apprentices were young boys (I didn't even try to picture what job they might be performing for him). Allen's openness about who and how he was came to be one of the qualities I admired about him the most. He made no pretensions about his sexuality or his desires. If he wanted someone sexually, he said so. That person could say yes or no. Also, he was one of the first gays to come out publicly in our culture, and because he was famous he made it all right for other ordinary people to come out. Sometimes the Naropa scene seemed a little icky to me, but no one was forcing me to be there. One night at a party at Allen's, I looked over to see him standing totally nude on his balcony having a conversation with someone. After a few seconds, I chuckled and realized, *Oh, that's just Allen.*

I wasn't sure what I could *do* for Allen. One woman sent a picture of herself in a chef's hat and offered to cook for him. He snatched her up right away. I decided to write a letter reminding him he had looked at my work and notebooks before, praised my work, encouraged me to write (He had indeed—that's when I had begun to take myself seriously as a writer), and now I wanted to be his apprentice. I offered to help type his notebooks. I knew he had copious notebooks full of journal writing, notations, and dreams; and now, because he was Allen Ginsberg, everything was important and needed to be typed and preserved. I also knew I wasn't much of a typist, but I didn't mention that.

When Allen interviewed me, he wasn't too enthusiastic. He said he had already selected several apprentices (all young boys and the cook, I found out later). He was a little unsure what to do with this 30ish woman. "I've talked to you before about your work." I nodded. "Oh, come along then," he said with his funny grin. So I was invited "in."

Allen always was interested in the content of my work. He thought the ideas and images were intriguing, but he was puzzled about my form. "You can't break a line like this. If someone asks for a line of Barbara Schmitz's poetry and they read one line of this, it would make no sense." I'd nod. I wrote a long poem about Bob's and my sexual relationship. I knew it was either extremely good or extremely bad. Allen loved the idea of it but ... "I don't know. It's just not working."

I bemoaned that mostly I wrote short poems.

"What's wrong with short poems? William Carlos Williams wrote short poems on his prescription pad. Emily Dickinson wrote short poems!"

He gave me an assignment I'm not sure I've fulfilled. Write a poem to make myself cry.

I learned to write an hour or two without stopping, to just write—not worry about spelling, punctuation—just get it flowing, get it out there. *Not to Censor*: You can always choose whom you show it to later, but censoring stops the flow and inhibits you from approaching certain material. People often remark about how honest my writing is. That honesty is the main teaching I received from Allen Ginsberg.

One day when I was coming out of class I was feeling particularly blue. Bob and I were separated for the summer; he was studying at the Gestalt Institute in Cleveland. Allen looked at me and said, "Come over for dinner." I wanted to take a bottle of wine and couldn't remember where exactly the Liquor Mart was so I wandered around for about forty-five minutes and was late. Allen said, "I was hungry so we started. Do you eat meat?"

I was a vegetarian then, but I said "Yes" before I realized it and soon had a huge hunk of steak on my plate with a baked potato. I took a couple bites of potato and sliced off a couple pieces of meat. As I was eyeing them, the doorbell rang and Peter Orlowsky led in a young man with long blond hair, wearing a white shirt and black pants. He had come to talk to Allen.

Allen motioned him to a chair. "Do you want to eat?" Allen asked. He shook his head. "Do you want wine?"

"Not until I drink the new wine," he answered. *Uh, oh. Here it comes,* I thought. And he began. He had come to preach to Allen.

Allen cut his steak, chewed, watched his guest politely, and interrupted his Gospel spiel here and there to ask a question or two. He was not belligerent or defensive about this attempt at conversion.

Then Gregory Corso barged in demanding to know when he was going to get paid. Allen said he didn't know; he would try to find out. Gregory proceeded to grab the salad bowl and consume the rest of the salad with his fingers. The Gospel young man seemed to have run out of steam. Allen asked him, "Anything else?" He shook his head no and bent to put on his shoes, and Anne Waldman flounced in wanting to know Allen's schedule and was he free on Sunday. Allen asked "Why?" a little gruffly.

"Because I want you to give a benefit reading with me for Marpa House" (the student Buddhist dormitory). At this point Allen began to yell. "I've got no time. No time to sleep. No time to screw. Somebody always wants something!" His face was flushed red.

"It's your own fault," she retorted. "You think you have to run everything. Your phone number's in the Boulder phone book for God's sake!"

Allen seemed spent from his explosion and hung his head. The New Wine man let himself out. "Thanks for dinner, Allen," I said quietly getting up to go. Even Gregory Corso set the salad bowl down and went out the door ahead of me. Allen's totally giving spirit and generosity often left him used up and exhausted.

I tried to type Allen's notebooks, but I didn't make much progress. Usually I worked on them late at night when I'd finished my other assignments and wasn't going to a Naropa party. But there was one page no matter how hard I tried I could not read. I had gotten pretty good at reading most scribbled handwriting from my years of teaching English. Finally, I had to give up. I took the notebook to Allen and pointed to the page.

"Oh that." He laughed.

"Yes!"

"Well ... I was stoned and riding in a rickshaw and writing with my left hand."

"Sounds like fun," I said, "but do you want to tell me what it says?"

"Oh, sure," he said cooperatively. He picked up the notebook, held it close, squinted at it, and read it off. He really did know what it said.

PART TWO: WITHOUT A MAP

One of the last times I went for an appointment when Allen was going to talk about my poetry, there was a note tacked to his apartment door.

> Barbara Schmitz
> Gone to Rocky Flats for arrest.
> I'll call you later.
> Allen

I smiled, nodded, and copped the note. I couldn't resist saving a little piece of history. That summer (1977) Allen and the other Beat poets (and whatever students cared to joined them) were protesting the moving of nuclear waste from Rocky Flats by train across Colorado. The plan was to have a sit-in with chanting and reading poetry on the train tracks when the train was coming so they could get arrested and supposedly create some news coverage about the situation. Again, because it was Allen Ginsberg, it did. Anyone who went to the event was supposed to receive training in nonviolent resistance first. The protest and arrest went smoothly as planned.

Allen had just happened to have stayed up all night the night before writing his "Plutonian Ode" which he proceeded to read in court.

O heavy heavy Element awakened I vocalize your consciousness to
  six worlds
I chant your absolute Vanity. Yeah monster of Anger birthed in fear
  O most
Ignorant matter ever created unnatural to Earth! Delusion of metal
  empires!
Destroyer of lying Scientists! Devourer of covetous Generals,
  Incinerator of Armies & Melter of Wars!
Judgment of judgments, Divine Wind over vengeful nations ...
...
I turn the Wheel of Mind on your three hundred tons!
...
My oratory advances of your vaunted Mystery!

(From *Collected Poems: 1947-1980*)

He claimed to have more files on the C.I.A. and F.B.I. than they had on him. One newsman said that anywhere anything was happening in the late sixties and early seventies Allen Ginsberg was there. I always tell my students that he was a fine example of a great American because he held America to her ideals.

One time at a party Michael McClure asked him who his apprentices were. I was sitting at the table with them. He rattled off all the names of the young men and forgot me. "Oh yoo-hoo, Allen, and me, remember?"

"Oh, yes," he said, "and Barbara Schwartz." Several times he introduced me as Barbara Schwartz. I thought that was okay. Maybe he was mixing me up with the poet Delmore Schwartz, who had a fine poetic reputation.

After another dinner with Allen and company, he suggested we all attend a showing of *The Last Waltz*, a movie about the The Band and the closing of the Fillmore West with music by The Band who backed Dylan in the sixties and seventies and many of the other rock stars who had performed there. So we trooped through the Boulder streets to the movie theater, a gang of "angel-headed hipsters" led by Allen in his white shirt. He still had his big beard then. He donated his salary back to Naropa, gave much of his money to a fund for young writers, bought his clothes at the Salvation Army, and as we approached the ticket booth, he asked, "Anybody need money?" I shook my head. Others put out their hands.

I ended up between Allen and his old-time lover, Peter Orlowsky, in the dark theater seats. Peter didn't recognize a single performer or group. With each change of artist, he'd lean across me and whisper in his loud voice, "Allen, Allen who's this?"

When Emmylou Harris sang in her sweet high voice in a long blue gown, Allen leaned across me over to Peter and said, "In this scene, Peter, men have to be men and women Madonnas."

Allen thought Lawrence Ferlinghetti in a high hat reciting a funny version of the Lord's Prayer was corny. And at the end, when Dylan had sung "Forever Young," and The Band was playing the "Last Waltz" with a couple waltzing across the empty Fillmore stage, Allen got tears in his eyes. Staring straight ahead, he said, "This makes me sad."

The writer Natalie Goldberg and I met in Allen's class. Years later, in 1997, she was driving across country. When she heard on the radio that he had died she pulled off the road and called me. We talked for a few minutes, sharing memories of Allen, and then she said Allen had written a small poem about the Buddha's passing that described his own going.

> LAND O'LAKES, WISC.
>
> Buddha died and
> left behind a
> big emptiness.

(From *Collected Poems: 1947-1980*)

My mind never knew what to do with Trungpa; he wouldn't slot into any category. I disapproved of much of the atmosphere surrounding him. There were drunken parties and much promiscuous sex which he was said to promote. If he fancied the wife of one of his followers, it was purported to be an honor for the follower to turn her over for Trungpa's pleasure. I'd heard of the incident with the poet W. S. Merwin and his wife reportedly being stripped and insulted at a seminar with Trungpa. On the other hand, I'd found his lectures mostly deep and profound, full of common sense and compassion.

At one lecture, he was so drunk that Ginsberg had to translate—not from the Tibetan but just trying to make Trungpa's babbling more comprehensible. Still, at that lecture he said something I always carry with me. He said in his small whispery voice that people's tears were precious pearls, and you didn't get to treat any human being like dirt.

I never did quite figure out what his "crazy wisdom" was all about, but it scared me: the alcohol, the sex, all of it seemed to be playing around with fire. Bob and I were fascinated by the potential sexual opportunities but were afraid of all the chaos and all the suffering. I decided Trungpa's scene was too high voltage and dangerous for me. I was grateful for the meditation, liked some of his teaching, but knew I needed to find a more appropriate teacher for me.

I had a hard time leaving Naropa. I felt so free there. I got attention. Men liked me. Women liked me. I was starting to write. I was having an adolescence: drinking, smoking marijuana. I had been so serious and so young when I married. I didn't want to go back to teaching, to boring Norfolk, but I did.

THE MILAREPA RANGERS

Always thought that I would be a Ranger
Knew I could make it if I tried,
...
And when I retire I'll write the gospels
And they'll all talk about me when I die ...

(To be sung to the tune of "Jesus Christ Superstar")

The Milarepa Rangers were a group of wild far-out friends who met every Memorial Day Weekend at Bob Johnson's Missouri River home for companionship, spiritual seeking, and partying. The companionship of these dear ones finally filled the spot for community left empty when I left the Catholic Church.

When we went to visit Adam at Naropa that first carnival summer, Dr. Johnson, speech instructor at Wayne, who had now become our good friend, went too. He visited relatives in Colorado, and then we all met up for a tour of the Glory Hole where gold was discovered in the 1890s. This was Dr. Bob's old territory; his father was a Colorado miner. We bought a pan and panned for gold at the Glory Hole stream, not finding anything but having a lot of fun swirling the water around and peering into the pan for anything that glittered in the sunlight. As we drove

Dr. Bob Johnson, Padma

through the mountains, we got intoxicated on the beauty of clear sky, aspens, peaks with still a little snow, crisp mountain air, and being together. As we drove past the Coors brewery, Bob in the backseat with me hollered, "If we were some sort of formal group we could have a tour with beer!"

I could almost see a light bulb materialize over Adam's head. He was taking Buddhist courses and was deeply into Tibetan mythology. Milarepa was one of the important saints. He meditated in a cave, ate Nettle Soup, and turned green.

Bob Johnson was living on the Missouri River in Ponca hanging out with the cowboy Boozer Gang, riding horses over the plains à la the Texas Rangers. So Adam combined the two images and arrived at the Milarepa Rangers, christening all of us right then and there with Tibetan names from the lineage. My name was Green Tara, the Compassionate Savioress, and Bob's, Tilopa, Naropa's teacher. Adam became Naropa and Dr. Bob, Padmasambhava, Milarepa's teacher. In the backseat, I started gonging on the gold pan with a stirrup and became the official gonger for the Milarepa Rangers. Thus, we proceeded down the mountain in fits of hysterical laughter and wild gonging, sans beer. (We never made it to Coors Brewery!)

We were famished, so we drove straight to Tico's in downtown Boulder. In the middle of the crowded restaurant, Bob Johnson rose and proposed a toast to the Milarepa Rangers in his most dramatic Shakespearian voice. It went like this: "To the Milarepa Rangers. Long may they ride. Far may they ride, and FAR OUT may they ride." Patrons of Tico's enjoyed it immensely, and the Milarepa Rangers were born.

Dr. Johnson, who had become Padma, decided that every Memorial Day weekend would become the Nettle Soup Festival at his home on the Missouri River in Ponca, Nebraska, which was soon christened the Sacred Toad Ashram. Padma says the ashram got its name because he awoke one morning after a night of partying on a sandbar on the river. He opened one eye and saw a toad staring at him. When the toad jumped into the river, Padma realized he also was a toad and jumped into the river. He further added that powdered toad skin applied to the back of the knee is a psychedelic.

Every Memorial Day "The Rangers" — you have to be initiated to belong — gather to camp and sing and pray and play for three days. Padmasambhava makes the nettle soup; the nettles are tender then. It is delicious; other ingredients like lentils and vegetables and spices are added. It tastes different every year. Padma says it makes you clairvoyant, and if you want to become a Ranger you must eat some. Usually, there are fish from the river. Everyone brings food to share — one person or two taking charge of a particular meal. There are various workshops, meditations, activities for children, and a prayer service on Sunday followed by a secret initiation ceremony—half serious and half in fun—whereby new Rangers are initiated. It involves being blindfolded, and includes imitation sounds of horses galloping as well as sacred chanting. It almost always rains. We get stuck in the mud. A couple of years we camped on the island across from Bob Johnson's property and had to be ferried across by motor boat—tents, food, people, dogs. One year the weather was so bad we ended up having to be ferried back again to the mainland for shelter.

One Nettle Soup Festival we stayed on the island the entire weekend. On Sunday morning, I decided to walk around the island when Sara, about five years old, asked if she could walk with me. "Yes," I said, "but I don't want to talk. You can walk with me if you can keep silent. Can you do that?" The tiny blond girl nodded, her pony tails bobbing. So we walked silently through nettles and dandelions, across the sand, hand in hand in silence. Sara stopped to pick up a rock, a wild flower—showing her treasures to me, but remembering not to talk.

Toward the end of our walk, I started to hear a song, sort of an Indian chant in my head. It was more like I collided with it as if it were in the air of the island from centuries before, hanging there from some ancient evening when Indians sang around fire on this island in the moonlight on a summer night. I kept repeating it in my head silently until I got back to my campsite and I could write it down in my notebook. I don't have musical training, and I can't really sing, so the music was lost to me, but I still have the words somewhere. I knew Bob Dylan said he plucks his songs out of the air.

Back at the camp, Sara looked up, let go my hand, said, "Thanks for the walk," and ran off to find her mom.

The Rangers grew and grew. Folks told other folks. Some people came for the weekend and then wanted to join. One Ranger went to South Dakota to the University and a whole group of her friends from there came and joined up. Anyone could come for the weekend, but if you wanted to become a Ranger you had to ask two Rangers. And we maintained there were two requirements:

you had to be spiritual, and you had to be a little crazy (after all, part of this business came out of Trungpa's Crazy Wisdom). It was a community of friends who gathered around Bob Johnson's sweet, wise, fun-loving spirit.

As long as I've known Bob Johnson, whenever anyone has called him on the telephone he always answers with a "Come right over, I'd love to see you." And he is often surrounded with all sorts of people, many of whom would have trouble fitting in in regular places. Padma is nonjudgmental—his love extends to everyone.

New Rangers had to be "novitiated," wear a string around their neck for a year or until it fell off, (sort of like Tibetan Buddhist strings given by Karmapa or the Dalai Lama), come back the next year for the secret initiation ceremony, eat Nettle Soup, and receive their Tibetan names. Once someone got pissed off, wrote a letter and said they didn't want to be a Ranger anymore. (The letter was quite a presentation—drenched in patchouli oil, stuffed with feathers and glitter.) We held a meeting and decided "once a Ranger always a Ranger"; you can't drop out, sorry, out of luck.

During this time, Adam, always the vanguard with New Age ideas and teachers, took Bob, me, and Dr. Bob to Lincoln to do yoga with Siri Chan, a Kundalini yoga teacher he had heard was there. We were startled that he was so young and that he had such electric blue eyes. His eyes were glowing blue fires as if someone had placed light bulbs behind them. He was dressed in traditional Sikh clothes—wrapped turban, flowing white shirt and pants—and immediately began to lead us through a yoga routine. The yoga was profound for me. At one point bending down in a prostrating pose, I felt as if all my worries and woes were being lifted away. He taught us the powerful "breath of fire," pumping air in with your stomach and exhaling strongly through your nose. Dr. Bob was coughing badly from bronchitis and smoking but had such a deep experience he quit smoking. Not only that. That yoga affected Padma so, he later went to Mt. Madonna in California to study yoga with Baba Hari Dass, began to practice yoga regularly and deeply, and became one of the few students to receive secret teachings from Hari Dass.

Hanuman Wall at Sacred Toad Ashram

In the late '70s, he broadcast a television show on yoga from the Wayne State television station. Adam continued to practice yoga and taught it in the park in Norfolk for the City Park and Recreation. I did yoga with Padma, Adam, and on my own for many years through the birth of my son in 1979. I even did a special section on Padma's TV series on yoga for pregnant women.

Baba Hari Dass gave Bob Johnson a Hindu yoga name as well, Raghubar Dass, and he became very interested in Hindu mythology and the story of Hanuman. In fact he became so intrigued he decided on top of a cliff at the Sacred Toad Ashram, up a winding path, to build the Temple of the Laughing Monkey to Hanuman, the Hindu god. It is a small rough-hewn octagon with stained glass windows laboriously made by Padma, representing the chakras, the energy points in the body that yoga attempts to awaken.

The temple sits atop a knob overlooking the Missouri River below, surrounded by elm and cottonwood trees that make a leafy green canopy for sunlight to filter through. One Ranger has built steel benches into an amphitheater in the hillside beside the temple.

Inside the temple is an altar with photographs of saintly figures, from his teacher Hari Dass to Jesus to John Lennon. People bring pictures and objects and leave them. There are candles, incense, and spider webs. And a carved sculpture of Hanuman from Borneo. Outside the low, arched door the inscription reads, "Enter the temple seeking nothing, and you will find bliss." And, of course, a gong. It's wonderful to climb the hillside path with the railroad tie steps and sit quietly inside. The energy in the temple is calm and sweet, much like the tiny temples of India.

The Rangers have waxed and waned like the moon. Some have come to the celebration for a year or two and then have gone on along their way. A few core members (many of them were Dr. Bob's students from college) have remained over the years and have become friends who visit him, the ashram, and each other several times a year.

The Nettle Soup Festival has become an approach-avoidance activity for me. I like having the community. I don't always approve of the drinking and partying that goes on at the Festival. I wanted the gathering to be more of a spiritual retreat. Many of the others desired something more like the Rainbow Gathering — the hippie gathering of the tribes. Some thought we could do both. As the Festival seemed to become more of a party in later years, I tended to stay away or go the last day for the morning prayer service on Sunday and the initiation of new Rangers.

I got tired of camping in the rain and the mud. Of pushing out stuck cars. Of cooking and cleaning up. Of not being able to sleep because it was noisy. Some of the Rangers got on my nerves.

I'm sure I got on some of their nerves. I wasn't sure I wanted marijuana smoking in the camp with children there even if it was discreet. Later when I met Pir Vilayat Khan, the head of the Sufi Order, he suggested I live in a commune—that it would be good for me to be around people I disapproved of. Seemed I was being offered this opportunity right in my own community and missing it.

Padma taught speech at Wayne State, was married to a Russian ballerina, and tried his hand at acting, dancing, and painting. He always envisioned having many fine arts performances at the temple—even had a beautiful stage and fire pit built outside. He has had enactments from the life of Hanuman, poetry readings, Indian ceremonies, flute concerts, fireworks, even a wedding, and would like to have more of these kinds of happenings.

As he has aged, Padma has asked that the Temple and land be left to the Rangers. We've had a couple of meetings, but we can't seem to get the group to agree or even to get the whole group together. Nothing is resolved. But in those early days the "Far-Out" Rangers did help assuage my longing for community I'd been looking for since I'd left the Catholic Church. I loved the outrageous antics, silly ceremonies, and deep friendships, but I didn't feel like I was doing any serious spiritual work. I still needed something more.

OLD MAN RIVER   (for Padma)

died in his room with his devotees
two tired old dogs and a cat who
liked to walk across his withered body
A view of his river
Moving always someplace else
out the window
Frozen garden and koi fish
sunk deeply alive in pond outside
Wooden eagle's eye steady
on the river

The temple he built to the monkey god
moved to sacred Indian land
His gaze now from a mountain top

in some other world
His laugh had split its sides
worn to bits from years of chuckling
at the absurdity
And in the end he dwelt in silence

He had been burned
His forehead pierced
All of his possession lost
and then more returned

His door and arms swung wide
not caring who the world said
you were Just loving who
you were with him

Jai Jai
    Old one
    Dear one
Honored father whom the monks
ministered to, did ceremony for
Who loved silly secret rituals
Made Nettle Soup and Borscht
Who loved his wicked horse Hot Pants

Who lived in the mountains
Loved the plains
Who did yoga
Had visions
Namaste Excelsior Hallelujah
Who acted in Shakespeare Sang
Pistol Packing Mama with New Guinea natives

Who married the Russian ballerina
Who danced and danced
until he could walk no more
then painted vivid thick goddesses,
landscapes and woodpeckers

Who desired to be Nothing

Friend, Guru
Who figured out how to stay,

to be, to die beside his river

Old Man   Old Man River
Moving   Moving on

TEA READINGS

The Catholic Church did manage to give me one last spiritual gift. My officemate at the community college had come across a nun painting what she called "psychic portraits" at the local mall (sort of an inner understanding of what she saw looking at you). After Sister Doris had done his portrait, my colleague invited her to teach a class at the college. Her "Managing Stress" class was added to the Continuing Education curriculum as he and I both signed up. She explained to my colleague the "Stress" title was only a disguise; the class was really about developing psychic abilities.

Doris taught us to count backward from ten to one to enter a trance state (similar to meditation), then to visualize a laboratory, with a male and female guide. We invented a ceremony with these guides and then were able to ask them questions. It is to this laboratory one goes to get the information to do their psychic work.

The class learned quickly from Sister Doris' lively, funny, easy explanations. Doris had her own natural psychic abilities and in addition incorporated techniques she had learned from Silva Mind Control. She revealed she often taught her elementary school students these meditation and psychic skills.

In her Advanced class participants arrived with the names of friends or relatives who were ill. We were asked to visualize what was wrong with the patient and then to imagine a cure for them. I was quite surprised when entering my laboratory with my given name to have my head snap backward. "There's something wrong with her throat," I said. And then, "Something in her gut." The contributor revealed my patient had something that kept her from swallowing correctly as well as intestinal problems. I never found out whether my visualized cure for her worked.

Sometime later I was visiting Bob Johnson at the Sacred Toad Ashram. At that time Padma's elderly parents were living with him. As I finished telling about Sister Doris' class, Padma remarked, "Now you can give tea readings!"

"Oh, I don't think so."

"Of course, you can," he insisted, carting his parents' tea cups over to me. So I swallowed, picked up each cup and counted down, entering my laboratory. I let a bunch of words stream out of my mouth. Both his mother and father insisted what I said was very accurate and even included images from their childhoods. We all sat quietly in amazement for a few minutes.

After this, I noticed the readings began to come as rhyming poems, pouring out almost faster than the receiver could write them down. I felt the person wanting a reading could either ask a question which would receive an answer or just receive a general reading. I would ask my guides to specifically address something for that person. I don't like rhyming poetry, so I had to get my ego out of the way and just let the images I saw turn into words and wash through me. I also began to add a disclaimer that I didn't know exactly what they were or how they worked, but if they were helpful that was great. They were often oracular, full of symbols. The recipient was often puzzled. "Put it aside for a while, look at it occasionally, and it might make more sense as time goes by," I'd suggest. Sometimes friends would let me know the reading did make sense later. I'd also advise that I wasn't sure about time—I didn't know if I was speaking about present, past, or future. Time in the transcendental is different and relative.

Later Shahabuddin assured me of the genuineness of the readings and strongly encouraged me to do them for others, sometimes sending someone to me for a reading.

PART THREE

Landing

FIRST SUFI CAMP

Our first exposure to the Sufis came with the movie *Sunseed*. A friend told us about this sampling of Eastern teachers who had come to the West and that it would be shown at the University in Omaha. Ever since we had been doing TM, Eastern teachers and meditation had been attracting us. Balthazar (this we learned later was his Sufi name), with a mass of brown curls and jokes and smiles, accompanied the movie and led a yoga workshop. This yoga, like the Kundalini experience before, was quite amazing. In the middle of prostrating in one posture I felt the weight of years of burdens being lifted from my body and wanted to weep with joy. I was flipped into an ecstatic state. My heart and body were weight-free.

While I was doing my TM practice in a friend's apartment, between yoga and the movie showing, a vision of a painting suddenly appeared which seemed to be a Picasso and definitely had a Cubist theme. I got to observe the work of art from an aerial view so I could contemplate it from every angle simultaneously. I was being given a private lesson on understanding Cubist art, "seeing it from every angle all at once." The drawing I made of it in my notebook resembled a diamond with its many facets reflecting light. (I later learned that the name Vajra had to do with diamond-like clarity.)

We were enthralled with all the teachers in *Sunseed*, but there was one — a teacher called Sufi Sam, Murshid Sam Lewis, not only a Sufi sheik but also a Zen roshi and an ordained rabbi — with whom I fell in love. He was cooking for his disciples and, as I remember it, using an egg recipe with precise measurements. In a moment of exuberance he said, "Oh, the hell with it ..." and threw all the rest of the ingredients into the bowl. At that moment I knew that whatever that person had I wanted. Balthazar reported that the Sufis were having a camp that summer in Woodstock.

Sufi Sam had passed on, but some of his students would be there. We would be welcome.

We had never really camped. My husband likes motels and comfortable beds. We bought a second-hand maroon Ford van that we christened Argonaut and decided we would journey (my husband more reluctantly than I) to Woodstock. Argonaut wasn't such a good vessel. It sputtered and lurched along until it finally broke down on the Ohio turnpike. We had to get towed! We eventually limped into Woodstock in the pouring rain. What's with Woodstock? Does it always rain there?

We drove up a muddy mountain. We had bought some camping gear—but we were first-time campers and envisioned that perhaps we could live out of our van. That would be a little uncomfortable but not too bad. We had a *tiny* pup tent—it was supposed to sleep two but just barely. It made no accommodation for stuff—clothes, toiletries, books, snacks. We peered out of our nice van at the registration man standing in the soaking rain. "Where's the camp?" we asked, looking around for a building or two. A mess hall? A latrine? A meeting hall? To our right through the rain stood several people on a wooden platform holding up some big beams. "They are just building the dome," intoned the person with the clipboard, gesturing with his chin toward that dismal scene. "Get your gear, and we'll drive your van to the parking lot."

"Can't we stay in it?" Bob pleaded.

Clipboard shook his rain-soaked head. "No room for vehicles. Get your gear."

"How are we supposed to put our tent up in the rain?"

Clipboard shrugged then brightened. "We'll give you a piece of plywood for the bottom. Help keep you dry."

"What about our stuff?"

Maybe he didn't hear. He didn't answer. "Camping's that way," he pointed and handed us a small piece of plywood.

We started to tie bags to our backpacks. I added a dishpan I'd thought to bring along for face and clothes washing. We loaded our arms and started to trek in the direction our guide pointed through the rocks and trees. In the steady rain all of our gear was quickly soaked. Stuff was banging against my back; my arms ached from everything I was carrying. I wondered why I was carrying it. Where was I going to put it? All around us was mud. Bob had gotten way ahead of me. I couldn't keep up, and suddenly my feet slipped out from under me. I went over backward like a turtle onto its shell and was stuck in the mud. I yelled loudly enough that Bob finally turned around, came back, and pulled me up. I'm sure it must have looked funny, but I wasn't able to laugh with him. I have to give myself credit for not crying, but I said quietly, "Let's not try to put our tent up. I'm not so sure I want to stay. This is miserable."

He nodded. He was glad I was the one who said it. Bob had mostly come here to please me.

We found a semi-dry patch of dirt under a tree, piled our stuff there, and went in search of anyone we might know at this camp. We found one friend from Omaha who'd been to Sufi camps before. She suggested we stay until Pir Vilayat, the head of the Sufi Order, arrived; we might feel better about the camp then. We agreed to wait.

A couple hours later a shiny car with Pir in the backseat drove up the muddy road. We were standing on the side, trying to get a peek at this saintly man to gain some comfort, some clue perhaps about what we should do. He looked peaceful in the glimpse we got of him, but it was still raining. We turned to each other, walked to our gear, and asked to be taken to our van. We decided we weren't ready to stay this time, in the rain.

Getting warm and dry later at the Howard Johnson's in town that song with the Biblical verse came to me, "Turn, Turn … to everything there's a season. / A time to sow. A time to reap / A time for every purpose under Heaven." I knew our time for the Sufis would come. I just hoped the next time it wouldn't be raining.

LAMA MOUNTAIN

Naropa got me started on my writing practice, and I began doing Buddhist sitting occasionally after sitting in class with Ginsberg and doing his sitting assignments; but Trungpa's community and his style weren't exactly right. As with the Milarepa Rangers an element was missing. The Sufis were a fork in the journey happening concurrently with the Buddhist scene in Boulder. The first summer on our way to study at Naropa, we decided to attend a week-long Sufi camp at Lama Mountain in New Mexico. There's something about Lama that makes you feel homesick—a great lonesomeness on that mountain looking down on the Rio Grande winding its way far below. The breathtaking majesty and beauty of the New Mexican barren terrain and immense sky makes you feel small and in need of comfort. Happily for us, the Lama staff decided we could camp in Argonaut. We took solace being surrounded by the walls of our van with our books, clothes, and extra food stuffed underneath the platform Bob had built for us to sleep on, although one smartass woman in Boulder described it as "a French whore house" because the carpet and paneling were red.

Lama is beautiful—the main meditation hall is a spacious dome with a star skylight and gorgeous hardwood floors. In the famous two-storied Lama kitchen the "Big Mamas" of Lama cooked us scrumptious vegetarian meals. One of the most coveted Karma yoga chores is to get to work along side the Lama Mountain cooks in their heavenly kitchen preparing a meal with food mainly from the garden. Hundreds of ash, aspens, and various evergreens cover the mountain top. Campers wind their way along small paths through meadows of wild flowers to the outdoor meeting places. Facilities include a tiled communal shower and sauna, various retreat huts, and a whole separate study center for people who come on scholarly pursuits. Tucked away is a Lamasery, a small store that sells Lama-made jewelry, prayer flags, books, and even chocolate bars if you are dying for a sugar fix.

PART THREE: LANDING

Lama was founded in the sixties as a spiritual retreat where seekers could go to be instructed by teachers of all religions. Ram Dass was one of the original teachers and founders. His now legendary book, *Be Here Now*, which inspired so many in the early seventies, was printed by the Lama Foundation.

Everything about the setting and the format of the camp was ideal. Pir Vilayat dressed very elegantly and formally in rich white, cream, or brown robes which accented his silvery hair and beard and creamy tan skin. He was the archetype of a gentle, sweet, and saintly leader. I often imagined that being in the presence of Jesus must have been like being with Pir. A feeling of fierce strength also emanated from his being; I knew he would take on the Devil if he needed to. I was surprised that my inadequacies were called forth in Pir's presence. "Oh, my, Pir Vilayat! I am not worthy." I felt akin to the woman in the Bible who stated that she was only worthy to touch the hem of Jesus' garment but knew that would be enough to cure her. I never exactly felt like I'd sit down in a bar and buy Pir a drink.

Before we'd left home I had a disturbing dream that continued to haunt me. I dreamed there was a baby sleeping in our attic, and a large bunch of people were trying to come into our house and up the attic stairs. I kept warning them to stay back and said if they started to come up the stairs I would kill the baby. I awoke very upset. Would I even consider doing something like that?

From the first day I felt strange. *All these people here are good people except me. They don't know how bad I really am inside. If they only could see me truly, they'd be horrified.* (Perhaps an extreme version of transactional analysis — "You're okay, I'm not okay.") I now know this is a quite common occurrence for beginners on the spiritual path — the "freak-out" at the first retreat, but no one told me then!

As the week went on things got worse. After meals, volunteers would be requested for cleanup and other jobs. I'd want to raise my hand to help, but it just wouldn't go up. I didn't volunteer to help with anything. What was the matter with me? Of course, I was doing the Karmic yoga duties I had officially signed up for:

work in the kitchen and child care. I hurried to the front of the line when it was time to eat so I could get my food first. All the time I was watching myself act this way and was appalled.

I started to go to our van by myself more and more, even to skip a lecture or two—to use the shower then because I knew nobody would be there. One night I asked Bob to bring me some food back from the table. He had asked me before what was wrong, but I wasn't able to tell him, so he had shrugged and hugged me. This time my melancholia seemed to flip him into a fit of ecstasy. "Oh! You are so silly!" he laughed. And then he laughed some more and went off to the dinner table swinging our camping dishes over his head. Of course, this made me mad and even more sad. Ever had someone tell you to just cheer up? My confidence had shrunk completely away.

One of the first nights at dinner I heard one of the campers telling a friend about his journey to see the Dalai Lama. He explained that the whole trip really wasn't ultimately about seeing the Dalai Lama, asking him a question, and getting an answer; it was about the changes he went through on the journey to get to the Dalai Lama. The first day of the retreat I had signed up to have a private session with Pir Vilayat. From what I understood you were supposed to have a question ready to ask the teacher when you had your session. I was worried. I couldn't think of a question. I couldn't think how to ask about what was troubling me. What was I going to do? I couldn't just sit there like an ignoramus in front of this great man. Maybe I would be able to think of something as the week went on. My appointment was on the last day. *Maybe I could just ask him about my dream. No! that would be stupid!*

On Friday morning Pir was coming to lead us to the Maqbara, the Tomb of Sufi Sam, on top of Lama Mountain. We were to have our last morning meditation there. His white robes were shining in the morning sun. He proceeded up the mountain, but I ran out of breath. I had to stop. I was disgusted with myself. I was a young woman; he was an old man. How could he just walk up the mountain like that? I didn't know Pir very well then and didn't remember that he lived part of the year in the Swiss Alps where he was a mountaineer. I was from the flatlands of Nebraska.

PART THREE: LANDING

By the time I got to the meditation site, Pir was already seated crossed-legged in front of his followers, his face slightly tilted toward the sun, looking as if it were being bathed in bliss. The campers were sitting before him with similar looks on their faces, and Pir was saying, "On this last morning of the retreat we are in ecstasy." I gulped and sat down. I wanted either to run screaming from the mountain or rush at him and yell, "Ecstasy? I don't know what the fuck you're talking about. I'm in pain. Pain. Can't you see?" But I sat. And sat.

Finally, Pir said it was time to file past Murshid Sam's grave. I was somewhere in the middle of the line. I noticed people were touching their heads to a stone at the foot of the grave, then moving up to the headstone to say a short prayer. None of them took very long. I wasn't particularly thinking or feeling anything; but suddenly, when I knelt at the foot of Sam's grave, all the week's sorrow, all my life's sorrow it seemed, welled up in me, and a spontaneous plea flew from my heart. *Help me! I'm out here all alone!*

Immediately I felt myself enveloped in big, soft arms, hugging me, holding me like one holds an infant, with as much tender love and complete acceptance as can be mustered. I could almost hear the words, "It's all right!" It seemed as if I were in this posture a long time, but when I stood up no one looked impatient or as if I had overstayed my turn.

Everything appeared slightly transformed as I descended the mountain. The campers seemed friendlier. The man beside me was grinning. "Did you get initiated?" I asked. When one decides to become a Sufi formally, she picks a teacher and asks for initiation into the Sufi Order. At this time the seeker is often given a name. This was a big marker I wasn't sure I was ready for. I didn't know much about initiation then. It's not like converting or joining a religion where you stand up, declare your intention, get baptized, and are welcomed into the church. Not so black and white, initiation is a subtle opening of the heart, a tiny step in the direction the soul needs to go.

The fellow camper smiled and answered, "Yeah, I guess I did," and I realized he also just had a spontaneous experience. A spark had kindled, a small heart-opening had occurred.

It was lunch time and after that I would have my session with Pir Vilayat. After lunch without thinking I jumped up and began washing dishes and then remembered to ask the time. I handed the dish to the woman next to me. "I've got to go." She smiled.

I followed the path through the trees to where Pir Vilayat sat. His young beautiful wife, Taj, sat beside him. (I didn't know until later he also had another older wife, but that's another story.) He nodded. I nodded. I sat.

"Oh!" I suddenly remembered. I was supposed to ask a question.

Instead of a question out of my mouth came, "I'm lonely."

Pir looked sad and said, "I'm lonely too. You know a spiritual teacher is very lonely." I nodded.

Pir asked what I did for a living.

"Teacher."

He nodded again. He suggested living in a commune maybe with some people I disapproved of. He gave me some spiritual practices, mantras, to practice. I breathed a big sigh. So did he.

I went through the trees looking for Bob. I felt light. The sadness was gone.

Help had come on top of the shimmering mountain with the Rio Grande snaking its way through the misty canyon far below. We packed up the van and went down. On to Boulder, Naropa, Chögyam Trungpa, and the Buddhists.

While we were attending Naropa, we sometimes attended Sufi dancing on Sundays. There was an active Sufi community in Boulder. The dances were inspired by Murshid Samuel Lewis whose arms had reached out to me on top of Lama mountain and who had been a mureed of Hazrat Inayat Khan, founder of the Sufi Order of the West and Pir Vilayat's father. The story I was told was that "Sufi Sam," as he came to be known, had a vision in the seventies in which he was directed to teach the hippies. Sam was a feisty guy with a mind of his own, and reportedly he spoke back and said he didn't even like the hippies. Nevertheless, he was told, that was his assignment. So he began his weekly classes for the flower children of San Francisco.

About the same time, he began receiving visions of "the dances," meditative movements to prayers and sacred songs from all the world's religions (somewhat akin to spiritual square dancing) which he taught to his young students. The "Sufi Dances," now known as Dances of Universal Peace, have been conducted for over thirty years in many parts of the worlds. They are often a first introduction for people to the Sufi path and are a very high form of movement, blending words and melodies from every spiritual tradition.

Sufi dancing offered me my first opportunity to look deeply into another's eyes and see this being beyond a personal level. To take each person's hand, to sing to each, even though I was afraid to sing, and the nuns told me I'd *never* be able to carry a tune. To look deeply into each open flower face and to sing anyway, and then pass on to the next glowing unfolding being and the next. To do this with each one; all of them, the same. My husband no more special than anyone else. All of them, the Beloved. *Ishq Allah, Mabud Lillah.* God is love. Lover. Beloved.

We would leave this dancing very high every Sunday ... and not from drugs; but it hadn't occurred to us it was a path, our possible path.

The writer, Elizabeth Gilbert, recalling her journey of healing and growth includes food, romance, and finding a spiritual teacher. Speaking to her reader in *Eat, Pray, Love,* she says,

> Your job then, should you choose to accept it, is to keep searching for the metaphors, rituals, and teachers that will help you move ever closer to divinity. The Yogic scriptures say that God responds to the sacred prayers and efforts of human beings in any way whatsoever that mortals choose to worship—just so long as those prayers are sincere. As one line from the *Upanishads* suggests: "People follow different paths, straight or crooked, according to their temperament, depending on which they consider best, or most appropriate—and all reach You, just as rivers enter the ocean."

Shortly after the encounters with Pir and Ginsberg I began reading and teaching Carlos Castaneda, the rage among young people in the early seventies. Castaneda, an anthropology student from UCLA, had found and studied with a Yaqui medicine man. *The Teachings of Don Juan* was the first of a series of books full of esoteric instruction. Don Juan, who lived in Arizona and Mexico (though newsmen tried unsuccessfully to ferret him out), had taken Castaneda, a white, middle-class, intellectual for his apprentice; and because Castaneda was slow and stubborn, Don Juan finally had to blow open his perception by using psychedelic plants. As might be imagined, the series was well received by the counterculture. An abundance of teachings about consciousness and spirituality could be found in these books in an amusing, unique, and palatable form.

Carlos often played the skeptical buffoon to Don Juan's fierce magical instruction. For example, after ingesting psychedelics and experiencing himself as a bird, he asks Don Juan repeatedly, "… but was I *really* a bird, Don Juan?" Not able to believe his own transcendent experience he kept after Don Juan to confirm its reality. My whiny self could identify with this dilemma. Despite mystical occurrences my mind would persist with, Yes, but I want to KNOW GOD.

The indelible teaching from the series for me was Don Juan's insistence that Carlos must find "a Path with Heart."

Without even being quite aware of it happening, these Sufis with their acceptance of all prophets and all religions were seeping a little at a time into *our* hearts, cracking them open without the full knowledge of it dawning on our souls. We were busy going about our lives, thinking we were still looking.

I don't remember very much about the first time I met Shahabuddin Less. Jan Potter, a sociology teacher from Blair, Nebraska, who had been at the Woodstock Camp, had become his student and brought him to Omaha for a lecture. She had made the strange and funny arrangement of renting a room at a bank for the evening event. I believe that was the first time I saw him, but my memory of the encounter is very foggy — no lightning flashes! I can't recall the topic or any particular exchange. It took a while for Shahabuddin's energy to penetrate through my thickness. As Chalice (Jan's Sufi name) said when she saw me after my first trip to India, I came back then without a lot of my "baggage." It seemed I had several layers to peel away until my vision got clear enough to see who Shahabuddin was.

Chalice brought Pir Vilayat to Omaha. After his lecture in a Unitarian church, anyone who wished could see him individually. Out of the whole van full of friends we had driven as usual to the event, only Bob and I asked for a private audience.

Pir asked if I was doing any other practices or working with any other teacher.

I said I was doing Transcendental Meditation.

He replied quickly, "I don't want to interfere with that."

"Oh, this wouldn't," I said, shaking my head, wanting to make a commitment to him, to the Sufi Order. I had wanted to ask for initiation at Lama Mountain, but it had taken me too long to work through my negativity. I wasn't sure what initiation entailed exactly but later read that Hazrat Inayat Khan said, "Initiation is like shooting an arrow at a point one cannot see; one only knows one is going into action ... a person may have to take a step off in an opposite direction."

Pir, in a gorgeous, white robe, took my hands, looked deeply into my eyes with his brown loving ones, and called the line of saints and prophets to ask for my protection and illumination. I didn't realize until later that this ordinary encounter was an initiation.

Our hungry friends were waiting in the van and wanted to stop to eat on the way home. I wasn't hungry. I sort of sailed above the talk and activity. They even ordered sundaes with chocolate syrup. Kathy was laughing loudly. Someone besides

Bob did the driving home. The Grateful Dead blared loudly from the van speakers. I felt quiet and content.

BABY?

My gynecologist in California in 1970 looked like Rock Hudson and asked me among other questions if I'd had anal intercourse. It took me a few seconds to focus on him saying he asked all his patients such questions so they would feel comfortable asking him anything. I wanted to know when someone would know when she wanted to have a child. He looked directly into my eyes with his deep dark ones and said, "Oh, you'll just know."

This answer threw me because there was always that clear knowing inside me about almost everything that I lived my life by, and he had been so adamant about this issue. I kept waiting for the gong to gong or the buzzer to go off announcing, *Okay! Now's the time for you to have a baby!* It didn't happen.

The years went by. We moved to Nebraska. I taught English at Northeast, attended Naropa, started writing seriously, and had some introduction to Sufi practices. I finally began polling my friends and family who had children—and eventually people I knew even casually—asking them why they had chosen to have children. I began to ask people who didn't have children why they had chosen *not* to have them.

The more I thought about it, however, the more confusing the dilemma became. This was a problem that seemed unsolvable with my head.

Bob and I loved the freedom of lifestyle offered by being able to take off as soon as school was out in the spring, attending Naropa in summers, and traveling to places like Taos and New York. We didn't think a child fit so easily into how we traveled, often sleeping in our car in odd places. We didn't make a great deal of money in our community college jobs; but with no family to support, it hadn't been an issue. I was just developing as a writer and struggling to find time for my writing career along with teaching. I also felt trepidation about my parenting skills. I hadn't grown up around any little children. I was the baby in my family and had few younger cousins or kids in my neighborhood. Neither of us felt like something was missing in our lives.

I kept asking Bob why people had children, trying to puzzle it all out when suddenly he announced at our ages of thirty-six and forty that he had decided that we *should* have a child. I was surprised. He had decided, he said, that we had the resources to share with at least one other being. We had the love, we had the finances, and the comfort. So we had the responsibility to share and give something back, to pass some of this along.

Bob's pronouncement made sense; but, I still didn't have the feeling I'd been waiting for that my gynecologist had assured me I would have. No matter. Sometimes you just plunge ahead and take a chance.

We had read some recently published research about determining the sex of your child. If you wished for a boy, have sex immediately after the egg is released because the male sperm can get to the egg faster or some such thing. Bob suggested we try for a boy. So one sweet afternoon in March in 1979 shortly before St. Patrick's Day, Bob was reading in the waterbed, and I was reading just beside it. I've always been able to feel the egg release from my left ovary. It's a sharp painful twinge. "Ouch!" I exclaimed.

"What?" asked Bob.

I thought, *Do I really want to do this? I'm going to get pregnant?* "Move over," I said, "We're going to make love."

Bob says he remembers calling a being from the ether. He did practices more informally than me but always seemed to have the right one at the right moment. *Ya Alim* (the one who knows the innermost heart of all creation) he called out to a soul to come as we made love in the spring sunlight with a slight breeze through the open upstairs window.

PATH OF LIGHTNING

TAKING A CHANCE

I hold the unknown in a blue blanket
up to the car window as we drive down
main street with our newborn
                        firstborn.

"Look," I say, although *they* say
a baby cannot see.
Already I know the books are useless.
He stared deeply into his father's eyes
as he floated him in warm water
and smiled when I kissed him on the cheek.
"This is your hometown," I say,
speaking to him the same as I have
all along from conception —
the afternoon I felt the egg release
and dove anyway into the bed
tossing my hands, fate, and my legs
                        in the air.

I didn't know for sure then.
How do you ever know?
Walking up the wedding aisle,
my head slid open and grace
poured in and not until then
did I know
it was right I should marry
this man   now
now.

But, this child will take some time.
I'm holding him up high to the window
cooing
because beneath him slowly
but surely I am sinking.

(From *How to Get Out of the Body*)

The next weekend Bob was finishing up some of his Gestalt training in Cleveland and had gone to the St. Patrick's Day parade with a friend there. An artist friend had stopped to see

96

me in Norfolk—an artist who was always complaining about his lot in life and how hard his life was. For some reason he brought up kids and said, "Whatever you do, don't have kids! Your life will never be your own again. You'll never be able to work. You'll have to take care of them twenty-four hours a day. You'll never be able to get anything done!"

I set the coffee mug I was carrying down on the kitchen counter, turned around and said, "It's too late. I'm pregnant." Knowing it for the first time as I said it, feeling a little worried, but not too much.

Bob called later that night and told me about the parade and then asked how things were at home. "Oh," I said. "I'm pregnant."

"How do you know?" he asked.

"Just do," I said. And I did and I was.

Having a child turned out to be one of the best decisions we ever made. Writer friend, Natalie Goldberg (who oddly has no children) says, "It's joining the human race." Having Eli opened my heart. When I first laid eyes on him I was puzzled. I didn't recognize this person. I didn't know who he was. I had talked to him inside my womb all through pregnancy. I had even called him Eli early on. There was a short period where Bob's father had announced he didn't like that name so I thought, *Well, we can't call him that if his grandfather doesn't like it*; but, right after his birth, holding him in my arms looking into his eyes I had announced, "This is Eli."

"What's his name?" asked Sister Salasia, the fabulous angel nun who had seen me through the drug-free Leboyer birth.

"Eli Jacob," I stated proudly.

She wrote out his full name and slapped it on his clear plastic bassinet which stayed in my room with me, a first in the Norfolk hospital, one of the many firsts I had insisted on: no internal fetal monitor, the Leboyer birth (floating him immediately after cutting the cord in warm water), baby rooming-in. I also was the first to use the birthing chair. The hospital was all-a-flutter awaiting the person with all these demands.

97

Slowly we bonded. Breast feeding was easy and lovely. No bottles, no formula, no fussing, just carry the kid along. Don't pay attention to the doctor who says only feed him every three hours. Don't pay attention to most everybody except the three of you.

Eli talked to me quite clearly the day of his baptism at two months. "Where's Dad?"

I answered, "He went to the drug store."

Eli said, "Oh," and commenced breast feeding before I, astonished, thought, *He couldn't have said that!* And then he didn't talk again for two years.

We lived in a blur of bliss, breast feeding and snuggling and cuddling like cave dwellers in love and primordial huddle; me unhappy only about forgetting my dreams, from being awakened so much for night feeding. Days and nights drifted past, Eli in our bed most of the time. I fretted some I wasn't writing very much, wasn't sending manuscripts out, but "down I forgot as up he grew" (e.e. cummings). Writing became secondary to the intense joy and labor of raising a small child.

SUFI CAMP AGAIN

We drove across country again, this time in a not-very-reliable Topaz. The car should have been reliable; we'd only had it a short time. It had been a showroom model and was about a year old when we bought it. Bob couldn't resist the Topaz because it was cute and red, but it turned out the transmission was going out.

The Sufis own land with buildings (!) in upstate New York. We had a building to sleep in, plus a kitchen and meeting facilities. This was a week-long retreat, and by this time we had a four-year-old child. We were accompanied on this trip by our son, Eli. He liked the idea of the camp; and although he was sometimes reluctant to go off in strange places with people he didn't know, he took to the various camp activities and seemed happy enough to be with the other kids for parts of the day so Bob and I could attend lectures and classes.

PART THREE: LANDING

Shahabuddin Teaching

Shahabuddin was teaching; he was the main attraction for us. He had come to Omaha several more times, and we had attended his seminars. We were drawn by his wisdom — a deep knowledge of not only Sufism, but also Buddhism, Judaism, and cultures and spirituality of many peoples of the world. He was warm, funny, and kind, even though he had the appearance and spirit of a fierce warrior. Shahabuddin is not regularly handsome. His hairline is receding, his nose is largish; but his intense dark eyes penetrate into your heart from his radiant high-cheek-boned face spread with his joyous, mischievous smile. He will gaze into his mureeds' eyes for a long time not turning away. He is a most beautiful human being. And I could now recognize his affectionate, intelligent voice anywhere.

When he smiles at you, it's a loving, compassionate mother smile, unconditional love. He is utterly pleased with you just the way you are. I loved looking at his face, listening to his voice.

Ziraat was also supposed to be a part of this camp, an aspect of the Sufi Order we had heard about. Its metaphor had to do with farming, but we had not had a chance to learn about it yet.

Shahabuddin led Sohbet, spiritual discourse with teachings, stories, answering questions in the mornings and afternoons. Bob and I were both delighted to be in his company, soaking up his presence, taking in the teaching. Often with Shahabuddin I would be deeply inspired with his words and then walk away and in a few moments be unable to remember any content of the talk. After a while I stopped being distressed by this forgetting and just enjoyed being with him. One of the teachings of Sufism is that much is given in this tradition by "transmission," by just being in the teacher's presence.

The only obstacle to my family's happiness was the food. I'd been a vegetarian since before Eli had been born but was having to make concessions to my finicky young one's tastes at home. I was in Heaven with the vegetarian health food meals here. Bob was having trouble with all the lentils — they gave him gas. And Eli! Eli didn't recognize most of it, didn't like the look and smell of it, and simply refused to eat it. That would have been okay for a day or two, but his refusal to eat went on for three days until he was a screaming beastie. We had cereal and a little milk (in the dwindling ice of the cooler), but that was soon gone, and I had a starving child.

People had gossiped around camp about staying out of the kitchen when Mirabai was cooking. Mirabai was a great, rotund cook but did not like the order or her command of her kitchen disturbed. Desperate, I timidly cracked open the door and shuffled into the fragrant room, imploring as I slid toward this immovable presence with hands on her hips, "Excuse me, Mirabai, I know you don't like people in your kitchen, but I have a child who doesn't recognize this food and hasn't eaten and is a mess, and I was wondering if you might have something he might recognize."

She looked around the kitchen, grinned, said in a deep voice, "How about a banana?" and stuck it out toward me like a lance.

Eli didn't particularly like bananas, but I decided not to bring that up and grabbed it. "Do you think you might add a kid-friendly item to the dinner menu?" I grew bold enough to ask. She *was* smiling.

"Does he like macaroni and cheese?" asked the same deep voice.

"That would do it." I bowed, hung on to my banana, and skedaddled from Mirabai's kitchen unscathed.

Eli gobbled the banana.

That afternoon we were supposed to go into the sweat lodge. Sweat lodges (a Native American spiritual tradition) are dome-like frames completely covered with tarps or blankets to prevent any light from entering and to prevent any of the steam heat from the extremely hot rocks from escaping. We were made to understand that this sweat was to be especially hot and was *not* mandatory.

The ceremony would consist of several rounds after entering, beginning with sitting in silent darkness, then praying out loud, bringing in more and more stones to intensify the heat and purification, and finally emerging into the light. We were free to decline reentry if we became too uncomfortable. I'd done sweats before and knew the intensity was not just in the heat from the rocks but also from the emotional intensity of everyone's outpouring of prayer and petitions, which become so overpowering you feel you cannot stay one second more and will need to bolt out of the heat and dark into the air and light. I also knew that if I'd make myself stay past that moment, usually the next moment or two would be when the leader would open the flap and lead us outside.

I decided to do the sweat, and Shahabuddin decided we first should let the kids try if they wanted. They could leave whenever they wanted — only one heated rock was brought into the center pit and the flap of the lodge door remained opened. Eli said he wanted to leave, and then so did all the other kids. "That's fine,"

Shahabuddin said. "They tried it." He added that usually the most sensitive have to leave first.

After the children left, we entered stooping and crawling through the low lodge opening, moving to the left, praying out loud to "All My Relation" ("Mitakuye Oyasin") — not just humans but everything alive. The white hot rocks were added one at a time. Traditional sage was used to slap the stones, and a sweet acrid smell permeated the dark dome. Because the sweat lodge was properly built, no light prevailed in the total darkness — just heat, smoke, sweat, and sage scent.

After a short period of silence, the prayers began to arise from our hearts. Everyone prayed aloud in turn for those most in need, extremely ill relatives, friends in desperate places. Some prayed for the world situation. One woman threw her pack of cigarettes into the fire pit. Not only was the heat searing and almost unbearably hot, but so were all the predicaments of those being prayed for. Scorching intensity! ("All pain and prayer ..." Black Elk.) The prayers became more fervent, more rocks were added to the pit, sparks flew higher.

The sweat lodge was crammed full of petitioners. I was squashed into the front row with one leg partially hanging over the pit with white hot rocks. Embers flew up and lit on my knees biting into my skin. My mouth and eyes were full of smoke and heat. I couldn't breathe. My skin was burning. Pouring sweat. Pouring prayers. Melting bodies. Melting hearts. I'd never make it to the end. I'd have to go outside.

Then Shahabuddin said, "Now we'll open the door. I want you to go outside and lie on the ground. (It was raining now outside!) Then open your eyes and look up and you will see an angel."

Oh sure, I thought, moving as quickly as I could to the door. It was the first time I didn't mind being rained on, lying on the ground with hardly any clothes on. *I'm supposed to see an angel,* I remembered. I looked up to a tree branch above me. There she was! In a light blue loose gown sitting on the branch of the tree with her back against the trunk. She had brown curly hair, had her legs crossed, her chin in her hand and was looking out over the valley. *I guess that's where angels* would *be*, I thought, on tree branches. Shahabuddin called us back to the lodge for one more round of prayer.

Someone asked me later if we compared angels. "No," I said, rather surprised. I didn't think of it. I just remember walking back with Shahabuddin and being really excited that Mirabai was making macaroni and cheese for the kids for supper. She even made mashed potatoes.

We did get initiated into Ziraat at the camp. Murshid Hazrat Inayat Khan who founded the Sufi Order says of Initiation that it is taking a step forward — taking a leap of faith which facilitates the students' unfoldment and assists them in meeting life's challenges. (Many different initiations are possible for Sufis. There are different aspects of the Sufi Order, like Ziraat, the Brotherhood, and others that mureeds can belong to if they wish.) Ziraat is a branch of the Order using the metaphor and images of farming — everything in the mind has to be "plowed under" — the good and the bad so the earth is turned over, fresh and ready for new seeds to be planted.

Symbolically much of what is being plowed up in the mureed (student) is negative qualities like prejudice, antagonism, and jealousy which are obstacles to spiritual growth. Guides emphasize that *everything* not just the negative must be turned over by the plow so that no impediments remain to prevent positive attributes from sprouting.

There is a very short ceremony which is enacted in Ziraat which consists of a dialogue between the initiate and the Great Farmer discussing the Farmer's work: ploughing, planting, sowing, and reaping. All of this is metaphor for spiritual work. In the address of the Great Farmer it is said that "the soul is working out its perfection to express itself in humanity."

Mureeds interested in Ziraat may be drawn to work for the ecology of the planet as well as work spiritually on themselves. We received the braided rope of Plow Persons — the first stage in the process. The stages go from Sower to Reaper to Farmer.

The children watched the Initiation; they could be initiated if they wanted. I wished deeply for Eli to choose initiation but did not push or encourage. I wanted him to take a step into this spiritual bounty and receive the blessings I was feeling, but I decided it must be his choice. He didn't ask for it, although two other children did. I heard one child explaining it to another. "What does it mean?" "It means you'll always come back." *How wonderful.* They had captured the essence of the whole camp, of Sufism, in their own words, at their own level of understanding. I think they meant they'd always come back to the camp, but I chose to think they meant also to this blissful time together in "this home of our souls."

The mechanics of the Topaz did not work well on the way home either, and we were not comfortable driving through the dense trees of forested New York and the East. We couldn't seem to see above us and get a view of sky. We breathed more easily as we drove haltingly toward the Mississippi and the big blue Midwestern horizon, praying the car was going to make it. Although the transmission went out, it was still under warranty, and the Ford Company replaced it when we got safely home. Our spiritual transmission was working well.

INDIA

Shortly after the New York camp, I attended the workshop where I told Shahabuddin I couldn't find a good teacher in my small town, and he made the remark about getting a bad one. Even though I had been shocked by his remark and puzzled, I was very drawn to him and the Sufi teaching, and I continued to attend his seminars and retreats every time he was offering something close by. He continually advertised his tours to exotic sacred places: India, Bali, Turkey, Nepal; and he told enchanting stories about the trips and travelers. Not imagining I'd anytime soon have the money to make such a pilgrimage, I'd sigh and daydream about doing it *someday.*

PART THREE: LANDING

Somehow, all of a sudden it seemed, in the mid-eighties, it felt like "my time." Shahabuddin was advertising a trip to India. We were going to buy new living room carpet and, Boy! did we need it! Our pukey green, fifties, shag carpet was worn-thin and looked horrible; but Bob said we had lived with it all this time, so if that's what I wanted, I should go on the trip. It seemed as though I'd always wanted to go to India; it had been the thing to do for the flower children in the sixties and early seventies. I had been listening to Shahabuddin say in his seminars that for Sufis, sooner or later "pilgrimage" is assigned. I was going on mine.

However, I should have never *said* it was going to be my pilgrimage. The universe conspired to make the trip as difficult as possible as soon as I announced that intention. Kothrenada, Shahabuddin's wife, called to tell me the trip was so tiny, all women, that Shahabuddin wasn't going. "Did I still want to go?"

I was very disappointed Shahabuddin wasn't going; I had dreamed of traveling in India with him after hearing his stories of saints and mystics in his seminars. I was nervous and scared—I was leaving my husband and young son at home, and now I would be traveling with total strangers, but I was determined. I was going on my pilgrimage.

It wasn't until I had been home for a few weeks that I realized *had* found what I was looking for on this journey.

The way the trip started should have alerted me to its coming difficulties. Our flight out of Chicago was delayed six hours because of mechanical difficulties. Kothrenada had suggested meeting me in Chicago so I wouldn't have to fly alone, and I was very glad to have her company over the long wait. I become extremely anxious in airports about missing flights, finding gates, getting lost. I felt protected and secure with Kothrenada; and although we are both quiet people and both more so without our mates, we got to know each other over a nice dinner provided by the airlines as we sat in O'Hare International Airport for hours. I was especially glad she was there since we also missed our connecting flight in Germany, and she had to confront airline personnel when they were about to send our luggage on without us. Kothrenada proved to be a knowledgeable and savvy guide in many ways, brave enough to exchange money on the Black Market for us. I believe she brought a videotape machine into the country for the family we stayed with (very against customs rules: India wanted to develop its own technology), but she only hinted at this. Reza and her six-year-old son, Nur, comprising the rest of our tour, coming from Boston, had to fly on to Delhi without us.

The flight from Frankfort on was extremely bumpy. Nauseous and vomiting by the time we landed in the humidity of 118-degree Delhi, which was waiting for the monsoon, I felt no better when Carmen Hussein, who ran the Sufi Hope Project in Delhi, met us, took a look at me, sick and green, melting in the heat, and instructed her helpers to get us inside the air conditioning of the airport. I went inside but couldn't tell there was any air conditioning. *Now I'm in for it,* I thought. *I just signed up for a trip to Hell.* And the heat was on.

We boarded a domestic flight immediately, a propeller plane, to fly north in the Himalayas to the town of Manali, city of the ancient fertility goddess and a favorite hangout of hippies in the seventies. Manali was reported to have had excellent marijuana in the "flower child" days, so if we'd been interested in that we could have most likely scored a stash. The stewardess passed out cotton for our ears, along with hard candy. Kothrenada, who had to watch my motion sickness on the long oceanic flight before, suggested I take some Dramamine. "Oh, what a good idea," I replied.

And we were up. For about twenty-five minutes. Then we came down. Small planes in India still weren't flying by instrumentation, and the weather was bad. We'd have to rent a car to get to Manali. From the time I left home until I could sleep lying down, take a bath, and change my clothes, was three and a half days. My body was still vibrating from the grinding of the plane over the ocean; but I had taken the Dramamine, so as we proceeded up the Himalayas I'd nod off, wake up to see a monkey outside our taxi window, then later an elephant, and nod off, wondering about this chosen "pilgrimage."

In a hotel bed at last, I could not sleep. Already we had seen families living on the streets, cooking with a can of Sterno, preparing to sleep on the sidewalk, many beggars, some of them children. The teeming Indian life had quickly shattered my sense of security. Yes, I had a house and insurance, but such scenes of daily Indian life (and death, we'd driven past a dead horse with its stiff legs like flagpoles poking into the air) brought home the fragility and brevity of life. I became convinced I was going to die in India. How would they get my body home? I fretted over and over all through the night. The fear and anxiety washed over me in psychedelic-like waves. Finally in the morning Kothrenada's sweet face and voice reassured me. "Oh, that happens all the time when people first come to India. You should have awakened me; I would have held your hand."

"Now you tell me," I laughed.

It's called culture shock. I'd been so excited about going to India I hadn't considered the experience might accentuate my anxieties and neuroses, especially since I'd left my support system at home. In fact, that's exactly why Shahabuddin loves to travel with his students. He knows it's a pressure-cooker that can lead to growth—you either have to give stuff up or go nuts, especially in such a difficult place to travel as India.

I got plenty of opportunities to practice. Since we had been delayed coming, Kothrenada suggested we add a couple of days to the end so we could go horseback riding in the Himalayas as was promised. My schedule was set at home for pickup in Omaha by my husband and son. There were no cell phones yet; I didn't know how to contact my family, nor did I want to lengthen my stay away from them two more days. I started to cry. Reza asked to speak to Kothrenada in private. Apparently, my sobbing was spoiling her "vacation." (Kothrenada comforted me as she and I were pulled by a tiny man in a rickshaw through an Indian street filled with cars, motorcycles, buses, and cows.)

Another time we were in a store when the clerk began to pull iron bars across the front. I looked up and said, "I hope we're not getting locked in." Nur, Reza's six-year-old blond son, looking up excited, asked, "Are we getting locked in?'

Basti Boy

Reza, with her brown hair sticking up, brought her skinny arms to her hips and began chastising me, "Don't do that. I'm trying to teach him not to panic." I wish I had told her I was only human, not perfect, but I hung my head instead, feeling like I had screwed up again. Maybe I could have explained I was without my family and she was here with hers.

One night in Delhi I went out with Kothrenada to get chicken and bread from a restaurant to bring back for dinner. Outside the door she pointed to a square on the sidewalk and said, "An old woman used to live here but she died." I stared at the bare sidewalk and tried to comprehend what she was telling me.

"Where?" I asked.

"Here." She pointed again to the concrete square. My head started to swirl, and I felt sick. I'd been in India a few days, but I still wasn't used to people making their homes on the sidewalk. When the taxi drivers picked us up early one morning to take us for an excursion into the mountains to a hot springs bath, Carmen told me they had it pretty good; they could live in their taxi cabs. "That's pretty good?" I questioned.

"Nice little roof over their heads," she pointed out, contrasting it to those who lived on top the graves in the Basti, the terrible ghetto where the Hope Project is located. (These squatters and their cardboard homes couldn't be bulldozed from the graves because the cemetery was sacred ground.) I just couldn't get used

PART THREE: LANDING

Homes Built on Graves

to this surreal order—the rickshaw drivers sleeping next to their rickshaws, stepping over sleeping children on curbs, not giving to one beggar unless you were prepared to give to all of them who were going to materialize.

But, toward the end of the trip, a last evening in Kashmir, right before we returned to Delhi and then home, several of us were stuffed into a small Indian taxi going downtown to get some batteries, Michael Jackson was blasting on the tape player, and we were speeding through the evening. I looked out the window at men with their backs turned urinating into the streets and suddenly everything felt normal. I felt as though I'd always lived this way. I was just about to leave India!

And Indian food was good: dal, a lentil dish, palak panir, spinach with chunks of cheese. Since no one else drank beer, I always got the whole "fifth" bottle for myself with dinner. Breakfast, however, was usually something to skip or just down and go on: hard-boiled eggs, burnt white-bread toast, and a pot of tea. With such a breakfast we faced the trials of journeying on to Ladakh.

We'd made a brief stop in Kashmir which was mostly lovely—stopping on elegant wooden houseboats left over from the British days, being rowed across Dal Lake to an ancient rose garden. The most traumatic situation was being denied entry into a mosque by a black-nosed, loud-voiced man (presumably because we were women) who then demanded a donation from us. Another experience, not so traumatic but rather amusing, occurred when staying with Carmen's in-laws in Kashmir. I had asked a maid where I might dispose of my sanitary products, and she directed me across the road, which turned out to be a huge pile of refuse. I was slightly alarmed when I noticed the house had no screens, and flies and insects seemed to come and go at will.

Although Ladakh belongs to the Muslim state of Kashmir, the people are almost entirely Tibetan Buddhist and consider the Dalai Lama their spiritual leader. It is said that if you wish to know what Tibet was like before Communist rule, go to Ladakh. Buddhism started there before it migrated to Tibet. Ladakh is bordered by Pakistan, China, and Tibet; and by land there is only one road winding through the Himalayas to this magical place which, at the time of my pilgrimage, was only recently opened to Westerners after being unavailable for many years.

By this time in the trip Reza was starting to lose some of her bossiness and grew friendlier. Kothrenada had lost her hair brush, and her thick, long mane of black hair was wild and unmanageable but still very beautiful. And I was beginning to lose some of my anxiety. As we started to ascend the high Himalayas I grew more and more ecstatic.

We had to wait two hours for the army caravan to make its slow way with truck and equipment through the mountain pass. In the meantime, a head in a pink shawl (I think it was a man) poked into our taxi window to inquire if we would like to buy musk: "deer balls," the voice explained. I made a face. "Oh, yes!" Kothrenada exclaimed. It was the sort of present her son would love.

The army tanks trundled through; we could go on in the rain.

Our driver smoked, flicking his butts out his open window while I nervously eyed the gasoline can without a cap in the front seat between us. Suddenly Reza's voice from her back seat perch proclaimed, "NO SMOKING IN HERE!" I hung onto my little taxi seat while peering into the caverns of the Himalayas far below the edge of the winding mountain road. Our driver turning completely around to glare at Reza bellowed, "You want me to drive. I'm gonna' smoke."

Nur's whine cut through the fumy air, "I don't feel so good, and," he added, "my tape player doesn't work." His urgent "I'm gonna' throw up!" cut short Reza's patient lecture about him playing the tape recorder too much. In tandem, Kothrenada and Reza rolled down the window, held his head out, and we drove on as a sick Nur vomited out the taxi window.

A small stream of melting glacier water had run across the rutted, rocky road. The taxi ahead of us was stuck. Our driver stopped our taxi and hurried to help push the other car out. Our vehicle was soon stuck in the same spot, so their driver halted and came to push us. What a way to go to Ladakh!

In about an hour we stopped for food. It was served in a tent beside the road, and to my surprise, the meal was green beans and potatoes, much like the food from my father's garden. Food so familiar, so far away from home! I inquired about a toilet and was directed to a rectangular wooden building about the size of a house. There were no windows, no door, no lights. As I approached the entrance, the pungent stench was nauseating. Stepping inside I realized the "house" was one large room with a wooden floor with piles of feces here and there. I could not see very far inside. I didn't want to step much past the entrance; however, there were male soldiers passing by outside, and I needed to go. Feeling around with one foot inside, I managed to slip just out of sight and do my business as fast as possible, grateful for the Kleenex in my backpack. If I had come to India to dump my garbage and "shit," going to Ladakh had to take the prize for toilets; and this toilet had to be the worst of the Indian "bathrooms" on my pilgrimage. Just after this, someone pointed out the cave of the great Buddhist saint Padmasambhava in the distant mountains.

We drove on to Ladakh remembering to work on consuming the entire case of water we were told we needed to drink to avoid altitude sickness. But I felt wonderful. The high Himalayas agreed with me.

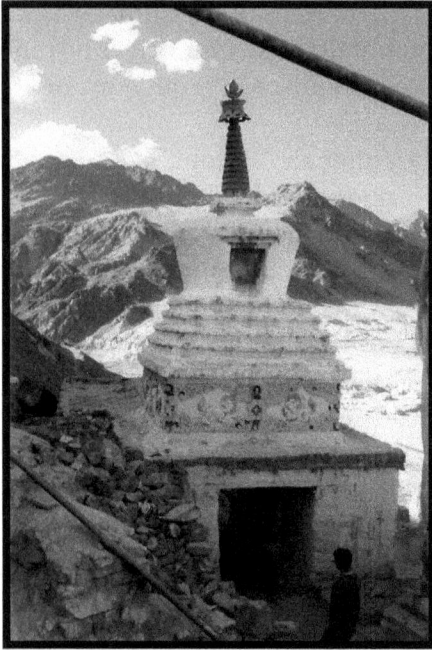

Ladakh Stupa

Many beautiful stone and adobe stupas dotted our path as we wound our way higher into the mountains. Until the first or second century, no images were made of the Buddha; instead stupas—structures that resemble upside down bowls, often with symbols representing the chakras painted on the pointed tops—stand for the Buddha or Buddhism and often make up wayside shrines. Some are simple structures; others are more decorated or ornamental. Some of my favorites in Ladakh were made out of the rich adobe-like earth of the countryside and decorated with the turquoise of the territory, and they glittered against the bright blue Ladakh sky.

The monks at the monastery at Ladakh were delighted to see us and, bowing and smiling, made us tea. I was shocked to see some very young boys, perhaps six or seven years old, in scarlet monk's robes; but we were told by our guide that poor parents often leave very young children at the monastery because they cannot feed them. After tea the monks told us there was a beautiful view of the valley through a little anteroom and up a ladder onto a roof. In the circular room were piles of feces covered with toilet paper. I guess someone had decided the dark, out-of-the-way place made a good indoor toilet. We trekked on through the leavings and up the ladder, and there was indeed a most glorious view of the verdant rice-growing valley below. It occurred to me that this was an appropriate metaphor for this trip to India—trek through some shit for a nice reward.

In the way of this pilgrimage fate allowed us only one afternoon of touring in Ladakh. Our guide was a sweet, knowledgeable Buddhist. He took us to a shrine illuminated with flickering butter lamps but still so dark we had to use flashlights to see the ancient thanka paintings. One statue of a female deity was said to be so powerful it was only uncovered once a year. As I stood in front of the butter lamps, I started to feel as if I had been there before. Even stronger than

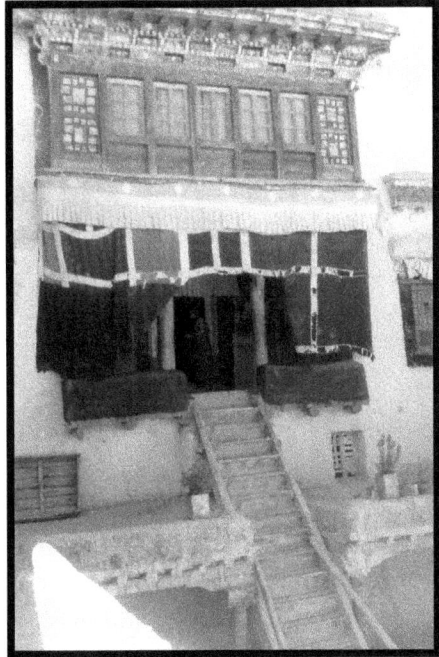

Monk Waiting at Stair Top

that, I felt as if this were my home. I turned to Kothrenada. "This is all very strange," I said, "but it's very familiar. I feel as though I belong here." She said perhaps it was similar to the Catholic Church, but I felt it was much deeper and older than that, like some ancient connection, as if I had been here meditating centuries before. I studied a thanka of one of the wrathful deities; she had a fearsome scarlet visage. "Why is all that money hanging on the cord in front of her?" I asked, turning to my guide.

"People think if they leave an offering, she will remove their fear."

I reached into my purse. I wondered how much money I would have to leave to get rid of all of them. All of my fears. Forever. *But I'd need to get home!* I laughed out loud and left a big bill. Outside at the entrance was a huge depiction of the Buddhist Wheel of Life. I studied it closely, noticing the display of all the suffering souls who seemed to be creating their own pain, all

Ladakh Buddha

going around and around this mandala representing the Buddhist cycle of birth, death, and rebirth. For the first time, I realized how psychological Buddhism is, and it truly made sense to me. I saw how I created most of my own suffering with my own mind, by my own desires, wanting what I didn't have or couldn't attain and clinging to what was passing or lost. And then not appreciating what I had in the present. *"Wow!"* I exclaimed as I stood gazing at the bright thanka painting. The guide looked at me and smiled. He saw I was having a mini-satori. More like I was getting hit by a Mack truck.

We were looking forward to lunch at our guide's home the next day and another day of touring—another monastery, a museum. I had seen a silver and turquoise necklace I had liked in a shop in town, but I couldn't make up my mind. I told the shopkeeper I would come back tomorrow. He told me I'd better buy it today! I had laughed, but by late afternoon tanks started pouring into the city. Our taxi drivers, Kashmiris, had been worried and nervous all the way there. There had been rumors of Buddhists throwing rocks at the Kashmiri taxi drivers. Now the Muslims were said to be storming out of the mosque (it was a holy day), brewing for a fight. The tanks were coming in to keep the peace. The tourists were restricted to their hotels.

PART THREE: LANDING

There went the rest of our tour of Ladakh! Would this tiny conflict get on the news at home? Would our families be worried about us? "Probably not," Kothrenada said. After a day in our hotels (Kothrenada did our colors—which colors go best with our particular hair and eyes; I did psychic readings) all the tourists in town gathered. The Ladakh police agreed to escort us in a caravan, leaving at 6:00 AM the next day, until we were safely out of the territory. Kothrenada cautioned us that our taxi drivers did not particularly care about our safety; we were pretty much on our own. When we asked our driver what the conflict was about, he said he didn't know, but he would fight if he had to. This attitude that someone would fight when he didn't even know why he was fighting was puzzling to me. English and American tourists and their drivers met in the town square at 5:45 the next morning. We waited and waited. Finally at 6:30 we proceeded out of Ladakh without the promised police escort. Ah, India! We wound back through the mountains without incident.

Back in Delhi, I had not yet been to Hazrat Inayat Khan's tomb, and that was the real reason I had come on this trip. I wanted to pay homage to the being who had brought his teachings of light and love to the planet, the teachings that were beginning to help me find my way. This was the teacher who had taught Sufi Sam, who in turn had reached out to me from his grave on Lama Mountain. And I guess I was looking for something here too. There must be some of that light, love, and grace in Hazrat Inayat Khan's burial place; whatever was there I would gladly receive.

I put on my best dress, also my longest dress, which dragged in the dirty streets. Carmen pointed out that this probably was a bad choice. And I had to agree as I watched a pig with circular tusks eating garbage off the curb. Carmen had come from Germany to administer the Hope Project, the Sufi charity project and school located in the worst part of Delhi where the garbage is dumped. The people there collect and sort the garbage. This is where Hazrat Inayat Khan, who founded the Sufi Order, wanted to be buried.

Carmen gave me a tour of the school and then left me to go by myself to the burial site. (Kothrenada, Reza, and Nur were off on their horseback riding.) "There it is," she said, pointing in the direction of the beautiful structure.

Hazrat Inayat Khan's tomb is a lovely open-air space with a marble floor and filigreed walls that let light filter through. There is a tree growing through the roof. The tomb was constructed around it. The prayers Murshid composed are inscribed on the walls. His tomb, covered with a golden cloth, is above ground (as Muslim tombs are) with columns that support a golden canopy arching over it. The cloth itself is often strewn with fresh rose petals.

As I walked inside, I found four men working and chatting, doing some kind of repair on the wooden columns or canopy over the tomb. How disappointing that I couldn't be there by myself! The climax to my pilgrimage wasn't what I expected, but I sat and tried to quiet my mind. Immediately, I began to go over how much money I had left. I knew I needed some for tax at the airport, but I wanted to give a donation to the school. The Hope Project was teaching basic education and occupational skills to children of the ghetto to lift them out of poverty. "Teaching them," Carmen explained, "to fish their own fish."

Stop, I had to say to my mind. *You came all this way to India to be at Murshid's tomb. Figure out the money later.* Finally, I just sat for a few minutes. I didn't have any kind of mystical or memorable experience.

It was only after I'd been home for a few weeks and one of Bob's friends inquired if I had found what I had been looking for in India that I recalled leaving the tomb slightly disappointed to walk through the Basti back to my hotel. In front of me a woman with raven hair and wrapped in a royal blue sari climbed out of a cardboard box. She turned and looked at me. Her eyes smoldered with fire. She placed her hands together in prayer position, bowed, and spoke, "As-salaam alaikum" (God be with you).

I knew what to reply. "Wa-alaikum salaam" (and with you), but I stood frozen and stared. Here in the poorest, dirtiest part of India was this vision of beauty blessing me! Truly I felt as if I were seeing God. And she and I were the same. She smiled into my eyes and glided down the street full of rubbish.

I told Bob's friend, "Yes, I did."

Before I left for the airport to fly home alone, I sat in Carmen's Delhi apartment watching television with Carmen's maid. This was a new maid; the previous one whom Carmen had loved dearly had to be let go because she missed too much work. That maid had to stay home too often after a rain to protect her drying soaked possessions (she lived on a roofless tomb). The TV was tiny, the color sort of bluish/red, and the show was in Hindi. I'm pretty sure it was a soap opera; it resembled something like "As the World Turns."

My flight out of Delhi was screwed up. *Of course,* I thought, *coming and going!* Carmen asked the taxi person to stay with me. He was worried I would miss my connecting flight in Germany ... again? Finally, he picked up my suitcase, yelled at some people, insisted adamantly at a ticket counter, threw my suitcase on the luggage belt, and handed me a new ticket. "There!" he said. I wanted to give him a good tip, but I couldn't figure out the money so I did nothing. I asked him if he liked his job. He said if you were fortunate enough to get a job that was the job you were going to have the rest of your life. It was all right, but all the flights left Delhi at night so he never got to see his friends because he always had to work at night. My flight finally left at 2:00 AM.

A movie was advertised. The man beside me murmured, "Choices, choices. Movie or sleep?" I looked at him as if he were crazy. "Sleep," I pronounced. I hadn't slept in India — either from being asleep in the daytime from the Dramamine then wide awake at night or just sleepless from time change or anxiety. Partying college boys on the Germany flight said they had ordered me chicken because they couldn't awaken me to find out what I wanted to eat.

I was worried about getting through customs in Chicago; I watched the film instructions carefully because there wasn't much time to get through customs inspections and catch the

Omaha flight. All my anxieties came swirling up once again. I should have given the Goddess in Ladakh more money! As I was hurrying through O'Hare a stewardess beside me asked, "What country are you from?"

Momentarily confused I said, "Isn't this the United States?"

She laughed and said, "I thought you were Dutch."

Home at last, Bob said I smelled like India. He sat beside me as I slept and slept. When I woke I went to see Chalice who had brought both Shahabuddin and Pir Vilayat to Omaha. I had dipped into her group sessions she held in her home from time to time when I felt I could drive the two hour trip. I asked her for a Sufi name. I had made my pilgrimage. I felt like a Sufi now. She meditated for a few minutes and said, "It's Tibetan Buddhist." I said that would be right.

"What is it?" I asked, excited.

"Vajra. Transformation by the lightning bolt."

MORE CAMP

Then came the camp in Missouri. Sufis love camps. They have an affinity for meditating in Nature amidst plants, trees, along streams. Not too long after I'd come back from India, Bob and I attended a camp led by Shahabuddin in the wooded beauty of the Ozarks of Missouri. Usually there were accommodations for children, stories, hikes, and music, and Eli generally liked to be with the other kids, so Eli went too.

As an added surprise, Reza attended this camp, so Eli and Nur got to meet and play together.

Bob and I took on some of the child care, and I especially remember a gleeful afternoon with a procession all around the kitchen and dining room with a long line of kids following one of the adult helpers singing a silly song, "Follow Uncle Larry / Follow … follow his behind." And there was late night zikr (Divine remembrance, chanting the names of Allah, especially

La illaha ila allah—there is no deity but the one God) with accompanying movement with Shahabuddin; sweet and intense while the children slept. And our family was allowed to sleep in our van!

At this camp I tried to concentrate very intensely on Shahabuddin's lectures. As when I was first with him, if I listened very intently I could mostly follow what he was saying and could generally understand the teaching. However, I would not be able to recall later any of the content. Sometimes I would take notes, but then I felt as if I were missing things coming from his lips, and I usually did not study the notes later anyway.

During the first break, I noticed Shahabuddin studying Bob and me. I looked at him. "Interesting couple energy. You should do more couple things," he said. I did not drink coffee regularly then but was drinking a cup to try to wake up so I could concentrate more. I noticed Shahabuddin was drinking coffee too. He had said he did not use caffeine. So he left me wondering all through the next lecture session about that and what he meant about the couple remark.

At the next break, Shahabuddin looked at us again and suggested we enroll for his Midwest Intensive Weekends being held in Minneapolis over the next two years. Every other month we'd come to Minneapolis for a weekend. We'd have to make a commitment not to miss any. He assured us we were ready for it.

Bob was not as committed to Sufi teaching as I was, and taking the seminar would involve two years of driving eight hours each way every other month to Minneapolis. We had a young child. What would we do with Eli?

I said, "I don't think … we couldn't make a commitment not to miss any …"

Shahabuddin moved closer to us. "Well," he said, and added his now-famous confidential statement, "Don't tell anybody," (Sufis take care of tender fragile hearts. Shahabuddin has to be particularly careful. Often I find him saying, "Don't tell anybody this or that" so someone won't get hurt feelings if she feels excluded from a particular event or situation) "but you guys don't have to commit to it all; you can come whenever you can."

One of the most wonderful qualities about Shahabuddin as a guide is his intuition about when to give his student space. By giving us permission *not* to make the commitment, we were able to take the Intensive Weekends and attend the complete set of teachings. Bob only missed one time when he was very ill; I didn't miss any. As events unfolded, someone always stepped forward to care for Eli, and once or twice we were able to take him with us. The two-year Intensive did, as was advertised, "change our lives." Our practices deepened, our understanding of the Sufi teachings expanded, and we bonded with the other students making good, deep friendships: some of the participants were from Minnesota, some from Wisconsin, and a few of us drove all the way from Nebraska. The Intensive Weekends, unlike typical workshops, were held in private homes.

Besides doing practices and receiving the teaching over this time period, we hung out with the other Sufi students during breaks, prepared and ate meals together, and basically slept on floors, couches, or wherever we could, in sleeping bags. The people who were in our Intensive group are very dear to us, much like family, perhaps closer. Whenever we see each other, often after long periods of time because we live in different parts of the country now, our arms and hearts immediately open to each other, and our faces light up with the joy of reunion.

THE INTENSIVE SEMINARS

The Super-8 Motel on the edge of Minneapolis was our Friday night oasis. We'd crash there after our long drive from Nebraska after our work week, and then we'd proceed to our weekend Intensive on Saturday morning. Our usual destination was a beautiful home in the woods on the St. Croix River offered to us most weekends by a couple in our group. So we'd all arrive on their doorstep carting sleeping bags, pillows, food, notebooks, prayer cushions, and the other stuff we thought we'd need for overnight and two days.

PART THREE: LANDING

The format began usually with all the participants speaking about themselves, where we were in our lives since our last class. Then Shahabuddin would teach from Hazrat Inayat Khan's writing ostensibly but more spontaneously—from what arose from his heart, which is traditionally Sufi teaching called sohbet or spiritual discourse. Shahabuddin had selected a topic for each weekend; however, we happened to be meeting the weekend of the beginning of the first war with Iraq. That weekend we just did Universal Worship Service over and over, praying for peace. (The Sufi Order Universal Worship Service consists of lighting a candle and reading from the text of each of the world's religions and perhaps singing a hymn from each.) We'd ask questions as they came up. Shahabuddin would give us some sort of answer. We'd do practices—chanting and prayers where he felt they were appropriate. We'd have breaks for teas and snacks, breaks for lunch and dinner. I often thought it was boring sitting around in between the times Shahabuddin was "on." People drank tea and chatted, cooked dinner. I was so used to filling every minute of my time, teaching, writing, raising my child, that I never *just* sat around. It took a while for me to see that *simply* being with the others in this way was also a part of the Intensives, and the deepening of our relationships over these two years because of this time spent together become precious. The Intensives have brought me some of my closer friends. Bob got angry once because one of the other participants told him to stop moving around so much during one of the meditation sessions because he was bothering her concentration. Later, they became close pals.

Sometimes we'd continue with formal class or practice into the evening. Sometimes we'd get up at 3:00 AM to pray in the sweat lodge (outside in below zero Minnesota winter!). One time Bob wore his clothes into the sweat lodge, and they were frozen by the time he returned to the house at 5:00 in the morning. Sometimes we'd be awakened at 4:00 AM by a lone violinist stepping over the sleeping bodies for prayers or practices.

We'd usually do a Universal Worship Service on Sunday. Sufism as founded by Murshid Hazrat Inayat Khan acknowledges all prophets and all religions. He teaches that each message came

121

into the world and its culture when it was needed, and each predicted the one that was to follow. A Sufi, it is said, can worship at any altar. A person who performs the prayer service is called a Cherag and is ordained to do so.

Besides the formal study, much took place on many levels during the Intensives. During one session Shahabuddin mused aloud, "I don't know if what I'm doing has helped anyone at all …?" At the next break I hurried up to him to tell him how much he had helped me. Since I had been doing Sufi practices, my mind chatter had calmed down considerably; my inner critics had quieted. I found myself in the present much of the time. I said, "Before I worked with you my mind used to drive me crazy."

He laughed and said, "Your mind used to drive *me* crazy!"

Then as usual, someone else wanted to ask him something, and I never got a chance to ask him more. I wanted to question him on what exactly he meant by that. I wanted to think he had some kind of psychic connection and could see what I was thinking, and now he could see how much I had improved; but that may not be what he meant at all. He may have only been making a joke, and I may have been gifting him with some kind of magical powers he does not have. But he left it to me to take the comment as I wished, which seems to be the crux of the Sufi teacher/student relationship. If the student is willing to take the teaching she must also be willing to puzzle out the meaning of this teaching as applied to her life. (It was interesting to me to look up the word "crux" and learn that it also means the Southern Cross constellation.)

I was surprised at one seminar when Shahabuddin spoke about what he needed. What he wanted right now he said was some friends. He needed some feedback. He needed some support. I flashed back to my darshan with Pir Vilayat on Lama Mountain, where instead of asking him a question I told him I was lonely. He told me he was lonely and that spiritual teachers were especially lonely. From this time on I stopped being so in awe of

Shahabuddin and started to regard him more as my friend, to try to think what I could do for him or give him instead of just what I needed from him.

Shahabuddin says there are two kinds of teachers: the kind who huddles over you, protects you, draws you to herself/ himself and the kind that's like the mother mountain lion, tries to get you grown, self-sufficient, and then starts pushing you away. He prefers to be the second kind. In the beginning, I used to get panicky and think I really needed and wanted him to tell me what to do. Although I had been having some success as a poet I was thinking I needed to go somewhere and learn how to write fiction. I wanted Shahabuddin to tell me if I needed to go in this direction with my writing.

At the next intensive weekend after he had asked for friends, one woman kept following him around pestering him with questions about her personal life. Every break she was there asking him what she should do. Finally in exasperation, Shahabuddin threw up his hands and said, "I don't know what you should do with your life. I want to go smoke with my friend."

Shahabuddin no longer smokes. He did at one time, but he'd just come from Bali where he'd been negotiating for a piece of land. He said everyone in the room was very tense, and it occurred to him to ask for a cigarette. Immediately about ten packs were offered in his direction. Everyone lit up, and negotiations continued smoothly. He had the remnants of a pack of Balinese cigarettes (cloves and spices mixed with tobacco) and was going to share one and have a talk with my husband who still did smoke. The woman went away to figure out her own life, I guess, and Shahabuddin and Bob went outside to smoke and talk.

It is so tempting to want Shahabuddin (or someone) to figure out our lives. If put on the spot sometimes Shahabuddin will try, but often people will get angry about his answers. I remember his telling a story about a couple who were trying to get pregnant. The husband asked him to please predict if it was going to happen or not. He pressed Shahabuddin for an answer, and Shahabuddin said no. The husband immediately became angry and continued to be angry and vengeful. I'm not even sure why we would think the spiritual teacher is supposed to have the answers to our lives' dilemmas. I've never heard him claim to be a psychic, only to be our spiritual friend. My friend Veronica was going through a very bad time and in desperation called him. He told her he'd like to talk to her, but he couldn't because it was the weekend.

"Oh, of course," she said and hung up and figured out her own problem. She laughs now telling me about it. She says now every time she wants to call him to solve a problem she tells herself she can't because "it's the weekend."

A FEW OTHER THINGS LEARNED DURING THE INTENSIVES

I should do what I want to do. I know Shahabuddin told this to me as a practice. I'm not sure if this was for others as well; I think so. He said I should do the spiritual practice, as I believe this pertained to other activities in my life as well, that I most felt like doing. In this effortless way, I would be perfecting myself. For me the perfectionist, who had always tried to do everything right in order to get to Heaven, especially what the "holy people" told me to do, this was too good to be true. I could do what I wanted to do? It took me some time to figure out what it was I wanted to do, starting with such simple things as what I wanted to eat. I think for women especially, who are often trained to accommodate everyone else, when given this freedom sometimes we find ourselves in an existential dilemma. But I am practicing.

On top of this suggestion, Shahabuddin told me specifically, I should go even further. I, who grew up being a goody two-shoes trying so hard to get to Heaven, should do something illegal every day. I don't often remember to do this one, and it's sometimes hard to find something illegal to do in a small town. Sometimes I used to drive the wrong way on campus for a short time in the parking lot (not too daring!) but, you get the idea! For balance, said Shahabuddin. It's not good to be too pure!

If someone is looking at my food, I need to give it to them or give them some of it. (As time has gone by I've seen that this giving relates to more than just food.)

I don't get to talk about people if they're not there. (I haven't been very good about keeping this, I'm afraid.)

Instead of criticizing someone, I should imagine the person he or she can become.

I should not react immediately to bad (or good) events. Let a few moments pass before I take in a momentous happening so the impression won't go so deeply into the soul.

If there's been a serious automobile accident that must be driven past, I should look away, not at the accident victims, so the impressions of the accident are not taken in.

Then there are the four C's: Compare Not, Complain Not, Criticize Not, and Condemn Not, which I believe came from the Tibetan saint Tilopa through San Francisco Sufi teacher, Joe Miller. If I really do these, there's not much left to talk about. I made a small sticky note with the four C's on it and attached it to a photo on my desk at work to remind me to practice them at school. I gave it a stab—glad I didn't have to report to anyone on how well I did them.

And many of the teachings I didn't think I remembered come to me when I need them (in Shahabuddin's voice) when the situation arises when they are pertinent. I can hear him speaking, telling me what I need to know in each specific instance. It's as if I have a portable teacher in my pocket readily available when necessary.

I incorporated many of the breathing practices and mantras into my walking routine.

WALK

Walk daily
or as often as possible
swing yer arms
        back and forth when you walk
Walk fast
Walk uphill some if possible
Feel the pull at the back of yer leg

PATH OF LIGHTNING

"Power walking is good for the thighs"
Do breathing practices while you walk

IN THROUGH THE NOSE   OUT THROUGH THE MOUTH
IN THROUGH THE MOUTH   OUT THROUGH THE NOSE

Walk past the hospital where your son was born
Walk past your doctor's office
Wave to Paul if he's in his yard
Walk past the nursing home where
your father-in-law and your mother died

Walk past peoples' flower gardens
  if summer
Notice flowers you'd like to plant
Walk in the cold and dark if it is winter
Watch *out for icy sidewalks!*

WALK WALK WALK WALK
IN THROUGH THE MOUTH   OUT THROUGH THE NOSE

Try to think positive thought as you walk
Breath in and out the chakras
Start with the crown
  Then the temples   third eye
    throat heart stomach
      Work down to the pubis
      In and out the hands and feet

Chant mantras while you walk
Not Oh, Lord, I am not worthy
Ya Ghani Let me be self-sufficient
Ya Mutakabbir Let me be a large person
Alahoakabar   God is Greater
Estafirla   Forgive me
Ya Sami   Ya Basir
Inner Sight   Inner Sound

Notice position of the sun
Clouds or not in the sky
Moon's visible too in early summer

ESTAFIRLA

PART THREE: LANDING

Smile and say hello to joggers,
bikers, other walkers as you
round the lake
Nod to Korean nuns in white habits

GOD IS GREATER   GOD IS GREATER

Stop in cemetery
Visit Reed suicide at 15
     Marty cancer at 49
     Roger health problems all his life

ALAHOAKABAR
ALAHOAKABAR

Walk past Dennis' house
Greet him if he's outside
Listen to his "Un, Un"
All he can say now after his stroke

ALAHOAKABAR

Walk past Brian's
    Ask him about stock market
    if he's outside

YA SAMI   YA BASIR

Notice grumpy Fred's, the custodian's, lawn
      full of rose bushes, geraniums in pots,
      phlox in barrels, wooden ornaments,
      hanging fire hydrants, beaded chimes

Get barked at by dogs while cutting down alley

NICE DOGGIE   NICE DOG

Walk past adolescent 24 hour supervised home
with drapes pulled tight
Where are they?

IN THE NOSE OUT THE MOUTH

Admire two story yellow house
  fence weighted down by vine
  orange flowers trumpeting

ALAHOAKABAR

It's your house!
Walk inside gate
Open front door
Call, "Honey, I'm home!"

YA SAMI YA BASIR

(From *How Much Our Dancing Has Improved*)

About three-fourths of the way through the two-year intensives, I began to feel despair. I couldn't explain it; things just seemed hopeless. It's not as if there were personal crises in my life. Everyday events were proceeding about as usual. At the next weekend retreat, I brought up the feeling of despair with Shahabuddin. He took it very seriously. "You are going through a Dark Night of the Soul," he said. But what he said next surprised me, although I felt it was accurate. "You asked for it!" he said. "You prayed for things to deepen. You prayed for things to accelerate, and now you've got it."

I sat in stunned silence for a few moments. *What'll I do now?*

Shahabuddin asked if anyone had a copy of a particular song with Hazrat Inayat Khan's words about hope and morning. Someone did. He stopped everything, put the song on the stereo: extremely glorious music yet very soothing and comforting, a metaphor about dawn always coming. And then he said, "You need someone to pray for you. Will someone pray for her? Don't say you will unless you're really going to do it!"

What really touched me was two of the men (there were only five in our group of about twenty) volunteered to pray for me. Shahabuddin said he also would pray for me. He suggested I read St. John's *Dark Night of the Soul* as well.

PART THREE: LANDING

In *Dark Night of the Soul*, St. John says the soul in this condition "finds not the pleasure and sweetness which it was wont to find, but rather affliction and lack of sweetness" and "it is aware only of its own wretchedness."

Traditionally the Dark Night of the Soul is viewed as a rather regular stage in mystical development. Many of the great mystics experienced this anguish in their spiritual questing. Evelyn Underhill in *Mysticism* defines some of its characteristics. God appears to have deliberately withdrawn His presence in the Dark Night seemingly never to manifest again. God's absence is more bitter because His presence has been so sweet to the mystic. The mystic is convinced of her own sinfulness and imperfection and overcome with a boredom and aridity, an emotional fatigue. There is an additional stagnation of will and intelligence. Finally, a feeling arises which seems can only be satisfied by death. Underhill feels that psychologically the Dark Night is a natural physical balance to the extreme high of the ecstatic state.

All of these symptoms seemed much more extreme than what I was experiencing. One woman about my age suggested perhaps I was having some kind of emotional hormonal response which I considered also. But, I had a genuine feeling of suffering.

A few days after I got home, Veronica, the artist and art teacher in our group, sent me a gorgeous piece of art. She said it was what she saw when she meditated and thought of me. A bejeweled golden sun and silver moon border a jade river with myriad ultraviolet triangular stars on a deep blue sky—all jewels pasted on—glitter and dance on this wonderful work which sits on my living room mantle surely guiding me through my Dark Night with all this light.

Shahabuddin had explained we would bond with the people in our intensives, but I didn't understand how deeply the connecting would go and that the bonding would be as much the purpose of the intensives as the formal teachings. My despair persisted for a while but gradually lessened, and slowly the dawn did come.

Our Intensives ended with a three-day retreat in a wooded state park in Minnesota.

We received individual wazifas (mantras) sent ahead by Shahabuddin who was arriving later. By now we had all gotten used to Shahabuddin arriving late or leaving early — off to some other retreat, some other group, some other duty, some other place in the world. The wazifa practices selected by the guide for the student are attributes the guide perceives as qualities that are emerging in the student. Many of the wazifas are one of the 99 names (qualities) of God, but Sufism uses phrases from other traditions as well. Reciting and meditating on the qualities enables them to be reflected and expressed more openly and freely in the mureed's life. (The literal translation of the Arabic word "wazifa" means assignment or daily ration.) The mureed is expected to recite the wazifa with devotion, sincerity, and perseverance.

At a retreat the wazifas are repeated for hours. We'd split up to say them out loud. Bob stayed in our van, and I went to our cabin where our friend Peggy found me. She apologized for interrupting me. I was happy to be interrupted. I had been repeating my wazifa for forty-five minutes and was bored out of my mind. She announced that her fiancé was coming on the last day, and Shahabuddin was going to marry them. "That's wonderful!" I said, jumping up and hugging her. I had mentioned to her before that I had thought about asking Shahabuddin to remarry Bob and me for our twenty-fifth anniversary, which was that summer, so now Peggy had come wondering if we'd want to get married with them ... "Are you sure?" I asked. "Maybe you want it to be just for you?"

"I think it would be wonderful for someone who's been married for twenty-five years to be married at the same time."

I hugged Peggy again, and we ran outside to the van to ask Bob.

After the exciting break, Bob and I went back to repeating wazifas until Shahabuddin arrived. Then we all agreed upon the weddings being performed at the very end of the retreat. I suddenly realized I wasn't going to be seeing Shahabuddin every other month, and I hadn't asked him to check the daily practices I had been doing. (Routinely the student gets a "tune up" with the teacher, repeats his practices for the teacher, checks to see if those breathing practices and wazifas are indeed the ones the teacher perceives are the most helpful ones the student should be doing.) I didn't even know when I might be seeing Shahabuddin again. I panicked. I wanted … something … something binding. I wanted to marry him too. I wanted some kind of promise. That he would always be there for me. Always guiding me. That I would always get to see him. That I would always be able to find him. Some kind of permanent connection. I hadn't yet asked him to initiate us. I hadn't asked him for a special practice. That's what I wanted. For him to see me as special. Hazrat Inayat Khan says the friendship between spiritual teacher and student is "the most sacred, it must be considered beyond all other relationships in the world." But, the retreat was over. I didn't say anything. And it was time for the weddings.

About an hour before the scheduled wedding time three women came whisking into the main hall and grabbed me and Peggy. I just had time to ask Mary Lee if I could borrow the attractive blue skirt she was wearing and accepted a shawl from someone else. I had only packed camping clothes. Peggy had brought a dress, anticipating the wedding. Suzanne, Kathy, and Jane collected makeup, lotion, a curling iron, perfume and had picked wild flowers and woven them into glorious wreaths to crown us with when they were finished fussing and fixing with us. I did not have attendants who fixed and fooled with me on my original wedding day like these women did. On my wedding day I did my own hair, put on my own makeup, got dressed, and went to the church. Now our "bridesmaids" hummed and danced around us—bestowing us with blessings and having a great party, creating a nest of female energy. "Look up, smudge the mascara a little, curl her hair under …" Then they danced us across the meadow to our grooms in the shelter house. Our workshop comrade who had awakened us with her gentle violin for our 4:00 AM meditation sessions serenaded us now as our wedding ceremony began.

The altar was set symbolically with candles representing all the world religions. Peggy and her fiancé performed Universal Prayer Service by lighting the candles and reciting a short prayer from each tradition. Shahabuddin married them first, stating that their union was destined to bring dissonant forces in the world together. (Chen, the groom, was from China and had been one of the students present at Tiananmen Square.) Then Shahabuddin paused. For quite a long time. "Are you going to say vows for us?" I asked, thinking maybe he was finished. "Let's let this one sink in first," he said and waited a little while longer.

Then he stood before us. I felt energy and light and love begin to pour through me and it all surged through my body as a flood of tears I couldn't stop. Tears poured down my face as Shahabuddin spoke softly.

"Your union isn't going to be what you hoped for, but it's going to evolve into something else completely. It's going to be something much bigger and develop into something you never expected."

The light began to fill the whole room. I remembered walking up the aisle to marry Bob twenty-five years before; I saw him standing at the front of the church looking small and scared, and at that moment the top of my head opened up and a funnel of light poured in.

Back then I felt like I was being flooded by Grace or the Holy Spirit, and I knew that marrying him was exactly the right thing to do and I was receiving blessing. This was very similar.

When Peggy sent us pictures of the wedding a couple of weeks later, there was a huge column of light cutting across the picture diagonally — you could barely see any of the people, only legs. My friend Pat took it to a photographer, and he said he didn't see how that could have been a developing error.

There was a cake. Someone had gone to town and found one. As Joanie played her violin everyone danced in circles, exuberant, wild dancing. Then suddenly the wedding was over, the camp was over, the retreat, the Intensives were over. Everyone was hugging. We all went separate ways. I slept in the back of the van as Bob drove home. He said he felt both like he was taking

his new bride home and as if he had gotten a new puppy. The
van broke down a few miles from home, but someone stopped
right away and picked us up, and we sent a tow truck without
even worrying about how much it would cost. And it felt like our
honeymoon again. We were young and new.

LIGHT IN THE WEDDING PHOTO

Pouring all around them.
It was the second time.
The first time was 25 years earlier in
the Catholic Church.
Their spiritual teacher marrying them
this time said the first one didn't count.
This one was the real one.

He (the teacher) was barefoot.
She (the bride) wore a crown of wild flowers
and borrowed a blue silk shawl.
The groom wore a grey t-shirt with
the globe of the earth on the back. *This
Is It* stitched in red over his heart.
They were camped in a park.

She cried in ecstasy.
She cried with joy and
the light poured down like
honey on the tableau of wedding.
On the ritual of marriage.
He (the groom) in his golden curls,
 still curling.

Both of them a little more round,
 a little more soft.
Knowing a little more about loving
and being blessed from the heavens —
a wedding gift — golden showers
from above. A little bit illuminating.

Light. Rays of love.
 Triangles of blessing.
Over their little wedding scene.

Caught even forever for the
scrapbook pasting in the photograph.
LOVE LIGHT LIGHT
       LOVE

(From *How Much Our Dancing Has Improved*)

Shahabuddin came to Omaha again; and since he was
staying with our good friends, Karl and Suzanne, we got invited
along the evening before the seminar to go out to dinner. Bob
drove the van. I was happily tucked next to Shahabuddin in the
back when I began to feel very peculiar. My mind felt jumbled,
disoriented, and racing like I was on some kind of drug trip. I
looked at Shahabuddin. "I feel weird," I said. "It's like I've taken
psychedelics."

He looked at me, nodded, and then laughed. "How do you
like it?" he asked. "That's how my mind is most of the time."

I took his remark to mean that I had somehow gotten a
"contact state of consciousness" by being close to him. But, as
with many times before, he did not elaborate further, and I did
not necessarily feel that I should question him.

We had a lovely Italian dinner, and on the way back to Karl
and Suzanne's in a fit of enthusiasm Bob put on a tape of Allen
Ginsberg nearly screaming his "Hum Bom" poem, "Whom bomb?
/ We bomb you / Whom bomb? / We bomb you! Whom bomb?
…"on and on. Shahabuddin soon tapped me on the shoulder,
shaking his head. I ejected the tape. Bob looked surprised.
Shahabuddin stated enthusiastically, "I like it that you like it,
Bob; but I just can't listen to it right now." I've tried to model
Shahabuddin's way of declining when I have to reject something.
He usually does it so gracefully you don't mind at all that he has
said *No*.

The next day the seminar was conducted in Steve's many-
roomed Victorian. I reveled in Steve's chocolate brownies and
breakfast in his plant room full of light with delicious coffee
and pastries and dear friends. Shahabuddin began to teach once
again in his warm penetrating voice and words of wisdom. The
weekend sped by.

PART THREE: LANDING

On Saturday afternoon he inquired if anyone wanted to be initiated, and my hand shot up. "Pir Vilayat initiated us some time ago," I said, recalling the quiet scene in the Omaha church, brief but powerful. Remembering the longing I had felt at the end of the retreat to be connected to Shahabuddin and the joy and blessings which accompany an initiation, I went on pleading my case, "I feel that you're our teacher. Shouldn't you initiate us?"

"Haven't I?" he asked.

"Into Ziraat."

"Yes," he said. And then the lecture and the afternoon went on.

The next afternoon, shortly before he was to leave, Shahabuddin began the initiations. He had done three and then looked around. "Anyone else?" He had forgotten! I raised my hand. "No," he said firmly.

I felt crushed. What had happened. *All right.* I started to console myself. *Shahabuddin knows when you are ready for an initiation. I'm not ready.*

"Both of you come," he was saying. "And I have to do it in silence."

Bob and I walked to him together. He took our heads in his hands and put them next to his head. He held them there, our three heads pressed close together like little children. We closed our eyes as he prayed there in silence, and the room elevated and my heart opened and I felt extremely happy and light. I guess that's what is called ecstasy.

I read later in Hazrat Inayat Khan's teaching that teachers practice Tawajeh, a method of receiving knowledge and power from the teacher in silence, a way that is considered essential and desirable. I did not know this at the time, only that I felt greatly joyous, and I now felt I had the deep connection to Shahabuddin I was longing for as the Intensives were coming to an end.

And then, in a moment, all this too was over, and Shahabuddin was leaving quickly again. Leaving early. Leaving as he usually leaves. In a flurry. To get to the airport. To catch a plane. To be on to the next place. To the next group waiting.

It was at this workshop that he gave us a most valuable secret to staying tuned, staying high. Take a gentle in-breath and remember. Remember how it was in this moment when you were in the present. Think back to what it was like. Then you can be there again. You can put yourself there again. You can stay there.

I often return to Steve's beautiful sunlit home and quiet glorious weekend when I draw in my breath. And the joy is there too.

People ask me how Shahabuddin became a teacher. This is the story as I remember him telling it. In the early seventies while he was attending law school at Columbia, he and a friend were experimenting with psychedelics. They were amazed by the depth of the experience and decided if a small amount of psychedelics could provide such a profound experience, a huge amount must do something incredible. So they ingested a gigantic portion of drugs. During that time, he heard the word "Sufi." He had never heard the term before; he did not know what it meant. A short while after the psychedelic experience, wondering what that word might mean, he found a Sufi group advertised in the *New York Times* and attended. During the meeting the members held a gong over his head, smelted with the blood of an ancient monk, and gonged it, putting him again into an altered state.

Continuing the search he went to a psychic who said she kept getting a word she thought was "Sophie" connected to him. Sophia is the Greek goddess of wisdom and a key figure in the Gnostic religion, where she is sometimes referred to as the mother of the universe or the bride of Christ. The traditional Sufis were wise sages who lived as outsiders and wore rough wool. This young Jewish man in New York returned to the group of elderly Sufi women who had been initiated by Murshid Hazrat Inayat Khan. They informed him of an upcoming lecture by Pir Vilayat, Inayat Khan's son, the current head of the Sufi Order, which Shahabuddin attended. (He said he understood every word until the lecture was over and he was on the street, and then he could remember nothing.) But, he had found his destiny and subsequently after law school moved to San Francisco, where he studied with Murshid Sam Lewis and Joe Miller, two powerful nontraditional Sufi teachers. Thus, he became a teacher himself in his early twenties.

Shahabuddin says God tells him he will take care of him as long as he keeps teaching. He has raised four children and now has a home in Sarasota, Florida where he has established Rising Tide, an esoteric school. And he leads tours to beautiful sacred places. He has been a teacher in the Sufi Order of the West for close to forty years.

Before I knew Shahabuddin, life never made much sense. There's a line in one of Murshid's prayers, "that we may know and understand life better." Living was always slightly dissatisfactory to me, like that old Peggy Lee song, "Is this all there is to the circus?" If the "getting and spending" were all there was to life, I didn't really want it. This journey on earth seemed ridiculous, like Macbeth's "player / That struts and frets his hour upon the stage / And then is heard no more."

Although I had loved the rituals of the Catholic Church as a child, they didn't answer the deep questions for me. My mind was always whirling and taunting me with worries and anxieties; it never quit. After I began the breathing practices and wazifas Shahabuddin prescribed, my mind quieted, and I became much more present and awake.

Even better than that, a soft joy came into my opening heart, and almost every day I woke up happy and contented, not looking for something else, not wanting more.

Shahabuddin and the Sufi teaching have been the most wonderful blessing. After the Intensives and the Omaha initiation, my practices and perceptions deepened. I began to notice beautiful things—trees, light, flowers, art—more intensely, without being aware until later that spiritual progress through beauty is a main Sufi practice. I began to feel that even if there were nothing more after this life, my life had improved so much (although nothing much had changed except my outlook), it was enough.

TURKEY

At the Omaha seminar, Shahabuddin announced he'd be leading an upcoming trip to Turkey. I had been fascinated with stories about Mevlevis—the whirling Dervishes—and often Shahabuddin read from the poetry of Jalálu'ddin Rúmí, the founder of the Mevlevi Order. A visit to Rúmí's Tomb in Konya was to be a highlight. At one of the breaks I said excitedly to Bob, "Shahabuddin's going to Turkey!" Bob wasn't very interested. "What's in Turkey?"

I answered, "Dervish!"

On the next breath Shahabuddin smiled and said, "The food is wonderful."

I thought that a rather peculiar remark, although I knew Shahabuddin loves to eat.

I didn't think we'd be able to afford the trip—certainly not two of us, anyway—but very shortly after this my mother called to say she had found a paid-up life insurance policy on me. It was exactly enough to pay for one person to take the Turkey trip. We figured we could manage to pay for the other ourselves. We arranged for one of my Creative Writing college students to stay with Eli, who was thirteen and excited about having Karl stay with him. They could play basketball and play music together. Karl played the organ and piano, Eli the drums. Eli was hoping he could have his girlfriend over. We saw a double rainbow as we left town, surely an auspicious beginning.

Jalálu'ddin Rúmí, who has become the most popular poet in America, was a religious scholar in thirteenth-century Konya, Turkey. One day a mysterious wandering monk, Shams, appeared and proceeded to toss Rúmí's scholarly work down a well. He told Rúmí he could have it back, but Rúmí was so taken by the mysterious stranger that he no longer cared about his research. He fell deeply in love with Shams, who was to become his companion and teacher. Shams is referred to as "the sun" in Rúmí's writing. Rúmí's students became jealous of the special relationship between the two and are reported to have killed Shams, throwing his body down a well.

PART THREE: LANDING

The Whirling Dervishes were founded by Rúmí who, grief-stricken for Shams, spun around and around a pole in grief. Rúmí's poetry was often spontaneously recited while he was in the ecstatic trance of turning; a scribe recorded the words. Often the dervish would pray and chant (and whirl) all night. Thus the famous poem:

> This we have now
> is not imagination.
>
> This is not
> grief or joy.
>
> Not a judging state,
> or an elation,
> or sadness.
>
> Those come
> and go.
>
> This is the presence
> that doesn't.
>
> It's dawn, Husam,
> here in the splendor of coral,
> Inside the Friend, the simple truth
> Of what Hallaj said.
>
> What else could human beings want?
>
> When grapes turn to wine,
> they're wanting
> this.
>
> When the nightsky pours by,
> it's really a crows of beggars,
> and they all want some of this!
> …
>
> (From *The Essential Rúmí*)

The Dervishes or devotees who whirl are arranged like planets around a central sheik or leader who portrays the sun. An important part of the Dervish attire is the high brimless hat worn at an angle during the turning. The Dervish posture is important—one arm raised at an angle with the palm facing the heavens, the other extended, palm down to conduct the blessing earthward. The circular skirts twirl outward, and the Dervish is expected to keep his feet on the ground even in his trance in which he twirls to ecstasy.

Istanbul is a modern cosmopolitan city. Women flash about in short skirts, heels, and blue jeans as well as the modified Muslim garb: short coats and scarves. As we rode into the city on the airport shuttle under the ancient aqueducts built by the Romans, we spotted gigantic banners advertising a Guns and Roses concert. "Can you get us tickets?" we hollered to Shahabuddin near the front of the bus. He laughed and shouted that he doubted it. On our way to change money and buy water we found what was meant about pedestrians "having no rights" in this city. We stepped very cautiously and quickly off the curb amidst the swirling mass of cars, buses, taxis speeding without heed to humans trying to cross a street.

It was Bob's first time out of the United States. Shahabuddin welcomed him to The World; but shortly after arriving and looking around, Bob was appalled by the trash in the streets and the layer of grime on the blue tiles. Bob who makes a speciality of polishing and shining beautiful things wanted to start cleaning everything. Since I had been to India and seen the squalor there, I wasn't too put off. Then our first morning at breakfast some of our group rushed in to say there was a gypsy with a bear outside whom we could photograph. We went outside to get the great photo. Being rather slow about it, we found that the others in our group had disappeared leaving us with a drunken gypsy who demanded $20 for a picture before we could determine the currency. As we stood stupefied shaking our heads *No* the gypsy grabbed a twenty out of Bob's hand and wobbled down the street with his chained bear following. Immediately after this

Bob, loving sweets and snacking, wanted to take some pastries to our room, and merely ordered them from a street stand without asking the price. We ended up paying $20 for them also and were caught up arguing about our old money issues. I was worried about spending so much money right away the first day, and Bob just wanted to have a good time. The same old shit on our nice trip. Shahabuddin's theory that travel would accelerate whatever we needed to work on was indeed happening!

Soon we were on our way to Konya, to the stone streets and Rúmí's gorgeous tomb. Landing on the military airstrip in Konya with soldiers with machine guns and bombers taking off was scary. We wondered for a few seconds if we were in the middle of a war. But the Turkish soldiers smiled and ushered us nicely to a bus, where other friendly Turks made room for us for the trip into Konya where all of our luggage was unloaded from the bus and reloaded into the trunks of taxis. With so much luggage there was no room for the passengers, and the trunk lids wouldn't close, so we paraded down the street behind the bouncing trunk lids to our hotel, located right across the street from Rúmí's Tomb which is now a national museum.

The next morning our group gathered in the hotel lobby where Shahabuddin inquired if we were ready for Rúmí's Tomb. Then he laughed and asked, "How can you not be ready?"

Shahabuddin paid our admission; we left our shoes on wooden shelves by the front door. Bob's were black Michael Jordan Number 23 tennis shoes. The women all covered their heads with scarves, and we were inside the huge, cool, golden tomb. Hanging lighted lamps rained by the hundreds from the ceiling. The dargah (tomb) is an art museum as well as a tomb and is full of calligraphic plaques with Arabic lettering and art. In the center is a huge ark-like structure: the tombs of Rúmí, his son, and his father, covered with elaborate woven metallic golden-fringed fabric with material wound on posts at the head of the tomb to represent the conical dervish hats. The atmosphere is calm, tender. I felt a very dear mood that might best be described as loving as an infant's nursery.

I began to pray asking that I might know the purpose of my life. Almost immediately an answer came, and even more surprising it came in the form of the Catholic catechism. In my mind's ear, I heard: to know God, to love God, to serve God.

When I was a kid, I could memorize like crazy. I won the catechism prize every year because I was so good with those questions and answers. Who made you? God made me. Why did God make you? To know him and love him and serve him in this life and afterward in Heaven. My most favorite prize was a blue plastic holy water fountain with a picture of Mary in it. My dad hung it up by my bedroom light switch and cut a small sponge so I could dip into the holy water and bless myself with the sign of the cross. I tried to keep holy water in it, but I would forget and the sponge would get hard and dry.

Rúmí's tomb was full of tourists from many nations. I heard German, French, Spanish, and Japanese. People flowed through the sacred place. Because our group was praying so devoutly, the other tourists started to find us interesting and began to study us. After a while, Shahabuddin, led us out. The proper way to exit a dargah is to leave facing the tomb, backing out of it. In the courtyard, someone thought to ask, "Are there special prayers we should be doing?"

"Probably," Shahabuddin said, "but I don't know what they are." "Personal prayer," he added. "Pray with your hands open. Ask for nothing. Receive everything."

I felt bad that I had asked for something. But not for very long. I hadn't known I wasn't supposed to ask, and I did receive. I didn't know what those Catechism words meant as a child. As a Sufi we're supposed to see God in everyone. That's the real living God. So I realized I had a big task: to know God, to serve God. Not to mention that third one, "love." Still, I was surprised when praying fervently at Rúmí's tomb in Konya, Turkey, to have the answer delivered in such a form.

We did Zikr in the hotel that night. Sufis say Zikr is the practice of remembering. La illaha ila allah—There is no god but God {IT'S ALL GOD}—with a circular head movement—suggesting annihilation of the ego. I remembered I had told friends at home I was going to Turkey to do Zikr with the Dervishes, but we didn't meet anyone in Turkey who was doing these practices. *We* were the ones doing them. I almost laughed out loud in the middle of the practice realizing *we* were the dervishes I had come to see.

The owners of a rug shop close to the dargah, hoping to show us a few rugs, had offered their place of business to us as an oasis for resting, gathering, and having tea. Shahabuddin asked if we might "dance" there after hours. This idea made them extremely nervous. When Atatürk modernized the country in the fifties, he outlawed dervish whirling and other dervish spiritual practices fearing the powerful dervish orders might hold back the modernization. Now when the Mevlevi whirl, it is done only in a cultural context, like a ballet performance. Tekkes, the dervish monasteries, still exist, but in secret; they are illegal.

The rug shop owner hung carpets over the windows of the rug shop and stood anxiously by as we did our Dances of Universal Peace. Valerie, whose birthday it was, (she had wished to see the dervish spin) whirled in the center of our circle as we sang Happy Birthday. The rug merchants, despite our urging, refused to join in and were very happy when we were finished and they could remove the rugs and tell us "Good Night." Again, I realized I was dancing with the dervishes, and they were us.

The widow of the head of the Mevlevi had agreed to see our group. As always when we traveled in Turkey, our group created a stir. Since we were a large group—about twenty including a baby, we had to hire several taxis. When lots of taxis pulled into a quiet Konya neighborhood and a bunch of Westerners started piling out, the Turkish kids gathered like bees. A couple spoke a sort of English. *Who are you? What doing here? So many?* They smiled and laughed. We laughed. I wanted to give them something but feared creating a riot like we did in India with kids hanging onto our moving taxi.

Suddenly, Shahabuddin is urging us toward the building; we're moving in mass through the kids, inside, up steep stairs.

I'm toward the front. As we take off our shoes, I hang back; I don't want to be the first inside. I want to watch someone else so I know what to do. A middle-aged woman is ushering us in. The widow sits on a bed, near a window, dressed in a print dress with a scarf tied around her head, like all the Muslim women here. She looks like any grandma in decades past back home. We sit on the floor in front of her.

Shahabuddin introduces his wife, Kothrenada. The widow greets her, hugs her, takes her hand, and then stares at her hand and talks to the middle-aged woman (her daughter) in Turkish. The daughter translates: says Anna (Kothrenada) shouldn't wear nail polish; she won't be able to get a good meditation. Later, back at our hotel, when someone in the group asks Shahabuddin about this, he shrugs, says people sometimes can't separate the cultural from the spiritual.

The widow asks Shahabuddin about her son Jalálu'ddin, heir of the Mevlevi Order who was sent to the United States by his father. *Is he well? Is he eating?* Shahabuddin assures her he is well. She says she would like to see him again before she dies.

Jo, a member of our group, tells her she is beautiful. The widow says we are all beautiful. She says being with us is like the old days. Would we like to do zikr? We all nod, and the daughter brings the sheik's beads—a huge strand that gets passed among us first. Everyone touches them. We chant together. *Ah, again, here I am in Turkey doing zikr with the dervishes.* Then the room recedes and we go inside sound, become the sound. We are very high sound. When we are finished, the daughter passes around a bowl of hard candy. In Hindu tradition, the teacher distributes Prasad, blessed food, to the disciples. This seems to be a similar custom. It's just a piece of wrapped candy, but it tastes so sweet and good melting in my mouth. Shahabuddin murmurs that he hopes everyone eats the candy.

The widow says she misses the old days, being with everyone and doing zikr, and she misses God; but she will be with him soon when she leaves the prison of her body. A door in my heart swings opens and I begin to sob, and all my grief and sorrow and ecstasy begin to pour out. Shahabuddin also tells about his

With Dede's Widow

secretary who died in a car wreck. She died with a smile on her face and was buried in a wedding dress. Suddenly, the intensity Bob and I have been having over money, the pastry, the bear; his threat to break his glasses, the festering of those old issues breaks loose. All of that comes pouring out, all down my front. But it's more than sadness. It's gladness. Highness. Everything. I can't stop.

Those who want to, file up to the widow for a blessing. She babbles over me in Turkish, touches my hair and neck like a sweet mother would. I've been purified, washed clean, then blessed. My crying stops. We bow, go down the stairs into the sun and Turkish kids, and on to the cemetery to where her husband, Suleiman Dede, is buried.

We must be bread crumbs. We're at the cemetery and here are the kids again. Following us. Following us everywhere, but we leave them now outside the locked cemetery. We have to scale the wall to get inside. Shahabuddin finds an accessible spot where a stepladder leans against the chest-high wall. He stands at

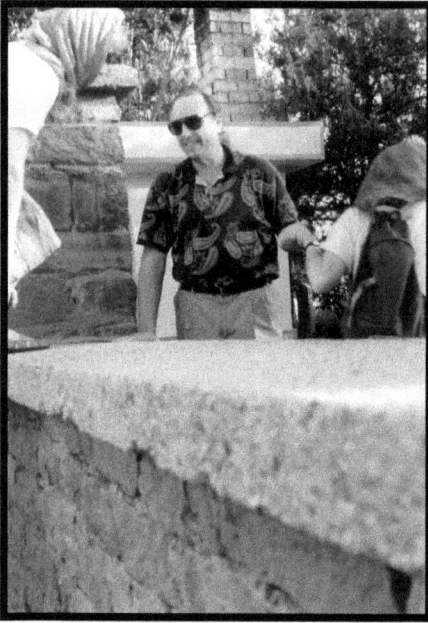

Shahabuddin Helps us to the
Other Side

the top, taking our hands, helping us across to the other side. Bob takes a picture of this scene. I have an enlargement at home. It's a symbol to me of what the spiritual teacher, especially Shahabuddin, does. He helps his students get to "the other side." And what I particularly love about Shahabuddin is he does not give us a rigid set of rules to follow with consequences if we screw up. He's just there at the top of the wall with his hand out, smiling at us, helping us all he can.

When my husband went over the wall, Shahabuddin said, "You know you were totally off the rhythm of the zikr from what everybody else was doing, but you didn't care, did you?" Then he grinned and gave him a little slap on the butt. That's about as much of a correction as we'll receive: a pointing out so we'll know we were off course but no put-downs or reprimands. Certainly no whaps with a big stick. Or maybe he even meant Bob was out of sync with everyone else but really right for him. You get to figure it out. And always the constant presence to aid us in our journey to the other side, always the smile.

No one cuts the grass in Turkish cemeteries; the weeds and grass grow as tall as people. There are concrete forms around the graves and concrete dervish hats on the tombstones. Once over the wall, we plowed through the grass, over rocks, passing towering plants, concrete forms, and tombstones. "Don't take too many pictures here!" Shahabuddin cautioned, so I left my camera in my

bag, although I was dying for a picture. We found Dede's grave —
the head of the Mevlevi, Rúmí's descendant — and paused briefly.
Then back went our snaky line of pilgrims through incredibly tall
grass, graves, wall, kids, taxi.

> In Turkey
> in the cemeteries
> the uncut grass
> on graves above
> grows long
> competing
> with the uncut hair
> beneath

We made one more stop that day, at Rúmí's cook's tomb in
the country tended by a sweet old woman who poured rose water
on our hands. Shahabuddin says in the hierarchy of rank at the
monastery or tekke, the abbot or sheik, is the highest and the next
in rank is the cook. We were told a wonderful story about Rúmí's
cook. Once when preparing food for Rúmí and his disciples and
honored guests, the cook ran out of wood. In a quandary as to
how to finish cooking the rest of the meal, the cook stuck his foot
into the fire to provide the necessary fuel. As the story goes, the
leg burned until the food was ready and then he withdrew his
foot which was miraculously whole.

Since Turkey was my first trip with Shahabuddin, it was a new
experience to hang out with him casually, unlike at seminars and
retreats. What a thrill to be travelers on a bus together! The tour
bus carried beer and soft drinks which we could purchase. Bob
decided to have a beer and asked Shahabuddin if he'd like one.
Shahabuddin nodded, so Bob bought him a beer. Shahabuddin
held his can of beer and walked the bus, remarking to the other
travelers happily that Bob had bought him a beer. I guess nobody
had ever thought of buying their guide and spiritual teacher a
beer before. He sat across from us most of the long bumpy ride

to Pamukkale, the ancient Roman bath site. I wanted to think of something to say. I was sure there must be questions I wanted to ask him, but my mind was blank. He was Shahabuddin. The Guru. The Sufi Teacher. That's how I was around Allen Ginsberg, too, when I first met him. In awe. Wanting to say something but tongue-tied. I'd wanted to be in his presence, be next to him. Getting to be close to Shahabuddin was like getting to be close to God; I wouldn't know what to say to God either.

The whole bus cheered when we rounded a bend and the blue Aegean came into view. When we arrived at Pamukkale at the top of a high hill where the once flowing bathing waters had now turned into tiers of white salt, the bus stopped a distance from our hotel. We could go touring here at these ruins where there was also a swimming spot, or we could proceed to our accommodations for the night. The busload of people was unable to decide. After a few minutes Shahabuddin announced playfully, "Well, I'm going swimming!" grabbed his suit, and was off the bus, leaving the rest of us hot and dazed sitting on our sticky bus seats. I read in Murshid Hazrat Inayat Khan's teachings that the mureed (student) should learn by imitating the teacher. Shahabuddin often gives great teachings like this in his ordinary everyday behavior. (Since we could not make up our minds, he did what he wanted to do and went swimming.)

After viewing the ruins at Ephesus, we went to Mary's House, which was discovered by a German nun who had seen it first in a vision and then gone to Ephesus. We had heard a lecture the first day about Christianity not being very well accepted in Anatolia until Mary, the mother of Jesus, was emphasized. The cult of the Earth Mother was a very strong part of the culture here so with the added attention to Mary, Christianity began to thrive. Later the Pope is said to have journeyed to this tiny cottage and confirmed that this place in Asia Minor had been Mary's home. Asia Minor was St. John's missionary territory, and Jesus on the Cross gave Mary to John to care for. "Son, behold thy Mother. Mother, behold thy son" are the words I remember hearing in the Gospel.

The house has only four small rooms but a strong sense of presence. Upon first entering I spied a wooden kneeler that I was immediately attracted to, something from my Catholic childhood, in front of a wall where a portrait of Mary purportedly formed by itself. The portrait is sort of bluish red and murky. I was more interested in the kneeler than the portrait. All those childhood years spent at mass kneeling and praying. I didn't even think to form a prayer, to begin to ask for anything. In my mind I heard the command, "Be kind." *OH!* again, I was surprised. Here's where I thought I might receive Catholic dogma or instruction from the catechism, but instead got a Rúmí-like platitude. "Be kind." Politeness and good manners are really the essence of Sufi teaching. Not only do Sufis try to see the divine in each human being, but also realizing how fragile the human heart is, they make an attempt to be careful of each person's delicate feelings. At the Christian shrine, I was receiving Sufi teaching. And later realized, finally getting it, Sufi teaching is "universal" teaching.

A spring thought to have healing properties had also appeared on this property. I went out into the sunlight, walked to the spring, reached into the water, and made the sign of the cross, touching my eyes and head, particularly the areas where I get my migraine pain, wishing for healing from my bad headaches. I have to report that the migraines are still with me. Shahabuddin asked the group later if we thought the place was really Mary's house, and everyone answered yes. He said he agreed. He felt that it was also. And I left firmly resolved to follow my instructions to treat my fellow human beings with kindness.

Later that night after dinner and shopping, Bob bought a belt I didn't think he needed, and we were starting to argue about money when I felt someone pounding on my back. It was Shahabuddin walking up the street with Kothrenada; they'd been looking at glass for his import business. Did he intuit the situation? I don't think so, but it was very interesting that he appeared at that moment. When I had complained to him earlier about Bob spending $20 on pastries, he shrugged. "Probably about the best $20 you ever spent" was his response.

The last day in Istanbul we had free time and felt confident enough to hail a taxi and give our destination as the Topkapi Palace, home of the Sultan during the Ottoman era. "How much?" we asked the driver. "The meter's running," he said, nodding toward the ticking machine. My sweet, friendly husband then started a conversation which we soon realized our driver was not capable of conducting. The driver reached under his seat and with sparkling eyes produced a Turkish/English dictionary which, he explained, his friend had given him. He asked us if we wanted to know his favorite English word. Indeed, we did. "Splendor," he pronounced, followed by a large grin. We smiled back "Wonderful choice" and stepped out of the taxi before the splendid Topkapi Palace.

We asked what the long line was. It turned out to be pilgrims waiting to see a hair of Mohammed encapsulated in glass. We fell in line also and viewed the one long wavy hair. "Well?" Bob asked. I didn't have any particular reaction.

Just then we were drawn by haunting chanting in an adjacent corner of the museum. In a dim space a cleric sat on a stool near a glass-enclosed room intoning deeply from what we supposed was the Koran. We were more interested in the atmosphere created by his sound than what was inside the room. (Our friend, Abby, from Bangladesh also on the tour, told us back at the hotel that the remains of Mohammed are purported to be in that room. Supposedly the sultan had them placed there to show his devotion. Of course, there's also the story of Mohammed ascending to Heaven on his steed.) We stood close to the chanting, out of sight of the chanter, for close to a half hour, awed by the beautiful sound, truly having an ecstatic experience. We toured some other rooms, loving the blue and white tiles, the art, although Bob was put again off by how grimy everything was and wanted to scrub walls and floors.

The cost of the taxi back to the hotel was double, rush hour traffic, but we didn't mind. We got back in time for our group gathering in Shahabuddin's room. He had on a caftan-like robe about calf length with a small rip in the side, his muscular hairy legs protruding. At first I was surprised by his attire; *he's holding the meeting in his pajamas?* Then I realized it was his sheik's robe, and an eerie feeling descended. *What was I doing there, in this swarthy man's hotel room in Istanbul, Turkey? Me, a little Catholic girl from Nebraska. Maybe this weird stuff and strange sounds were all a sham ...*

I took a breath. I let it out. I came back. It's Shahabuddin. My guide and friend. He hasn't ever steered me wrong. He wants us to speak about the trip, about some way we've been affected. I know he's going to call on me first. He does, and all I can think to tell about are our fights about money, about how much our financial issues surfaced here.

That's not what I wanted to say. I wanted to talk about something more spiritual, deep, and profound. But that's what was there, so that's what I said; and I surrendered to it and didn't fret about not seeming more spiritual. We moved on to someone else.

A woman jumped up saying she just *must* return to the Blue Mosque. Shahabuddin pointed toward the door. "But," she said, "I have no money left for cab fare." Shahabuddin told her his wallet was in his pants on the chair in the other room. She raced into the other room, then out the door with some bills in her hand as we all chuckled.

Back in our room, Bob revealed that he needed to ask for some practices; he felt like he wasn't done. "Go back," I encouraged him. He returned in a short time, smiling. He reported that Shahabuddin was standing there as if he were waiting and said, "I've been waiting for you for centuries."

Turkey makes you hungry. For breakfast there are omelets, hard-boiled eggs, scrambled eggs, cereal, bread, rolls, pastries, plums, figs, other fruits, feta cheese, other cheeses, salami, several kinds of olives, cucumbers, tomatoes, coffee, tea.

On the street for sale on almost every corner are the most fragrant non-rising ovals of bread. They're sold on small carts for a few coins, about twenty cents. Ahura, who's been to Turkey twice before, said she came this time to eat the bread.

I'm hungry at the Topkapi Palace. An ice cream cart in the courtyard provides ice cream bars but not like any I've had in the U.S. The one I select is vanilla ice cream with a big chunk of chocolate candy in the middle.

Also on the street are spits with sizzling meat turning, roasting lamb probably. And toward the end of our journey it's Eid, when the lambs are sacrificed, so we order lamb in a restaurant. It's succulent, juicy, tender. I think I've ordered a small portion and receive a huge amount.

Then there's Turkish coffee, always served in miniscule cups, half grounds and half potent as poison, thick as stew. The Turks cannot conceive anyone would possibly drink two, so whenever my husband, who is a coffee lover and wanted more than half a shot of coffee, would order two they would only bring him one. We had to order one for him and one for me, the only way he could get two cups of Turkish coffee at a single meal in Turkey. The only coffee alternative to a tiny cup of Turkish brew is Nescafé, instant coffee. The Turks don't seem to know how to brew coffee in a pot, but there's little to complain about in terms of the cuisine in Turkey. Vegetables, salads, legumes, all kinds of fresh fish are in abundance as well as sweets for dessert.

Unexpected accompaniments to the menu were beggars outside almost every restaurant, some mothers with babies in their arms; one night in a restaurant on the Mediterranean, my fish order never arrived during the whole meal and everyone was finished—I decided to go without; and one evening Coleman Barks, the well-known translator of Rúmí poems, was added to our dinner party in Istanbul (he is an old friend of Shahabuddin's). I was delighted to have him join our group although I didn't get to speak with him.

Shahabuddin was right to talk about the wonderful food in advertising the trip.

Back at home, thinking about the trip, it occurred to me that often at seminars or in Shahabuddin's presence mundane, trivial issues often surfaced. Apparently these old patterns and ways of being and doing have to melt away before the new or

152

more "ethereal" ways can come into being. I recalled somewhere Shahabuddin saying Sufism is merely doing the right action at the right time without having to think about it, which would involve, I supposed, getting rid of a bunch of stuff which would cause you to stand around debating about what the right action might be. I also recalled him saying "Being spiritual is having self-confidence" which I thought was odd at the time I first heard it, but now it was beginning to make more sense.

All kinds of interesting dreams flooded my nights at home. I dreamed I just about got pregnant in high school. Shahabuddin in my dream said any child I would have would be beautiful, but I wasn't ready then. In the dream he also implied that he had been my teacher and had been guiding me to where I was now for much longer than I had known him in his physical body. (This seemed to me very similar to what he had said to Bob in the hotel room in Turkey.)

In another dream people are on a very friendly bus trip, and then we are all supposed to find a sex partner and everyone goes crazy. Shahabuddin says (in the dream) that is the point—people go crazy when sex gets introduced into the equation. In fact, Shahabuddin did say something similar to that. People have their spiritual trips very well together, he said, until sex comes into the picture.

The effects of this Turkey trip continued to unfold for many months.

BALI

We had no intention of going on a trip to Bali with Shahabuddin. We had thought to visit his community in Sarasota where he was establishing a school, to check out Florida, visit him, and see some friends from other trips. After greeting me on the phone and hearing my plans, he suggested that our family instead accompany his group on their upcoming trip to Bali. I didn't answer. "Are you broke?" he asked.

"No-o-o," I answered, "but I don't know if we can afford a trip for the three of us to Bali."

Bali was one of the exotic places I had dreamed of traveling to ever since Shahabuddin had begun relating stories of the beautiful people with such open hearts. Their religion is a combination of indigenous native Balinese, Hinduism, and Buddhism and is relatively untouched because they did not allow Christian missionaries on the island. "I'll see if I can figure out a deal," he said, and we hung up. I went across campus to Bob's office to ask how he'd like to go to Bali. "Do you want to go?" he asked me.

"Well, I want to go someday. I don't know if we can afford it right now."

It seemed to be our time. We had a small inheritance from Bob's father. Shahabuddin figured out how Eli could travel "in country" free, sharing a room with us, a hut on the beach with his own son. We'd only need pay for his flight. Only Eli didn't want to go. He was involved with a circle of friends we did not consider desirable, and he also had a girlfriend we considered worrisome. We tried to entice him with great descriptions, almost threatened, and finally in a weak moment he agreed; so we bought three tickets before he could change his mind.

Right before we were to leave, my husband's stepmother died (Bob's father had passed away the year before). Her family agreed if we attended the visitation it would be all right if we were not present for the funeral since it was scheduled for the day of our Bali departure. As we drove to Omaha to catch the plane, the impression of Bernie in her casket was strongly in our minds. Eli asked why her body was pushed up out the casket at the viewing. I thought that was a very good question. I answered that I imagined so that even the people sitting in the back could see the corpse. All of us were silent knowing that for our family we'd prefer *not* to see a dead body in a casket. Later in Bali, I decided people must want to gaze one last time at a loved one, but I've never been able to relate to a dead body as the person I loved. What a contrast this funeral ritual was to the cremation we were soon to attend in Bali.

PART THREE: LANDING

The flight to Bali from California is nearly as far as Australia, twenty-two hours. The only stop, Hawaii, is very brief. With swollen ankles and feeling very weary, we landed in Denpasar as Eli looked out the window, delighted with the palm trees, exotic foliage, and stone sculpture. "This looks like Indiana Jones," he said. We were met by grinning Nura, dressed all in white with white baseball cap. He drove us where we needed to go in his van, even slipping money to cops at certain points when a bribe was expected. He ferried us to Melati Cottages in Ubud which offered bamboo furniture, chickens strutting about, and a fruity drink with a parasol. I was starting to think I was in an Indiana Jones movie myself. We soon leaned "Galong ... galong" for "walking" to answer the many inquiries for a taxi as we had chosen to walk the short distance to town, just around a short irrigation ditch, past some ducks, out to the road, past a restaurant, and we were nearly there. On the single main street all kinds of merchandise hung in open-air booths for purchase.

The first afternoon Shahabuddin turned the tour loose to shop downtown, except our family. He knew we needed extra help. He accompanied us shopping. The long trip and jet lag were taking its toll. After a few minutes, I exclaimed, "I'm just too tired!"

"I know what you need," Shahabuddin grinned. "A little sugar, a little caffeine." He ran around the corner, returning with bottled Coke. I reached for the bottle and gulped it down, much to Bob and Eli's amazement. I *never* drink pop. Our shopping went much better.

SPREE

The skinny young man in the Bali shop
       grabbed my shoulder
       and a dress off the rack.
"Just your color," he grinned
     shoving us both into a dressing booth.
"My mother sews these."
"See," he recited, pulling the curtain tight,
    "There she is."

Turning, I saw cocooned on the corner bench
    a nodding, wrinkled woman.
Stifling a scream, I tried on
    the greenish gown,
    didn't agree the color was for me;
    but sneaked a peek at Mom's cross-stitched
    face and bought the dress anyway.

Bob is amazed that I'll do something when Shahabuddin presents it that I'd never do if he suggested it. Sometimes I'm amazed, too, but I trust him so completely that I'm willing to break through my concepts and rules and do something out of character, and it usually is "just what I need."

The first night we walked for what seemed like hours to go to the temple; it was a special six-month celebration. We had to be warned continually to watch out for holes, for ditches, for absence of curbs. There are no safety regulations in Bali and consequently many accidents. There were no lights either; and we were following our on-foot guide, a diminutive schoolteacher, who walked as fast as anything, dodging dangers in the dark. We walked past shops, bikes, motorcycles, kids, skinny dogs, bridges, women going to temple dressed in their lacy tops, tightly wrapped sarongs, men in little caps, huge bamboo pyramids balanced on the women's heads. We watched a procession of Balinese taking the gods to the river for purification, boys in temple clothes with huge swaying banners rushing by in the dark, giggling. No one was mean or threatening, like you might feel at night in an American city. The whole mood was joyful. More dogs. Dark and light shops. We went up stairs. Across a bridge. Coconut palms swaying across the night. Rosemary and Diane told how last time they were in Bali, a young teenager girl had fallen down a hole. Workers had to cut down a palm tree and lower it for her to hang onto to pull her out.

Finally, we arrived at the temple, where the girls from Melati Cottages waited with our offering outside. Inside, the temple seemed a combination three-ring circus, acid-trip, decorations, wreaths, mysterious fabric piles, huge piled offerings of bamboo,

Going to Temple

fruits and flowers, iridescent parasols, groups gathered talking, incense, noise, buying, selling, all happening at once. My mind went to sensory overload. Get sprinkled with holy water, swallow it, sprinkle it on our heads. A priestess kept pouring water in our outstretched hands. Finally our guide closed Bob's hands or the priestess would be there still pouring water; the priest or priestess pours water as long as you keep your hands outstretched.

How does one become a priest in Bali? You start performing the duties of a priest and if anyone comes to you, you are a priest. If no one comes, you aren't. It's as simple as that. Temple service is simple also. You hold a flower in your hand. The priest takes the flower and gives you a piece of blessed rice, which you stick on your forehead. You open your hands, make a prayer of thanks, receive a blessing of holy water.

"That's it?" said my son the last night, when we took an offering to the Temple of the River Spirit, which was on the

157

land where we were staying. "That's it," I said. "No sermon?" he asked. "No sermon," I said. He grinned. He could go for this kind of church. We learned the Balinese worship entailed five simple phases: Empty yourself. Pray to the God of the Sun. Pray to the God of the place you are staying. Ask for forgiveness. Give thanks.

When the Temple service was over we went to eat at the Lotus Cafe, which supposedly had Western food, but because it was so late the menu was sadly depleted. Unfortunately we weren't informed until we'd placed our orders and waited half an hour. I ended up with a vegetarian plate, and Indian food arrived. Suddenly the taste of curry brought me back to India, the culture shock, the homeless, the poor, and the suffering. Extremely late at night we found our way back to the Cottages and slept the deep sleep of exhausted travelers who had finally landed.

Nura transported us the next day to LaLa Linga where Shahabuddin was buying land, a cliff above the Indian Ocean. When he and Kothrenada had come here on a vacation, as the sun was setting it had occurred to him to try to buy this property, but it had not been for sale. Shortly before they were to leave, however, the land became available. The Balinese generally do not sell land with temples on it to foreigners, and this property had two temples, one to the River Spirit and one on the other border. With the wonderful piece of land seemed to come the equally wonderful staff, who would build lovely bamboo huts for each group of visitors (and take them down when we left), cook and serve meals, tidy our huts daily, and make forays into town to fetch anything the guests needed.

When we got to the land Shahabuddin so loved which was to be our home for the next two weeks, bordered by the Indian Ocean joined by the Balian River, Eli looked around at the few bamboo huts constructed on tall poles and exclaimed, "What do you expect me to do here!" After his fit of anger passed, he discovered he could body surf in the feisty Indian Ocean with Vadan, Shahabuddin's son, play cards with Vadan and

Shahabuddin (or "Vadan's dad" as Eli called him), even stroll across a meadow to Bob's Balian Beach Bungalow where Bob had hamburgers (of sorts), chocolate cake, darts, and even a television that got a few scratchy stations. One night the men, Nura, his older brother Oka, Eli, and Vadan, got to go into the city. This was very exciting for Eli because there was no age limit on the sale of alcohol in Bali, and he was on his own without his parents. The men went to a restaurant, a bar, and slept at a motel. Eli said he had a fine time. We didn't question him about the amount of alcohol he had consumed; we assumed he was safe in the older men's company.

We spent most of our days walking the beach of sparkling dark sand along the edge of the water or sitting quietly in our beautiful huts with blue plastic roofs. I brought notebooks and books but didn't feel inclined toward reading and writing. Sitting in a meditative quiet state seemed to be my main mode. (Even when I returned home I didn't return to my habitual writing routine. Finally, I began to want to write but not as compulsively as before. I had taken in some of Bali's deep peace.) Every morning we walked down a tree-lined path and bathed with the Balinese in the river and tried to dry ourselves with our towels that were still wet from the day before because of the humidity. Each morning we waited a long time for our breakfast orders which got all mixed up. Usually no one got what she had ordered so we just ate what was set before us because we were so hungry, and everyone laughed happily.

The Southern Cross twinkled in the sky at night. It took me a while to get used to the idea that it wasn't preparing to rain every night as the sky turned dark at six o'clock. We were so close to the equator that days and nights were of equal length. After dinner we'd make our way in the dark back up a small hill to our little hut where we'd listen to the roar of the Indian Ocean throughout the night. And, almost every evening a little rain pattered for a few minutes on our blue plastic roof. I'd awaken in the deep night unsure what the racket was. The roaring was reminiscent of a raging Nebraska blizzard in midwinter. Only the Indian Ocean going about its business.

Throughout the night from out hut we could see the lanterns of the fishing boats, small catamarans, bobbing on the ocean. Strangely, most of the Balinese cannot swim and are afraid of water. They believe the evil spirits come from the ocean. The good ones come from the volcano at the center of the island, and directions are given from that starting point.

We also noticed blue globules of light whizzing around, particularly, it seemed, around Bob. "What are those?" we finally thought to ask Shahabuddin. "They're the spirits," Shahabuddin replied, telling us they liked Bob. He said we also sometime might see someone standing there. "It's not real," he said. "Just a spirit." Once when Bob got up to pee, I looked up to see a turquoise-colored globe swoop up from the fishing village below, arc around his body and head, and then spiral away. It certainly wasn't a firefly.

The only aspect of Bali that wasn't so wonderful was the food. It was ordinary and boring and sometimes, it seemed, downright horrible.

THE MENU

Jaffal: squashed cheese sandwich, tomatoes and eggs inside
    sometimes
Fresh fish, brown sauce, spices
Chopped up chicken, tiny odd pieces, roasted with spices
Hot Dutch chocolate
Ginger lemon tea
Thick Balinese espresso
Vegetables, green beans with peppers (too spicy hot!)
Hard-boiled Balinese power eggs
Omelets
Hard white bread toast
White rice
Red rice
Balinese rice
Rice
Rice
Rice
American chocolate bars

PART THREE: LANDING

We were invited to lunch at Nura's family compound. One of the reasons Shahabuddin's trips are so exquisite is that he gets to know and love the local people so his groups are usually invited into local homes. The trip is like going to visit friends and family in exotic places! The Balinese live in compounds: the parents, then their married children and their children. Compounds, surrounded by high stone walls, are many-roomed, rather open structures built around a sooty kitchen, which is mainly a cooking hearth, and the altar. In every family someone is an artist who paints small pictures or does sculpting; someone is a tailor or a merchant; and someone tends the chickens, raises a few pigs, takes care of the rice paddy. It seems as if most family compounds are almost self-sufficient. When we visited Bali in the early nineties there were no homeless. Birth control is written into the religion.

Besides the altar in every compound where the spirits live, Balinese life is rich in awareness of and homage to the spirits. Some of these seem to be the ancestors and some to be the spirits of nature. Several times a day the women leave offerings of small woven bamboo mats with tiny servings of rice and some other morsels and flowers at the base of trees, in the courtyards, and at other spots in nature. The offerings are set in place quietly and reverently and then the offeree disappears. Often the food gets eaten by the dogs and chickens that roam the countryside. (Balinese dogs are not pets like American dogs — they are tolerated and fed scraps but not coddled or petted or seen as a beloved family member as in our culture.)

Much accommodation is made for the spirits in the temples and homes: brightly colored parasols with fringe are hung open so the spirits can dwell there. In the home, the rooms of the elderly and the infants are the closest to the temple because the infants just came from the eternal world and are still close to its influence, and the elderly are on their way there and are entering its influence. Noticing the offerings being made so happily and casually and seeing integration of spirit into the ordinary, drew us visitors also into the holy and joyous ritual of everyday Balinese life.

Family Compound, Oka and Children

The Balinese make much use of fabric, and colors are very symbolic. Black and white checks are very popular and represent the struggle between good and evil, which is perpetually being fought, neither side ever being victorious. In the mythical portrayals, puppet plays, and elaborate costumed dance productions, many of which last for hours and hours, there are no conclusions—good and evil go on and on, forever battling each other. The shadow side is acted out on stage for all to experience; perhaps that is why there is in actuality so little crime or evil doing in real life in Bali.

PART THREE: LANDING

Our group was asked to purchase sarongs, blouses or shirts, and little caps for the men for our visit to Nura's family because there was an altar in their compound, and Shahabuddin wanted to show respect for the family by having us dress in temple clothes for our visit. Nura's parents' eyes sparkled when they saw our group arriving in sarongs of every bright color, some improperly wrapped and some too short since most of us were much taller than the Balinese. For temple, the women also wore a black elastic girdle-like garment around their waists. We bought the largest we could find for me, but I was very thankful to get back to my hut and get that torturous piece of clothing off. I don't think Balinese women come in size Large! The Balinese women decided Eli looked so handsome in his temple clothes they picked a beautiful flower to adorn his temple hat.

Shahabuddin had told Nura to convey to his family to make a "simple lunch," but our group was fed a many-course meal, with many types of rice, of course, and most spectacular of all, each of us received his own coconut with a straw in it, probably handpicked by someone in Nura's family. Vadan remarked that Bali looked like an island of bodybuilders. The Balinese have remarkably muscled, sculpted bodies. The legend is that they are descendants of the lost tribes of Atlantis. (In actuality, the Balinese are descendents of high caste Javanese who fled from Muslim invasion in the sixteenth century, bringing their Hinduism, royal families, priests and artisans to Bali.)

One excursion off the land was to snorkel at one of the top coral reefs in the world. On our arrival the much touted coral reef appeared to be a muddy shore, and our family had our usual amount of difficulties. There was no instruction. Others jumped gleefully into the water. I am dreadfully afraid of water. Eli's equipment didn't seem to work, and Bob's moustache let water into his mask. He was also worried about me because someone had mentioned how soon the bank sides dropped away to very deep ocean. Shahabuddin tried to help but finally spread his arms wide, shook his head, and said, "You just have to get into the water!" and walked away leaving us. Bob gave his snorkel tube to Eli, who managed, he said, to see some amazingly colorful schools of fish. I swam close to the boat where I could touch bottom, seeing a few fish, and Bob sat in the boat taking in the scenery topside. Again, Shahabuddin taught us this day by example, telling us just to do something (make a decision), and then instead of hovering close by trying to make everything be all right, took off to enjoy himself as we should be doing.

We were very fortunate to be invited to attend a cremation ceremony during our stay. Sometimes a cremation might not occur until several years after the person's death, until the family has accumulated enough wealth to throw a party for the whole village. The person from whom Shahabuddin was buying the land was cremating his father. In fact, Shahabuddin's last payment made the ceremony possible.

We were invited to the son's house where we were served water in cardboard boxes, tiny bananas, watermelon, and coconut cake. The son told us, "This is a very happy day for me." After the refreshments were served, he announced, "It is time," and the gamelan players, all dressed in black, started gonging on their instruments with small anvils, making a tin-can pounding, clanging musical accompaniment to the parade of papier-mâché bulls. A red and gold many-tiered castle, several feet tall and as wide as the road built on bamboo poles, was frantically spun and carried on the shoulders of about ten young men. This huge beautifully painted castle would soon house the remains of the dead which would be cremated. Our guide, Darsa, said the cremation was mostly symbolic because it had been ten years since the man had been buried. The remains were brought from the temple wrapped in fabric, looking like a large tamale, and were passed up along a white cloth ramp while being touched by many friends and relatives as the remains were conveyed into the castle. The son climbed aboard the ramp, stood at the front of the castle, and showered rice on everyone down below.

Shahabuddin had told us earlier that the impression from the cremation would go very deep, and we'd be feeling the effect for a long time. The showering rice did feel remarkably like descending blessings! The procession marched to the burning point with much yelling and twisting about of the castle. Also much gamelan gonging. Upon arriving at the cremation site, the remains were brought back down along the cloth and placed inside the gigantic papier-mâché bulls. A dove was released symbolizing the freeing of the father's soul. The bulls were set on fire, and everyone stood in the hot midday Bali sun watching the bulls burn the remains.

Money is also sometimes burned at cremation. We were told that the poor are often invited to cremate their relatives at the cremation of a rich person, as a cremation is so costly, constructing the papier-mâché figures, hiring the band and serving refreshments for all. As the bulls burned, the carriers got to drink water, and some of the crowd dispersed. I flashed back to our stepmother in Nebraska. How different. How strange each ceremony seemed.

I had asked Shahabuddin if it would be all right for me to wear my visor along with my temple clothes to the cremation—with my perfectionist nature, I wanted to do the correct thing, but knew I needed to protect my fair sun-damaged skin from the scorching Balinese sun.

He looked at me, grinned, and quipped, "as long as you don't mind looking like a stupid idiot."

I almost got my feelings hurt, and I almost didn't wear my visor; but I decided I needed to protect my face and wouldn't mind looking like a "stupid idiot." Shahabuddin seems to know when he can say something that will wake me up, maybe toughen me up a bit, and not be taken wrong.

Shahabuddin makes himself available as spiritual guide as well as travel guide on these trips. Some people were doing a retreat at LaLa Linga and stayed mostly in their huts and tents doing prescribed practices. Some were on vacation. There was no compulsion to do one or the other; we were just all there together in this beautiful place. The day the men went into the city, Bob and I did a mini-retreat walking the Bali sand and doing wazifas and mantras. Shahabuddin gave us each new practices to do upon returning home and talked to us about giving Eli many new experiences to help overcome his fears which Shahabuddin believed Eli brought with him into his incarnation. Our mini-retreat consisted of reciting *Gate, Gate, ParasanGate, Bodi Swaha* (gone, gone, gone-beyond-the notion of gone) from the Hindu tradition, which we chanted together in big, loping, galloping strides almost skipping down the Bali beach. This practice was much to our liking — fun and profound.

We also had a class and teachings each morning. Shahabuddin had mentioned something about my maybe reading some poetry, and each morning I prepared, and each morning went by without his ever calling on me to do so. I finally decided that must be my practice for this trip, to give up the notion of being "the poet," to relax my ego as well as my body, to forget about getting attention for my poems and just be there with everyone else on the beautiful Bali beach.

The woman on retreat in the next hut was ill. I heard Shahabuddin tell Kothrenada she was "incredibly open," and I was envious. Shahabuddin called me to help him rearrange her hut when she stepped out for a few minutes, and I wondered what practices she was doing and what kind of a retreat she was on to cause her to go so far and render her so open as to be ill and dizzy (not that you *have* to get sick when you start to open — this was a particular circumstance). Even though I try hard not to, I am continually longing for someone else's more profound — I imagine — experiences than mine.

The last night on the land we put on our temple clothes to go to say goodbye to the River Spirit. His temple was a small wooden box with a straw covering on one end capped with what looked like an iron pot. The temple was about the size of a large bird house (big enough for a chicken). "Where does he live?" I had asked Shahabuddin earlier. He nodded toward the small structure. I never quite got it, *Inside that box?* I was wearing my sarong and walked by Shahabuddin's hut. "Barbara," he called to me. I walked closer. He was tying his sarong. His eyes caught the setting sun. I could hear the roaring of the Indian Ocean. The women were coming down the path with the mammoth pyramid of fruit we were taking to the temple for our offering, trying to balance it on their heads like the Balinese women. "Isn't this far-out?" he laughed. "Indeed, Shahabuddin," I laughed, also happy I'd taken him up on his invitation to *take the trip*. "It's far-out!"

Also far-out is that the Balinese can't understand the concept of child abuse. "What do you mean?" they ask. And they still can't understand when you explain it to them. Their newborn are treated as angels: Their feet are not allowed to touch the ground until they are four months old. The infants are handed from family member to family member until the celebration when they are landed on this planet, and for the first time, their feet set down on earth. We visited a museum about children's parties, for different stages. "A whole museum about birthday parties!" one of the women in our group exclaimed in the courtyard. The sign above her said "Please to have a pleasant sightseeing." At the Ubud market, a baby on its mother's lap blessed us, beamed love across nationalities, language, and concepts. Just smiled and smiled at us.

When the Balinese give you a gift, it is much like giving a May basket. It's presented in a bag or sack and left more or less anonymously, and they never ask about it again. They certainly don't expect a thank-you note. Nura and his brother Oka had made a special trip at our behest to buy all of us fluffy pillows for our huts. As we packed to leave, we had to mention to someone to tell the brothers that the pillows left in the huts were for them. They didn't say thank you, but we received special smiles as they helped us with our luggage to the van. Oka was the older brother. He complained once that Nura wouldn't help him learn English. Shahabuddin said there were all kinds of family complications; Oka being the older brother should be more successful, but apparently Nura had done better with his life and career. Bob tried to help Oka learn a few words and gave him a baseball cap before we left. He looked into our eyes tearfully and asked, "Mister Bob and Mrs. Barbara, you won't forget Oka when you get to America, will you?"

As always, when you travel with Shahabuddin, you bond. You share each others' histories, problems, joys. One woman had just gotten stood up at the altar only a few days before. She was an old friend of Shahabuddin's and Kothrenada's. They suggested the trip to Bali as a cure. They even ended up letting her sleep with them a couple nights when she was a complete wreck!! We learned about one woman's abuse as a child. Back in Melati Cottages at the trip's end, a few decided to stay several days longer. As I was hugging someone goodbye I felt a heavy weight on my toe, then terrible pain, and thought someone had dropped a camera on my foot. We stepped back. A flower pot had fallen off a ledge breaking my toenail and badly bruising my toe. While I hopped around in pain, Shahabuddin said quickly, "Nobody got hurt on this trip. You're taking the pain for all of us."

I thought about that for a minute and said, "That's not true. Eli got stung by an insect and his eye swelled up. He got his hand cut by the bug sprayer."

"Oh," Shahabuddin said, "you're right."

And I limped past the irrigation ditch, past the ducks, out to the road, bidding Bali goodbye in my heart.

I don't take literally everything that comes out of Shahabuddin's mouth. Shahabuddin has taught us himself, as per Hazrat Inayat Khan's teaching, if you disagree with something, just disregard it. There is no compunction in Sufism. It doesn't lessen Shahabuddin's helpfulness as a teacher and guide for me if he's off sometimes; I just shrug and go on. He speaks from his intuition; he's generally in the ball park; sometimes he's not. He's not infallible. I don't expect him to be. He has been known to say if you have enough faith you can learn from a garbage can. Sometimes it takes years and plenty of a mureed's faith to get the teaching.

Sadly, the discovery was made in later years that Shahabuddin and the friends who had invested in the land with him did not own the beloved property. The land had been "sold" to others as well. Reading Elizabeth Gilbert's *Eat, Pray, Love* I learned such property swindles tend to occur in Bali. Gilbert says the expatriates in Bali warned her.

> … you can never really be certain what's going on when it comes to real estate in Bali. The land you are "buying" may not actually "belong" to the person who is "selling" it. The guy who showed you the property might not even be the owner, but only the disgruntled nephew of the owner, trying to get one over on his uncle because of some old family dispute.

Back home I was showing Eli's girlfriend Bali temple photos, and she said, "Oh, they're superstitious."

"No," I said, searching for a way to explain the beautiful Balinese way of being. "It's more like they're able to live in parallel worlds at the same time, the essence of Sufism really. The spirit world is just as real to them as the material world. They are able to exist in both worlds at the same time, the offerings to the spirits, the parasols for the ancestors to live under are all very natural. It's nothing spooky."

She nodded. I remembered a time right after Eli's grandfather died. "We were at Eli's grandma's house right after his grandpa died, and we had tried to fix the bathroom facet but got the hot water one on wrong and it wouldn't turn off. Someone yelled for Eli to go to the basement to shut the water off, and he saw his grandpa standing there beside where his fireman hat and coat used to hang. I remember him coming up the stairs with his eyes wide telling me he saw his grandpa. And he had both his eyes; my dad had one eye removed because of cancer. And that was very real."

Eli was nodding, confirming this was so; and I think she got an inkling of this Balinese way of being, a slight impression anyway.

The fall after our Bali trip, I turned fifty. I had celebrated my birthday with a big catered party the weekend before my actual birthday with friends and relatives in our home. We had a sumptuous buffet of smoked salmon, salads, and a walnut wedding cake with a whirling dervish on top. There was a keg of beer on the porch, a full moon rising over Highway 81, wine in the kitchen, and a poetry reading in the living room. Now on the actual date, I got to be with my Sufi friends (many of them dear ones from the Intensives) and Shahabuddin. The seminar was held, as are most of the Omaha ones, at Steve's beautiful Victorian mansion built by the early aristocrats of the city. Sunday morning breakfast was coffee and pastries in the bright kitchen and sunlit plant room, and then everyone that was assembled along his board-room length dining room table started singing "Happy Birthday." Shahabuddin was somewhere else in the house, but as soon as he heard the singing, he came racing around the corner to join in, beaming. My heart flew open. *This is how much God loves me*, said my inside voice, *that he comes running to sing Happy Birthday to me.* The mystical stew of the teacher's act, my open heart, and maybe even chocolate gave me a moment of God-realization on the spot on my fiftieth birthday. *How lucky I am*, I realized. *I have this dear, loving teacher. I have the tender community of friends I longed for!*

In a short session I had with him later in the day, he told me I was sad because I'd only had one child, and now that child was almost grown. I didn't know if this reading felt right to me or not; but I would take his comment, like most ideas offered by Shahabuddin, and "hold it in my heart and ponder it." And then he told me he loved me "very, very much." I couldn't remember him ever saying it exactly like that before, and I decided it was a fine birthday gift indeed.

INDIA TWO

India was at war with Pakistan, but Shahabuddin kept reassuring us that the trip we were planning was still on, that we would be safe, but we would not be able to get into Ladakh. However, the price of the trip kept escalating, and the route changed — we flew west instead of east when we finally departed. The main conflict seemed to be occurring over the very road to Ladakh, the infamous army road over which I had taken the memorable trip with Kothrenada a few years earlier. I was very disappointed about not being able to go to Ladakh with Bob, but we decided we still wanted to go to Delhi and Kashmir with Shahabuddin. I didn't want to miss out on traveling with my teacher. I always learned much when traveling anywhere with him, and I dearly loved being close to him and absorbing some of his atmosphere. I also was no longer so in awe of Shahabuddin. I believed that we were friends.

The Imperial Hotel in Delhi cost $400 a night. It came with our travel deal. Carmen, who managed the Hope Project, suggested it. Shahabuddin said he'd never be able to work it into his package, but there we were. The showers had enormous, thick glass doors from top to bottom. We stepped inside a glass room with a marble floor to bathe. There was a huge bowl of fruit in our room, and an attendant in an old Indian army uniform complete with red-wrapped turban stood beside our door. If we stepped outside, he jumped to attention, "Sir?" "Madam?" wanting to help, wanting to fetch something.

I fell asleep okay that first night, but woke up about 3:00 AM wide-eyed; and for some reason I brushed my breast with my arm. What was that? I went back and took time to feel. It was a lump. Cylinder-shaped. Medium-sized. Very definite. I'd not noticed it before. Why would I find it now? On our first night in India? We were going to be here for two weeks. I couldn't do anything about it until I got home. Why wouldn't I have noticed it before I left? I couldn't spend two weeks worrying about it. I started to list all the things I'd done that I wanted to do: my son was grown; my poetry book was going to be published; I'd taught for a long time; and I had a good marriage. I wasn't afraid of death. But, I almost sobbed, *I didn't want to die yet. Not yet. Please.* There were too many things I loved on this blue-green planet. I turned to my beloved husband snoring softly, trying to be quiet in my misery. I didn't want to wake him. I wasn't ready to leave him yet.

Once again the first night in India brought me face to face
with my mortality. This time it wasn't culture shock like my first
Indian trip but something more tangible, right in my own body.
I told Kothrenada about the lump as we were getting on the bus
the next morning. She was reaching to feel it but some people got
between us. I determined to practice a Gestalt technique Bob had
taught me, one I used often when there was something I could do
nothing about for a while. I was fairly successful at bracketing the
breast cancer worry. (You place brackets around the worrisome
item or issue that can't be dwelt with in the present and stow it
away toward the back of your mind until it can be addressed or
resolved.) Finally, back at home I learned from a biopsy that it
wasn't cancerous.

We were given a tour of the Hope Project the next morning.
Our group stood in the courtyard of the charity project close to
Murshid's tomb with the pregnant mothers, the mothers with
babies in their arms, and the small children with their tin cups.
How could everyone look so clean, so well-groomed, so beautiful?
The Basti is nothing but a garbage dump. Everywhere are piles of
waste and refuse. What the people do here to hold body and soul
together is to sort the garbage. The women and children were
clean. Their clothes were bright and beautiful, the colorful saris
like multicolored jewels. I don't know how they accomplish their
laundry and perform their personal hygiene, but they are radiant
and shining. My Nebraska friend looked at their cardboard-box
homes built in the midst of the garbage piles on top of the graves
and shook his head. "We can just get on a plane and go back to
our nice houses." I nodded feeling sort of sick and looking for a
place to sit down. I couldn't find one.

The milk arrived in tall cans that looked like those Bob's father
used to pick up cream in from farmers' caves in Nebraska in the
forties and fifties. The Hope Project workers began to distribute it
with large dippers. The children waited—no pushing, no shoving,
just smiling—for the liquid to come to their cups. The babies are
weighed weekly, the weight carefully monitored and charted.

In the midst of this beautiful occurrence I remembered someone telling me that Shahabuddin was responsible for beginning the milk distribution and for the instigation of the Hope Project. Living in Delhi for a time, close to Murshid's tomb, he was devastated on his daily walks through the Basti, especially seeing the poverty of the children. Searching for some way to help, he consulted an Indian doctor about what could be done. The doctor replied, "If the kids could just have a sip of milk every day that would be a start." Shahabuddin announced, "Done," brought pitchers and milk, and the children started coming. Back home Pir Vilayat established a fund for the project, and it became a Sufi charity that was funded and expanded upon.

After milk distribution we were walked through the school, elementary for young boys and girls and skills school for older students. The project teaches mechanical training for young men and sewing and computer skills for women.

The building which houses the extended project was an old warehouse, grim and windowless. The teachers were bright and enthusiastic and the kids full of glee and energy in the dark rooms. In one room the young mothers sat with their babies. The teacher explained they had to teach the mothers things like not drinking water out of ditches so they wouldn't get sick. My friend Suzanne went to each pair of mother and infant, holding baby after baby with the most delighted look on her face.

Since we'd contributed money here, the Hope Project wanted to feed us breakfast, so we went to the courtyard and sat. And waited. And waited. (Bob was off photographing the beautiful people of the Basti.) I was musing about the surroundings not being as bad as when I was in India eight years earlier. Then, nothing mechanical worked. Everything broke down. And clerks made a point of not waiting on you. Finally, I remembered I hadn't had any dinner the night before. It sometimes happens when traveling with Shahabuddin. It gets very late and he has forgotten about dinner. Weary travelers sometimes decide to just go to bed instead of out for a dinner.

At last, large trays covered with silver domes arrived. I was so hungry I could have eaten plates, domes, trays. Breakfast was uncovered. Fried egg sandwiches on white bread! That was it. Nothing else. A couple of the women jumped up, said they were going back to the hotel, no doubt contrasting the rich abundant food available there with the meager meal before us. Shahabuddin nodded. I was too hungry to go anyplace. I tried to wait until someone handed me a sandwich. Mine was devoured in a minute. It tasted good too! There was one sandwich left on a plate. As I looked at it, I noticed Shahabuddin was eyeing it also, and I remembered learning in the Intensives if someone is looking at your food you need to give them some. Our eyes met over the tray. He gestured toward the plate. "Go ahead," he said. My mouth was watering. "I'll split it with you," I offered. We both grinned. I grabbed the sandwich and divided it into two, totally enjoying this odd and sweet communion with my teacher.

Back from the Basti and still hungry, Bob and I went into the Imperial Hotel to eat. We had to decide which of the restaurants to dine in. One restaurant was an old sailing ship from the seventeenth century dismantled and reassembled. So far we'd only had the breakfast buffet on the terrace, so much food spread out on long, low, white linen covered tables. Heaping platters of many colored fruits, piles of flaky pastry, coffee in silver urns. And we'd been in the lounge one evening when the band played old Beatles tunes, and we explained to nineteen-year-old Nathan about the Beatles coming to India to learn Transcendental Meditation from Maharishi Mahesh Yogi. No one believed being curious about TM was how we'd started on our spiritual journey.

Today, we chose lunch in the room with the grand piano and ordered an exotic eggplant dish. The young waiter asked what we'd seen in Delhi and was appalled when we mentioned the walls of the old city and the Basti. He was puzzled about why we would go to the ghetto. He started recommending museums and art events. We nodded and thanked him.

The food came. It was so much we couldn't possibly eat it all. Then from the grand piano came "Unchained Melody," the sweet haunting song both Bob and I had loved as teenagers when we didn't even know each other and were alone and lonely.

Laundry on the Street

Flooded by the dichotomy of the poverty we'd experienced in the Basti and the affluence of this Hotel with golden chandeliers and marble floors and overabundant food with attendants who wore elaborate costumes, I started to sob. "Get it together," Bob said gently. I nodded, trying to but not doing very well. "How about a cigar?" he said, handing me one.

I sometimes don't notice right at the moment, but Bob is as much my teacher as Shahabuddin, probably from the moment I made the decision to trust that my love for him would lead me to God. He is always beside me, clarifying, discussing, helping, redirecting me when I get mixed up or confused. Maybe that's why Shahabuddin initiated us together with our three heads held close at Steve's.

As we smoked our cigars, we talked over the trip so far and were curious about Andy; she had stayed in Murshid's tomb all night. She had come on the tour at the last minute. We marveled at how she got everything together — passport, vaccines — in two or three days. So taken by the energy in Murshid's tomb, she had asked if she might stay there all night. That morning when I saw her at the Hope Project looking radiant, I asked her how it was sleeping in Murshid's tomb. She beamed at me and said, "Well, I didn't really sleep."

Also at Murshid's tomb that morning we'd met Sherif Baba. We'd heard he was coming, a Turkish sheik with his translator. "Who's coming?" Bob had asked me. "Sherif somebody?" I said, not really knowing anything more. On Shahabuddin's tours much of the time the information doesn't all get passed along. You just find yourself some place you didn't know you were going to, the schedule makes a drastic change, someone new suddenly arrives. But when "Baba" took Bob's hand outside of Murshid's tomb, Bob said the hairs on the back of his neck stood up. "Who is *this*?" Bob asked me again. I had to admit I didn't know. But Baba and Bob took to each other; and despite the fact that Baba spoke almost no English, he and Bob started to sit next to each other and to send each other great beaming smiles.

We laughed too about how just after we had bought a six-pack of imported beer from Holland, counting out dozens of rupees, Shahabuddin strolled by in the lobby and pronounced, "Don't buy that imported beer here, it's too expensive." It seems beer was going to become a major theme of this pilgrimage/vacation.

Now, we retired to our very air-conditioned room to nap and found a warning from the U.S. State Department advising us not to fly into Kashmir tomorrow as planned. The notice warned that the war between India and Pakistan was escalating, and American tourists should not venture into such dangerous territory. We went in search of Carmen; her husband's family was having a wedding in Kashmir that we were invited to attend. She said they had called Aslam's family, and they had reported that there had been no change in conditions, so Shahabuddin's tour was proceeding; however, she took us aside to tell us that if we wanted beer in Kashmir, we'd better smuggle some in. Since Kashmir was mainly Islamic, we'd have to buy beer on the Black Market, and it was very expensive. She instructed us to give her a suitcase, and she'd stow some. We gave her my little soft-sided, black traveling bag with yellow handles—the one I took to India the first time; she filled it with a case of beer in aluminum cans.

PART THREE: LANDING

Because of the war, flying into Kashmir was scary. All the shades on the plane were pulled down. The stewardess called it a "blind landing." I was hoping the pilot could see! Security was very tight! We had to remove all batteries from our cameras and have our luggage very thoroughly checked before boarding. Baba and his interpreter, Jem, changed from their Turkish clothes to something more Indian style for arriving in Kashmir—so there was no immediate concern about Muslim terrorism connected with them.

Retrieving our suitcase from the baggage conveyor belt in Kashmir, we noticed it was dripping and smelly. Some of the metal cans had been smashed! We left a dripping trail across the airport, but even though we went through numerous security checks no one asked about the dripping suitcase. Perhaps we should have been more worried, but everything, even in the midst of a war, seemed light-hearted and fun. Somehow the suitcase later ended up at Aslam's parents' house. They are strict Muslims.

Once outside the airport, we were met by Shahabuddin's traditional wonderful local guides, with gorgeous leis of marigolds, the standard welcome into Kashmir. Our prodigious amount of luggage was loaded into vans, and we were transported toward the row boats which would take us to our houseboats on Dal Lake.

Kashmir had long been recognized as a vacation paradise where the wealthy Indians and the Brits were able to find relief from the heat of southern India. The people of Kashmir were not anxious to sell land to the British, so the British solved the housing dilemma by putting houseboats on the many lagoons and rivers. These beautiful, carved wooden houseboats have been converted into mini-hotels for tourists and are quite elegant accommodations. Guests and their baggage have to be rowed to their rooms. Habid, a seventy-year-old man, rowed Bob and me, Karl and Suzanne, and all of our luggage across the lagoon to our houseboat.

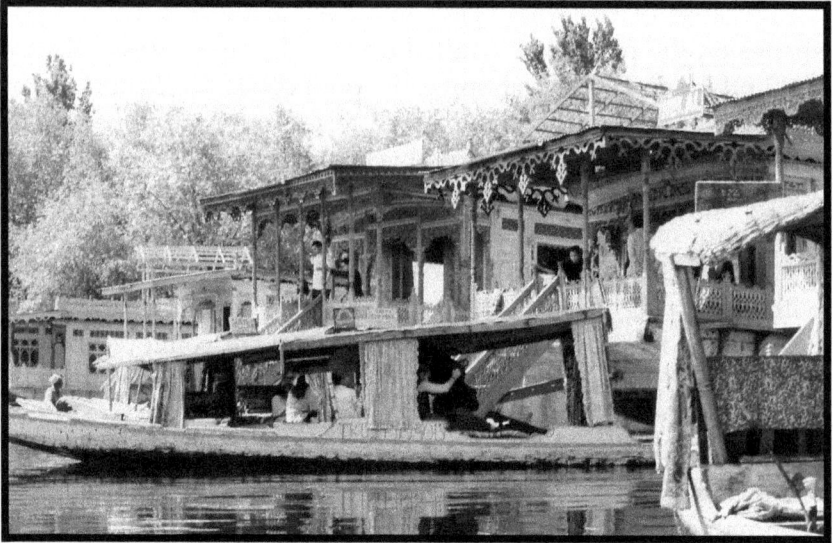

Kashmir Houseboat

The accommodations were exquisite with brocade draperies, Victorian furniture, and embroidered linens on the tables. Ours was the married couples houseboat with three bedrooms, three baths, a large living room and dining room. Our meals were delicious and family-style. We determined the time, and our houseboy carried the green beans, potatoes, and roast chicken in big bowls from the shed, where the cooks prepared food for all the houseboats.

The only annoyance was all the merchants on the chicharas (little rowboats) sailing up to our houseboat and even mounting the stairs into our living room. "Would you like to see my linen ... jewelry ... postcards ... I am a tailor." We learned to say "No, no, no, no, no, no, no" quickly. When our elderly boatman was rowing the four of us across the lagoon to the ancient rose garden of King Akbar, several merchants in boats were hanging onto our boat haggling, and our ferryman ended up rowing all of them. Karl told them to go away and to come to our houseboat tomorrow, which gave Bob an hysterical laughing fit for several minutes imagining all of these guys climbing the stairs into our living room. The sadness of Kashmir is that this beautiful land noted for its gracious welcoming people has been squeezed so by the conflict that the proud warm hosts had been turned into desperate hawkers trying to make a penny here and there.

The first morning of our stay taxis were supposed to come to the houseboats to take us to downtown Srinagar for a shopping trip. Shafee, who owned our houseboats and who, I found out later, was also a rug merchant, wasn't keen on letting this group of tourists get a look at merchandise anywhere else. We were supposed to wait at the rear of the houseboats for taxi pickup, but after one group had been picked up, Shafee saw me, my husband, and Charlotte standing there, and directed us around to the front, which of course, didn't make any sense; there were no roads there, only water. We followed his directions and missed being picked up. We waited and waited on the porch of the houseboat before we finally figured out we had been left behind. About that time Carmen's husband Aslam arrived, and I let loose with a long tirade at him as if it were all his fault. He listened quietly until I finished ranting and raving, then said he was sorry and would tell Shahabuddin. Immediately I was sorry for dumping on him and for getting so angry. It was only about shopping!

Bob, Charlotte, and I ended up spending the afternoon on the porch of the houseboat exchanging life stories. Turns out Charlotte had spent part of her childhood growing up on a houseboat and wasn't too happy about being stuck on one now. Also, all three of us were very disappointed that the part of the trip into Ladakh had been canceled, and now we were going to be spending more time in Kashmir. "On these houseboats!" grumbled Charlotte. I nodded in agreement.

When I woke up the next morning the houseboy said Shahabuddin was on the porch and wanted to see me. He had come last night, but I had already gone to bed. I brushed my hair out of my eyes and went to the porch in my pajamas. "What?" I said as soon as I saw him there drinking tea, talking to Suzanne. He turned and saw me standing there still sleepy and laughed. "Well, it isn't an emergency."

"I know, but what?"

"I just wanted to tell you your anger isn't personal."

"Huh?" I asked.

"It's this place. The war. The conflict. All of it. You are picking up on it. I was very angry yesterday. Then I figured out God wanted me to be angry. You were picking up on it too."

"I was embarrassed that I got so mad about shopping."

"It wasn't just about shopping."

"And I yelled at Aslam."

"He understood." Shahabuddin hugged me.

"Thank you for coming to tell me. I feel better."

He nodded. "You sure?"

He nodded again.

This explanation soothed my ego; perhaps even inflated it a bit. *Both Shahabuddin and I were picking up on things psychically!* But I don't know if I believed it completely. Maybe I was just stressed from traveling; maybe I *was* just having a fit. Maybe Shahabuddin was trying to make me feel better? No, I think he really believed what he was telling me. Now here was this oracular teaching once again, and I again was left puzzling about exactly how to assimilate it into my understanding of the spiritual journey.

Because our scheduled time for Ladakh was canceled, we had more leisure time in Kashmir, and, once I surrendered to it, living on the houseboats became quite idyllic. We decided as a group each day when we wanted to have dinner, and we had our family-style meal with our other dear friends, Casey and Nuria (with whom we had gone to Bali) and Karl and Suzanne, around the beautiful oak table in our dining room, always set with fresh beautiful mums and marigolds sold to us each day by the vendors. Friends from the other houseboats, all part of the tour, came to visit for tea; Basir would find a cake somewhere.

Suddenly, I had a community of friends and spiritual seekers. In Kashmir, India! The days became filled with community life, with some quite funny and absurd events. Nuria had had her nose pierced in Delhi, and it got infected. Kothrenada and Carmen had to operate! Nuria, who doesn't drink, downed a beer before the women began working on her with a needle dipped in alcohol. We drank beer on the roof of the houseboat as the full moon rose one night; looking across the water toward China. One friend explained the conflict between Pakistan and Kashmir; he felt Kashmir saw the Indian army as an army of occupation. We sailed in the chicharas with cushions and curtains to the ancient rose garden. Bob and Karl tried smoking Habid's hookah. When I got migraines, a woman who'd been in a terrible car crash and had her face completely reconstructed, did polarity therapy on me—the migraines vanished quickly. Bob went to some lectures of Baba's, translated by Jem.

Amber on Houseboat

One night I thought the houseboats were moving, but it was only a hallucination from taking my malaria pill. Our houseboy would walk into our bedroom unannounced to store things in the closet. Finding us in bed, he'd announce, "No problem!"

We made a few side trips by land in Kashmir. One was to visit mosques and tombs. The women had been reminded to bring shawls and scarves to cover our heads and arms. At one site, we'd all carefully wrapped ourselves checking to make sure we were properly covered, and as we were proceeding to the entrance, the attendants said something in Arabic to Baba, and he then spoke to Jem. The whole procession stopped. There was some discussion among the group—Shahabuddin, Jem, Baba, then Jem, Baba, attendants. Shahabuddin stepped out of line and to the side, saying softly, "If the women can't go in, I'm not going in either."

Bob translated this teaching further by quipping, "Why *would* you want to go to Heaven if there weren't any women there?" We talked quietly in the courtyard waiting for Jem and Baba to come out of the mosque.

We were also taken to a tomb, located on a side street in Kashmir, behind a blue wooden fence, that the locals claim is the burial place of Jesus Christ. The first time I was in Kashmir, I was asked if I would like to see Christ's tomb. I was thinking of some Sufi saint, somebody Chisti. "Christ who?" I had asked. "Jesus," they said.

"I'm confused," I said. "I thought Jesus Christ ascended into Heaven."

Some people believe that after the resurrection Jesus came to India, lived and taught there for several years, then died and was buried in Kashmir. The tomb is very unassuming. A casket covered with embroidered cloth is enclosed in wire mesh with one opening where you can reach into the space for blessing. There is an imprint of a huge foot in cement. Christ, or whoever is in this tomb, must have been huge, or had enormous feet.

I don't know who is buried there, but both times I've visited I've felt a calm peacefulness and that this was, indeed, a sacred place. There are no signs, no vendors (thank goodness), and no one would know that this was Jesus' tomb unless you were taken there by a guide.

Shahabuddin prayed. Baba prayed. We did a short meditation. I felt blessed and lucky, and I remembered Rúmí's poem.

> ...
> When the nightsky pours by,
> it's really a crowd of beggars,
> and they all want some of this
>
> This
> that we are now
> ...

Pounding Sausage for Wedding

The wedding could have been anticlimactic; after all, there was no ceremony, only the bride changing outfits, the women singing to her, and the men in the courtyard drinking tea. But, forty sheep had been slaughtered for the feast of which we were expected to partake. Bob and I were seated beneath a poster of Ayatollah Khomeini which read, *Death to Americans.* When we asked Carmen about it, she laughed, saying, "Oh, they just like the Ayatollah. The don't know what it says." The family videotaped us eating in groups — about five of us arranged around a large platter on the floor. The cook scooped rice, meatballs, and intestines out of his huge kettles onto the platters. We scooped up the food with our fingers. They asked how we liked the food. We chewed and chewed on the intestines, couldn't get them to disappear. Suddenly, Aslam appeared with a can of beer from his in-laws refrigerator. We looked up shocked. He laughed saying, "They won't know what it is!" Finally, as before the meal, pitchers of water were brought for us to wash with, and the platters were removed. "You have eaten nothing!" the hosts exclaimed as I smiled and Bob stuffed his handkerchief full of spit-out intestines into his pocket.

Since our beer had been taken to Carmen's relative's house we were happy to find beer in our own houseboat refrigerator. No one explained, however, that this was Black Market beer and at the end of our stay the houseboy presented Bob with a bill for well over $100, smiled, said, "You pay now, Baba" (the name he had begun to call Bob). Bob returned the smile and counted off the bills.

We set off from Srinagar for a small encampment in the high Himalayas. As the bus got close to our hotel in Gulmarg, riders on horseback appeared galloping after us, creating clouds of dust, whooping and hollering. With flapping bright clothes and decorated horses, the troop appeared more colorful than threatening. The bus driver laughed and assured us the horsemen were locals happy to see tourists, ready to serve us, carry our luggage, take us on horse rides, and provide us whatever we wanted and whatever they imagined we wanted. The bus got a flat tire making a last turn going up the incline to the hotel, all the more to the delight of our pursuers who scrambled off their horses, ready to take on the whole busload of luggage.

Shahabuddin had already instructed us that as usual he'd pay for the luggage handling as part of the trip package. We were not to get individually involved in haggling with people to provide services, too much potential for getting ripped off, cheated, baggage stolen, etc. A man, bent almost double, hefted Bob's gigantic suitcase onto his crippled back. Bob does not travel light; his luggage included a coffee pot, ceramic coffee mugs, binoculars, various snacks, medicine, lots of books, lots of clothes. Bob removed the suitcase, demonstrated the handle that pulled out and how the suitcase could be tipped and rolled on wheels. The elderly man watched, pushed the handle in, returned the suitcase sideways, struggled to heft it onto his bent back, and proceeded up the hill toward the hotel. We assumed he thought the tip would be larger if he carried the luggage rather than wheeled it.

I found myself trekking up the path beside Shahabuddin through a hillside covered with dainty purple flowers. "Wow!" we both said.

"What do you think?" he asked me. "Shall we stay here the whole time instead of moving?"

"I'd be for it," I said.

"Of course," he added, "we haven't seen the other place, and I'll lose my deposit."

"Oh, then," I began.

"No," he laughed, "you already made your decision."

The Sufi teaching is to make a decision. It doesn't matter so much if it is right or wrong. It is just important to decide, and then abide by the decision whether or not you like the outcome. Had I really decided for the entire group just like that? I guess I had. Well, I might as well enjoy it. The landscape was totally beautiful. Gorgeous Himalayas, fresh mountain air, purple flowers everywhere. Besides making the decision, the mureed is supposed to make the best of that decision within the confines of the choice. Ha! It would be easy to make the best of this decision.

Each room had its own wood-burning stove, a bed with a feather tick mattress, and a servant standing outside the door who was more than ready to be of service when you stepped outside. Since the conflict with Pakistan, tourism was nil, and everyone was desperate for business and work.

There was a Hindu temple we could see from our porch, a short walk across a meadow, and we decided that would be a nice enough venture for the afternoon. However, we were soon pounced upon by an ancient "guide" who showed us his official guide papers from the British days. He told us he once had met President Wilson. This produced an immediate argument between Bob and me. "We don't need a guide! We're going to walk across a field! We can see the temple from here!" The man stood grinning sheepishly. Finally he was employed, told to walk a few paces apart so we could have some space, and the three of us took off for the temple which was typically Hindu, red and garish, full of images, objects, plastic gewgaws and artificial flowers. It was glassed in; we couldn't go inside.

An Indian family wanted to take our picture and wanted to be in our picture. We were supposed to send them pictures.

Shahabuddin said, "You'll have to do it!" But we never did. We told the guide we wanted to meditate there for a few minutes, and he moved a few feet away. When we were finished he led us to a cemetery that we probably would have missed. British, died and buried in Kashmir. We read tombstones and looked up to see a dark-eyed, dark-haired man watching us at the periphery of the cemetery. Thinking back now Bob says maybe it was someone from the Taliban; maybe it was, or just a curious local watching the Americans, or someone else wanting the tourists' business.

Back at our hotel door the old man flashed his official guide papers and pointed to his whole-day guide fee. We shook our heads. "Nope," we said. "No whole day fee." I grumbled, "Give him a half day, and he's still ripping us off." Bob nodded. We went into our room and peeked out. A servant there moved slightly when he saw the curtain move.

We could have ridden to the top of the mountain; the horses and horsemen had all been arranged. Gentle horses, experienced horsemen, they hung onto their horses' tails. I'm not a horse lover. I'm afraid of them. I'd ridden a few times—but Bob loves horses. He's a natural rider. I can do it, but it's not really fun for me; but that's not really the reason I decided to walk. I wanted to see if I could do it. If I could make it to this Himalaya Mountain Peak (13,000 feet) on my own two feet. The other walkers were in terrific shape—Carmen the Hope Project woman, her 13-year-old daughter, Casey who works out, a woman from a Texas ranch, a young girl from Switzerland! "I'm walking!" I said.

The problem was my shoes. I have different sized feet and, I'd lately discovered, very wide feet. I can rarely find shoes that fit. I mostly own open-toed sandals, Birkenstocks, no tennis shoes. So for this climb I had to choose between my clogs and sandals. I chose clogs. (Bad choice!) Going up was not too bad for a while, although I felt like I was slowing the others. Some of the horsemen followed us. I asked Carmen why. "They think we will get tired and want to ride," she laughed. "Well," I said, indignant, "We said we were going to walk. Don't they know we mean what we say?" She shrugged. I panted. Huffed and puffed. Halfway up we stopped at base camp and met up with the rest, horsemen and all. Carmen's daughter said her legs hurt and she wanted to ride. The horsemen grinned in glee. *She's young*, I thought. *Young people don't always follow through on what they say.* We finished our Cokes and climbed on.

At the top I crawled onto a big rock, panting, and closed my eyes. Grateful to rest. Shahabuddin and Kothrenada passed out cheese and bagels. I was too tired to be hungry. Suddenly we were all gathering around a boulder, touching it and chanting. "This rock," said Shahabuddin, "is India, Pakistan … the whole conflict." Then we were praying. Praying for peace. Everyone's hands were on the rock. Everyone's eyes were closed. Singing. Chanting … Salaam. Shalom …

The horsemen asked what we were doing. Carmen's cousin told them we were praying for peace.

"They came all this way to pray for peace?" they asked.

Sanjay said, "Yes."

"It isn't even their country," they said with tears in their eyes.

Shahabuddin had explained before that Sufis go where there is war. Now he turned and walked toward his horse. "Let's go," he said. "This is what we came for."

I thought the way down would be easier, but it was harder. My toes slid to the front of my clogs. I stumbled around and got more stubborn. Carmen walked slowly with me. The Swiss girl leapt ahead like a mountain goat. Casey said I should have trained for this. I hate people who tell me what I should have done. Carmen asked about my shoes. I explained. "You probably would have been better off with the sandals," she offered. I nodded. I didn't know how I was going to do this, but the horsemen had gone on now. There was no way out but to come down off the mountain. Like laboring to have a baby. Texas woman gave me her hand when she saw me slipping. I slid all the way on the mud into a puddle. "Oh well," I said, getting up. "It feels good, cool."

Finally, there was the meadow. Carmen waved, went toward her cabin. I collapsed on my back. I didn't have to move. I could lie there as long as I wanted. Until I was good and ready. Until I felt like I could get up again and walk. I made it. To the top and back down again. Only because I was stubborn. Flat on my back, surrounded by delicate purple flowers and tall grasses, I gazed at the sky. How gloriously blue Heaven's dome was, how lucky I was, how tired I was. I decided I'd stay right there for the rest of the trip.

I was too tired to make the trek to the restaurant for lunch; and, of course, at lunch the announcement was made that dinner would be late that evening, so I was very hungry by the time I got to eat at nine o'clock that night!

We were delighted when we discovered we had an afternoon with nothing scheduled. Bob and I thought we'd just lounge about on our feather bed, but I had done a psychic reading for someone the day before, and the word quickly passed among the group. Everyone wanted a tea reading and lined up on the lawn outside the cabins for them. Bob brought me an umbrella, and I sat underneath beside the purple flowers, looking toward the mountains. Someone ordered tea, and I did one reading after another. I closed my eyes. I counted backward from ten. Then three to one, evoking my male and female guides. Then opened a mind screen and when images appeared I started to speak. The readings went on throughout the afternoon. Every time I looked up it seemed as though the line was growing longer.

Jem, Baba's translator had heard about the readings too. When our plane was landing in Kashmir he had rushed to my seat wanting a reading. We were waiting to deplane, people were standing in the aisles listening; it was hard to concentrate. "Oh, just do it," Bob urged. "Okay, I'll try," I replied. I closed my eyes, counted down, evoked my guides, saw some images, started talking. Usually the images come and go so fast I don't remember them. Apparently this reading created quite a stir unknown to me. It was full of images of death and dying in Turkey. Baba and Jem were supposed to go to Turkey after our time in India, and Jem was afraid the reading indicated something about Baba's death there. Jem talked to Carmen about it and even went to Baba. All Jem said to me was that Baba told Jem, Jem was going to get his ass kicked.

Some time after we got home from India, Kothrenada called me late one night to say she had gotten an e-mail from Jem in Turkey who was helping with the burials after the devastating earthquakes. Many of the images from the reading were occurring. She had called to confirm the reading for me. I didn't know what to think.

One young woman who had come with her boyfriend asked the next day for a second reading. I laughed. "Nope," I said, "you had yours. Only one a trip!" Still fellow travelers started coming to our houseboat and up to the roof where I just wanted to look at the full moon, drink beer, and talk. I was beginning to get just a little bit of an idea what Shahabuddin's life must be like all the time.

Our travel agenda started to go in reverse. From Gulmarg we returned to Kashmir. Shahabuddin reminded us before we went to the airport in Kashmir to fly to Delhi, then home, that there is always a "crash" when you leave India. "You get diarrhea, lose things, spill coffee on your mate, fight with your best friend. No matter how many times you've been and leave," he informed us. "So, go slowly." Just as he promised, I got diarrhea when I was trying to pack. Bob got sick on the way to the airport. We had to stop so he could vomit. I was glad Shahabuddin had given us some advance warning. Then there was security at the airport.

Going through customs leaving Kashmir wasn't bad for me. The women were searched by Indian women soldiers. They went through my notebook, looked at all my sketches, giggled, and waved me through. On the men's side, however, Casey said he told them his pills were vitamins, and they made him take one.

Nathan told me as he came through they made him drink some of the water in his bottle. I started to worry about Bob, still behind the curtains with his whole shaving bag full of medication. If they made him take all of that he'd have a cardiac arrest! Suzanne fretted that authorities might think Bob was a drug dealer with his many vials of heart medicine. From the airport lobby I tried to peer into the security area. We could see Bob's straw hat bobbing up and down behind the security screen. By standing on tiptoe I was able to glimpse the Indian guard with Bob's hat on *his* head laughing. Soon Bob walked into the lobby.

"How'd it go?" I asked anxiously.

"Oh," Bob said, "I gave him a couple cigarettes, a candy bar, told him I was an old man that needed my medicine, and he let me through."

Now I relaxed and waited to board for Delhi.

In Delhi, Shahabuddin asked what we were going to do before the plane left. Bob wanted to go somewhere air-conditioned. It was 118 degrees, and the monsoon hadn't come, so the humidity was suspended in the air, and he was sweating through his jeans. He had two bandannas he used for headbands. He'd wring one out, tie it around his leg to dry, and put the other around his forehead to keep the sweat out of his eyes. It was not a costume; it was a necessity. But teenaged Nathan, traveling with his mother, stared at Bob the first day at lunch and said in awe, "You were there, weren't you?" Bob looked back, puzzled. "You were at Woodstock, weren't you?" We both laughed. "Nope," we said. "But you're right, we're old enough to have been, and we like the music."

Now in the bus Shahabuddin leaned over and said, "*You* don't want to go someplace air-conditioned, do you?" I got what he was suggesting. "No," I said, "I thought I'd just stay in Murshid's tomb." He grinned. "I'll buy you a Coke, Bob," he joked, "if you stay in the tomb." Then he added seriously. "I was thinking of initiating you two there, but don't spread it around."

PART THREE: LANDING

I don't know how many times Shahabuddin has added, "Don't tell anyone!" after an invitation, but I understand the necessity. He has many mureeds. He can't take everyone to lunch. He can't cook dinner for everyone. He can't make a financial exception for everyone (or maybe he does?). If he is going to do an initiation, other people will want an initiation, and perhaps it's not their time.

When I was having such a difficult time with anger in Kashmir, Shahabuddin had told me he also thought I was going through some sort of initiation; and when he said that, I remembered an initiation in my dream. The belief is that you often undergo the initiation on another level; the one you receive on the earthly level is just an affirmation of the other state. So we decided to stay at the tomb with Shahabuddin, even though the heat was almost unbearable, and our clothes were soaked through, even our underwear.

I started to draw Murshid's tomb in my notebook, but I had trouble trying to make it go onto the page. And my pen exploded and I got ink all over my hands. I took another pen and started on the column at the head of the golden casket. It came out crooked, didn't look right, and then that pen too exploded. Shahabuddin shook his head, "I think you're not supposed to be distracted here." So I put my drawing materials away. "But you can wash," he laughed, and I went to the small adjacent restroom. When I came back I held out my ink-stained hands and said, "See? I didn't have to stay for henna at the wedding. I have my own designs." Shahabuddin took my palm and read it. "Oh," he said, looking at the thumb, "the crescent moon." Then he moved down my fingers, "A Hindu symbol, eyes coming through from the unseen world, a mystery." And the big slash across my palm he said was "Vajra," my Sufi name. Someone brought the Cokes he ordered, and we stepped outside into the courtyard and drank the cold, sweet liquid out of glass bottles. Shahabuddin said, "Here it is, 110 degrees and we are completely happy." It was true. The contentment spilled with the sweet drink down my throat and through my body and soul.

Back inside we sat quietly. He tried to tell the travel agent who Murshid was and about the tomb, but the travel agent wasn't really interested. He wanted Shahabuddin to read *his* palm. The agent left to negotiate some tickets to Bali. After a few minutes Shahabuddin said, "Wasn't I going to initiate you?" We nodded. I got up. "Not yet," he said. He retreated to the corner and began to sing very softly and sweetly "Sufi Inayat" over and over. The sound was so tender it reminded me of a loving lullaby. Just then the travel agent appeared in the dargah doorway waving tickets. Shahabuddin went out, talked to him, came back, and resumed singing. Again, the agent was in the door. Shahabuddin left again for another conversation. He reentered the tomb laughing. "That's really traveling between two worlds," he said, "but I'm ready."

I stood in front of him, and he pushed down on my shoulders. His dark eyes, so intense, deep, and open. I wanted to turn away, but I made myself keep looking into them, and if I have any idea what eternity will be like it will be like those eyes of Shahabuddin's. He prayed for my protection. He prayed for my wisdom. He linked me to the lineage of saints and prophets. He prayed that I find the purpose of my life, which is illumination. He blessed me. He hugged me. My heart quickened, and for moments the whole dargah was inside the heart of Hazrat Inayat Khan pouring through Shahabuddin's eyes seeing us and loving us. He then turned to Bob to initiate him.

Charlotte had gone to visit another tomb; she came in with a basket of rose petals. We scattered them over Murshid's casket like little children playing in water or snow. Others from our group started to arrive. Shahabuddin said, "We better say goodbye."

"Can't we say goodbye at the airport?" Casey asked. Shahabuddin gestured toward Murshid's casket, and I was washed with sweetness, love, blessings, gratitude. There must be other words to describe this newly sprung fountain radiating bliss from my heart, but my mouth didn't know how to sing them yet.

On the way to the airport I thought I saw a cow walking across the street, but I was so high I wasn't sure. I stayed so high all the way home that I left my notebook in the Amsterdam airport

PART THREE: LANDING

at seven in the morning. I called the airport trying to retrieve it; but no one had found it, and I had to let it go. Finally, arriving in our living room, I was twirling the prayer wheel from Ladakh we bought in a shop in Kashmir. Baba had blessed it, twirling it round and round smiling, saying in halting English, "Love you/Miss you." As I swung it around, it flew out of my hand and bammed into our coffee table, making two dents. Oh yes! Shahabuddin had said, "There's always a crash when you leave India."

DRINKING COGNAC

We're drinking cognac in the Amsterdam Airport.
It's seven in the morning on the airport clock,
but our tired bodies tick nighttime hours.

We drink beer we order in the beach
theme bar and sit at little tables high
above the airport crowd. Anything goes!

We've bought cognac, chocolate, cheese,
at the duty-free shops. Eating sweet rolls,
cheese chunks, devouring candy — all

dietary prohibitions forgotten, routines
all screwed up. We're broken-hearted
lovers wrenched away from beloved India —

Love we've met only briefly, fell for
deeply. Winging our way home now
far in the opposite direction like

bird flocks changing season.
Oh India! You remain, shrouded
in your misty Himalayas, vibrating

with color and car horns, wrapped
in the scent of strong spices, emanating
brown-eyed smiles and signaling

with little whiffs of human excrement.

(From *How Much Our Dancing Has Improved*)

PART FOUR

On the Path

PART FOUR: ON THE PATH

We had been to Turkey, Bali, and India with Shahabuddin, taken a two-year Intensive and many other workshops. For many years I did my Sufi practices every morning. I joked that I would not go anywhere or do anything else if I could not do my Sufi practices first; but it wasn't really a joke, and first thing every morning, I faithfully did the breathing practices Shahabuddin had taught us in seminars and then the wazifas he had assigned me personally. These practices changed from time to time as I would check in with him. The whole process would take me about an hour, so I gradually gave up practicing yoga because I did not seem to have time for both the breathing/wazifas and the physical practice of yoga. I no longer did the regular meditation of sitting and observing my breath either. My practices became specifically what Shahabuddin prescribed.

My general attitude toward life continued to be very positive and optimistic, and a general joy spread through my daily activities. My mind no longer yapped like a barking dog, and much of the time I met each moment as it came. I knew when I lost it and could stand back and see myself exhibiting my old behavior. *Oh well,* I thought, *I'm so much better most of the time.*

I had spent many Sundays being depressed—something about the open space of the day, yet the weekend ending and the work week looming put me in a blue funk. My overactive brain had been relentless in torturing me for years. I was always worrying about the future, stewing about the past, trying to be impossibly perfect. My mind would not shut up or leave me alone. Now, blessedly, much of this had given way.

I was no longer panicked about getting out of Norfolk. Shahabuddin had advised once that when I had everything just the way I wanted it in Norfolk, then I could leave. I more or less had put that goal out of my mind for the present and was busy engaging in my life. All of these attitude changes helped me know I had at last found the right path for me.

After the second trip to India and the initiation in Murshid's tomb, I had no doubts about being on the Sufi path. I knew that's where I belonged, and my heart was full of gratitude for finding Shahabuddin and the teachings of Hazrat Inayat Khan. I remembered back to a very early time, before I really knew Shahabuddin well but still called him to ask if I should take a leave of absence from my teaching job to go to Boulder for a semester. Bob and I were at a tumultuous time in our marriage. I didn't like living in Norfolk. I found Boulder and the writers and parties much more interesting and exciting.

Bob was outside planting a rosebush. Shahabuddin didn't know us well either. I think we'd done one or two workshops with him. He was quiet for a minute or two. Then he said he didn't think so. He said if I did, he was afraid I would lose Bob, and I wasn't ready for that. "Oh," I said. "Thank you." I went outside to report to Bob, and the issue was closed. I didn't go. It was that early intuitive wisdom of Shahabuddin's that helped keep us together.

My friend Suzanne says this story is an example of the way a good spiritual teacher-student relationship works. The student trusts enough to ask for advice and follow it. The teacher steps up to the plate, takes a risk and the responsibility to help the student in a completely honest way. It works, she says, if the teacher's a real teacher. I guess I was lucky that time. I think Shahabuddin has pretty much stopped telling people what to do with their lives!

And speaking of luck, in *Eat, Pray, Love* Elizabeth Gilbert says,

> The classical Indian sages wrote that there are three factors which indicate whether a soul has been blessed with the highest and most auspicious luck in the universe:
>
> 1. To have been born a human being, capable of conscious inquiry.
> 2. To have been born — with or have developed — a yearning to understand the nature of the universe.
> 3. To have found a living spiritual master.

Yes, for whatever reason, I was one of those amazingly lucky ones the sages spoke about for whom "destiny's molecules organized" and my "path intersected with the path of the master I needed."

Once Shahabuddin spoke about what we were all doing there together, in that particular room, at a particular seminar. He believed, he said, that our souls were all touched somehow by Hazrat Inayat Khan's energy as we were coming into manifestation. It seemed to make sense to me, and I was totally grateful to Hazrat Inayat Khan, Shahabuddin, and whomever on either side who had aided in this source of blessing.

THE WRITING

Save me, my Lord
      from the evil eye of envy and jealousy
      which falleth upon Thy bountiful gifts.

(From "Dowa" by Inayat Khan)

All this time I'd been writing, but I hadn't published much. My friend Natalie was famous. I still didn't have even a chapbook out. I had a few poems published here and there. When I heard about other writers' awards and publications I felt envious and wanted badly to be recognized. I knew it wasn't because my writing was terrible. My writing had gotten better over the years as I continued to work on it. I just couldn't seem to break through anywhere to have it seen. Something had to give. I couldn't stand the suffering anymore. Maybe I should give it up.

In meditation the answer came to me. I didn't need to give up the writing. Writing brought me many rewards. I got to live my life twice, reliving the events I was writing about, embracing and cherishing them another time. My memory was a lot better than most of my friends' memories because I was paying attention and taking everything in and then writing it down. Also, I had a wonderful written record of my life. I didn't want to give all that up, even if I never published a book. The only solution was to give up the suffering. The comparing and the competition, feeling the injustice of others' work getting recognition while mine was not. ("No Comparing" was one of the four C's I was supposed to be practicing anyway!)

Once I made that decision, much to my amazement, I was able to follow through with letting go. I was able to continue writing and not feel envy or jealousy toward my friends and others who were more successful in their writing careers. I believe my spiritual practices helped me surrender to the moment and my life as it was, instead of how I thought it should be. And, I finally made the connection that writing was my practice just as much as the wazifas and breathing techniques. When I was "on" I was connected with the Creative Life Energy. It was flowing through me to make art. The resulting product did not have to be published to be valued. I was indeed doing part of my life's purpose.

Eventually, after over twenty years of writing, publishing over a hundred poems in small journals, and the publication of two chapbooks, I finally had a full-length book of poems published. That too came with some delays (it wasn't done in time for the Nebraska Writing Festival as promised) and disappointments (it didn't win the Center for the Book award), but there it was in my hand, my very own book of poems! When I had given up the grasping, what I desired so much came to me.

We went to Shahabuddin's Rising Tide Institute for a weekend seminar one July shortly after my poetry book was published. Shahabuddin has always been a big fan of my poetry — he understands it deeply, is entertained and amused by it. I saw that there were several Sufi books for sale on a table in the corner and asked if I might display my poetry book as well. Shahabuddin nodded. After the first break, when everyone was settled, I looked up to see him holding my book, and he began the session by reading several of my poems. No prelude, just reading the poems. It was an odd and wonderful experience to hear my poems read aloud in a deep male voice, a voice so treasured in my heart. The poems took on a very different perspective. After several minutes of reading, he stated simply, "If you haven't figured it out, these are Barbara's poems, and the book's for sale."

At lunch break, peopled milled around the table, picked up the book, thumbing through it, asking how much it cost. I sold all but one. When I told Shahabuddin at the end of the day, he laughed and said, "Where's my commission?" I said, "There's one book left. You can have that!" He reached for it eagerly. "I know who I'm going to give this to," he said, "someone who likes Natalie Goldberg." Natalie had written the blurb on the back of the book.

During this time of my life, I would take overnight trips to poet Marge Saiser's house in Lincoln. We'd write Friday afternoon in a restaurant, have supper, write more Friday evening, usually a couple of times. We'd get up early on Saturday, have breakfast, go out for coffee with the Prairie Trout (Lincoln Writing Group), write some more, and I'd start home. One weekend had been particularly powerful. In fact, I'd had to get up out of bed to write a poem that kept coming when I was trying to go to sleep.

When I traveled in those days I'd usually listen to tapes from Shahabuddin's seminars, and some of them were tapes of Shahabuddin doing practices with his mureeds. Some of them were zikr, the Sufi practice of remembrance, "La illaha illallah hu; There is no God but God." In other words, it's all God. We'd been advised not to do this while we were driving, but Bob and I did it all the time anyway and often got very high. We hadn't had any accidents or near accidents, so we guessed it was all right.

I was on my way home, already high from so much writing and getting higher from listening to the tapes and doing zikr. Suddenly filled with a longing for God, I yelled out loud, "Let me see your face, Oh Lord," remembering the movie version of *In Country* where Emmett is up in a tree in a lightning storm and yells out something similar. Just then I passed a peeling white church on the highway I've passed many times, and painted on the side in huge faded red letters was the message, "God is within you." I knew there was something on the side of the church, but I didn't remember it said that! I thought that was a good answer so I tried it again. I yelled once more, "Let me see your face!"

Out of the corner of my eye I saw a fence approaching on my right and beside it the most enormous pig I've ever seen in my life. I didn't think it could possibly be real. It appeared to be nearly four feet tall. A ray of sunlight blazed down from the sky to the pig. Something was telling me, "THIS IS GOD."

If this were a movie, the most beautiful music would have surged up. The camera would have panned to the beauty of the clouds, the rows of corn glistening in the sunlight. Somehow the clouds were God's face, the corn his teeth. He *was* showing me his face. I asked and received. It was so simple and yet so astonishing. And I just kept driving down the highway, smiling a huge grin, chuckling, saying out loud, "Yeah, oh, yeah!"

At one seminar I had complained about living in Norfolk, Nebraska, far away from a Sufi community. I told Shahabuddin it was lonely there; there were no other Sufis. He looked at me briefly and then said, "You need to start something." There, now the responsibility was on me. I couldn't just sit and whine. I had to do something about it.

I had no idea how much effort this endeavor was going to take. I had to apply to be a Sufi group coordinator—fill out applications, send a full facial photo. I felt good when I was approved by Atum, the gentle Secretary General of the Sufi Order who, appraising my application, said he sensed I was a sensitive and aware person. Those were two qualities I would most wish to possess.

I called as many people in town as I could think of who might be interested in a Sufi study group. Then I realized I was going to have to prepare material. I felt woefully inadequate to present Hazrat Inayat Khan's teachings. In fact, I had read very little of Murshid's writing. I had always intended to and sometimes picked up a volume from his collected works, which we owned, but never got further than a few pages. I much preferred receiving the teaching through Shahabuddin. I reasoned that the Sufis say you receive Sufism through transmission—being in the presence of a master—Sufism being an oral tradition. And Shahabuddin always taught us it was experience, not concepts, that mattered. But I knew some of that was rationalizing.

As I began to read more to prepare, I sensed that Shahabuddin had done it to me again. In suggesting I "start something" he had forced me to study the teaching deeply in order to present it to the class. He was continually giving me what I needed when I needed it, though not always in the form I would prefer to have it presented.

Three or four people usually showed up for class. One woman came because she was lonely and just wanted some company. One couple came because they were curious and were checking out everything esoteric. One woman was genuinely into the teaching and practices. In fact, she did one practice so intensely she started to have a negative experience. I felt at a loss at how to advise her other than to tell her to discontinue doing it. She was the only one who came every week and continued until we had a fire in our house and had to live in a motel for six weeks; after that I didn't restart the group.

So, I could no longer complain that I didn't have a community. I had a tiny one that met, bimonthly, in my own home.

THE ART OF PERSONALITY

Shortly after we retired from our teaching jobs, Shahabuddin offered month-long training in The Art of Personality, one of Murshid's teachings, in Sarasota, so we packed up and drove south enjoying our road trip, never having driven through the Deep South before. I sang "Rainy Night in Georgia" to the motel maid in Macon who looked at me with a silly grin outside in the drizzling rain.

We got a good rate at the Calais Motel for a month in Sarasota. It had a swimming pool, a kitchen with dishes and pots and pans so we could do light cooking, and a bedroom with a door so one of us could move during the night when Bob snored. We were all set for a Florida vacation and some in-depth spiritual work.

Shahabuddin would take delight many days in moving our class from our usual meeting room to the beach. We would scramble for hats and sunscreen and reassemble in a few minutes on Sarasota's public beach, a stretch of glittering white sand next to the gentle rolling blue-green surf, a beach known as one of the most beautiful in the world. The white sand is crumbled Appalachian mountain rock and is carefully raked and maintained each morning by crews leaving it pristine and beautiful in the glorious Florida day.

Here, Shahabuddin assigned such practices as writing Allah on the horizon with our fingers, then with our eyes. Finally when we looked up, there was the word "Allah" sparkling in the air. (In our practice Allah includes "everything"; there is nothing that is not Allah, in contrast to the Islamic idea of Allah being God). Also, we wrote the word Allah and other wazifas in the waves, allowing the words to dance there, then be washed away with the outgoing water. I converted this practice to writing Allah into the branches of my backyard walnut tree when I returned to Nebraska.

The most intense beach exercise was "getting born and dying." Shahabuddin drew a long channel in the sand. He gouged a round circle at the top representing Oneness. The Astral plane was aligned directly below this under a horizontal line. We traversed one at a time from the Oneness space, through the Astral world, to the next plane, the Jinn—which Shahabuddin explained is where thoughts and inspirations, especially poetic and artistic inspirations, originate. Each of us flowed down the channel Shahabuddin had drawn there in the sand, down to the material world through the birth canal where Shahabuddin was waiting. He caught each of us as we entered the world, embraced us, and told us to go have a life for ten minutes.

Fortunately, I allowed myself to just follow the directions and not worry about what this exercise was supposed to *mean*. I began my ten minutes of life by enjoying the footprints I was leaving behind me in the sand as I walked to the ocean edge. Just as I was entering the water I looked up to see Bob, took his hand and we walked into the water together. Some of the younger members of our group dived into the ocean and swam. The sand, the glistening water and sun, the faces of the group, and especially Shahabuddin's and Bob's faces were shining, full of light and preciously beautiful because I knew that I had such a brief time to gaze at them and take them into my heart; very soon all of this would be ending.

In a few short minutes, Shahabuddin announced it was time to die. We went individually backward according to our ages moving our bodies without speaking from the material plane, through the Jinn plane, the Astral world, and into the Oneness—a line of human beings backing into eternity. As I enacted leaving the planet, I could see my dear friends standing in line on the sparkling white beach waiting to follow behind me. I truly did feel like I was glimpsing the world for a last time. My friend Nuria said she felt especially sad as she watched me leave the onlookers and my earthly life to return to the Oneness.

A tourist walking by just about crossed the channel Shahabuddin had drawn, but suddenly seemed to feel its intensity and looked up to see us all gathered around it. He looked startled and gave it wide berth. "No birth and death for him today," someone quipped, and we all drew close and embraced.

Shahabuddin did not offer much explanation for this exercise (other than "dying was easier than being born"); rather, he just gave us the experience. And, as with many of his experiential practices, it took some time to absorb. I believe he was allowing our spirits to experience our souls' journey into manifestation and back again.

We soon found out at the Calais that we had a neighbor from the seminar who lived three doors down. Khalil loved to cook; he loved to sing; he recited poetry. He very soon painted me a gorgeous t-shirt, "Oh, something about Nebraska," with an enormous cornstalk and an undulating sun over a glittering Missouri River. Khalil's belly laugh shook the theater seats and soon had everyone in the movie *Emile* laughing at the Sunday matinee we attended together. We weren't surprised to hear tapping on the door on Sunday morning or to see him standing there, his huge presence, in his bathing trunks, reciting "Condemn Not (one of the four C's) and Key Lime Pie?" bending from the waist and offering a beautiful pie he'd just made.

He had wanted to make a last trip to the beach when we were packing our car to leave but waited for us to get all our belongings in our car — (It took forever because as usual we had brought too much stuff!) — so he could sprinkle water on it and us, blessing us so we'd have a safe trip home.

And we haven't lost touch either. He calls us sometimes out of the blue. We just got a postcard from him from Hong Kong praising the wonderful food there. Khalil seemed to be part of the package; not only did we receive spiritual teaching in Florida but also new friendship. With this friendship I became aware once again that spending time with Shahabuddin gifts my life with interesting people and fabulous experiences. What blessings!

As part of the month-long class, Shahabuddin had been requested to give a cooking lesson. Khalil took the grocery list to the organic and whole food store so all the supplies were ready when Shahabuddin finished teaching his morning class. He looked around to see who wasn't there. Not everyone elected to study cooking. Husband Bob, for example, chose to do the dishes instead. I was there because I wanted to learn more about cooking and more about how Shahabuddin did it, and we all wanted to reproduce his results. His food is succulent, flavorful, spicy, everything food is supposed to be besides nutritious; but more than that, it is fun when Shahabuddin cooks. We wanted to learn about his state of mind as well.

One time at a seminar he invited Bob and me for lunch during a break (one of those "don't tell anybody else" times). I was feeling sorry for him having to cook lunch for us during his time off from teaching the intense workshop. "But, I like to cook," he said. As I watched him gracefully move about his kitchen with his cooking utensils and ingredients all the while having an animated conversation with us, I realized Shahabuddin did not approach his cooking the way I approached preparing our daily meals with a sense of duty and obligation. I needed to learn to be more present. I needed to enjoy cooking!

When I remarked how wonderful it was to have a spiritual teacher who cooked for his students, his reply was if the teacher doesn't cook for his students you need a new teacher. After our last intense meditation retreat was over, there he was out in the kitchen tying on an apron, reaching for a large frying pan.

"Oh boy," I exclaimed. "You cooking?"

"I am," he affirmed. "You eating?"

I nodded my head emphatically.

At cooking class Shahabuddin looked over the apprentice cooks and said, "Barbara, you're strong; you can stir the risotto."

Making risotto requires constant stirring for at least forty minutes. That wouldn't have been so bad, but I had to stir it *across* an open flame in front so I was not only slow cooking the rice but also my forearm. I'll do most anything for Shahabuddin, but after about twenty minutes of arm roasting, I had to ask that someone else take a turn. I can't remember why the burner had to be on, seems like another one didn't work or something. But for most of the lesson, I stirred the risotto feeling very much like Rúmí's cook with his leg stuck into the fire for fuel. I'd rather do this job than debone the chicken anyway.

Shahabuddin cooks like I heard Laurens Van der Post describe how Carl Jung cooked: "Not from a particular recipe, rather just having an idea in mind." He has some ingredients. He has some spices. He puts some things together and makes a delicious meal.

This day we had codfish baked with leeks and onions with some oil, crushed red pepper, salt, lemon juice, cilantro, and white wine. The chicken was dipped in buttermilk and egg and browned; then sugarless jam, wine, and lemon were added, and the dish was baked in a hot oven. The tuna was seared with herbs and mustard.

Risotto was cooked with red wine, Bragg's, and water, and then onion added. Parsley, butter, and pepper were included at the end. Shahabuddin also served salad greens with his great dressing: one part soy sauce, one part balsamic vinegar, three parts olive oil.

I'm sure Shahabuddin wouldn't mind a bit if you used his recipes. He'd add "Bon Appétit" and throw in some blessings. Speaking of blessings, Shahabuddin has also mentioned the ill-effects of eating food cooked by a surly cook, set before you by a grumpy waitress. "Best then to cook at home!"

Last time I saw him in Wisconsin, he told me he went to buy a new stove (He needed one!), and the store owner ran from the back and said, "You're a cook, aren't you?" Shahabuddin affirmed he was. "Why don't you buy a commercial stove?" the owner asked, which was much cheaper than the half conventional/half commercial stoves Shahabuddin was looking at. So the owner took Shahabuddin to the back of the store and sold him one of those instead. And I can see my teacher now smiling in his Sarasota kitchen, choreographing more glorious meals on his new restaurant stove.

The month-long class on The Art of Personality was very intense. It only met in the morning, but we had assignments and practices every day. We found ourselves so exhausted that we usually had to take a nap after lunch. The class and time sped by. On the next-to-last day Shahabuddin was going to do darshan. In darshan the teacher goes into a high state and does a spiritual reading on the student. It's been my experience that Shahabuddin does this practice rather rarely. Each person was to sit in front

208

of him with his/her back to him. Shahabuddin's eyes close; he enters a deep state of concentration, and slowly he begins to speak. The readings are like hearing poetry; rich with images, they demanded concentration on the part of the group and tired everyone.

After he had done a few, we were half collapsed and sprawled about in rather unattentive postures around the room. Shahabuddin stopped, admonished us, and then informed us that he was not doing this for our entertainment. Everyone came to attention, and he continued.

When it was my turn and I sat in front of him, he started to speak, then stopped. "I hate doing this," he said.

"What?" I asked surprised.

"It's just psychic stuff." I could feel him shrug. "But your mother's here."

"What?" I asked again. "She's right here!" he said again emphatically.

My mother never did discuss my Sufi practices or any aspect of my spiritual life with me once I revealed to her that I no longer went to mass. Even as the years went by and I tried many different ways to approach the topic, she'd stubbornly refuse any broaching of the subject.

Finally, near the very end of her life, the day she was being taken from the home in which she had lived all of her married life to be transported to a nursing home in my husband's and my hometown, she turned to me and asked, "Are you right with God?" I said, "Absolutely, Mother." "It's all right, then," she said. I sighed with relief, and she sighed. We hugged.

In addition to the conflict over religion, my mother and I were opposite in many other perspectives. When I was small she always wanted me to play with dolls. One Christmas I was asked what I wanted. When I answered, "A book and a prayer book," my mother replied, "Don't you want a doll?" "No!" I shook my head, standing firm, knowing my young mind. "A book and a prayer book." I got the books, and I also got a doll that I didn't play with.

My mother loved children's play. She loved domestic things. I made a vow I wouldn't be like her, although as I get older I see I am in many important ways, like persistence. But I didn't want to grow a garden, to can vegetables all summer, to cook and to clean. Her world seemed so small, so connected to a house, a city-lot garden. I wanted to travel, to see the world. I was a reader. When I was twelve years old, the city librarian told me I could read anything in the whole adult library. My mom read the newspaper and clipped articles she thought might be interesting to people. When I told my mother I was a writer, she said, "Who are you trying to be?" She thought it best to be humble, not too self-assuming. When I picked out a red winter coat for her when she was older, she said, "Oh, no, people might look at me." I laughed. "I like to have people look at me." When I was home getting ready to go out, she'd have to adjust a hem, a curl, a button. I wanted her to say I looked great. There was always something the matter, in her opinion, with how I looked. She was always trying to fix me.

I accepted that I wasn't the daughter she had been expecting. I didn't like to put my dolls around a card table and play tea party; I didn't like the blouses with bows she bought me. I was disappointing to her in some ways. I did see that she came to accept me. I did see finally that she loved me.

I was really surprised when Shahabuddin said she was there. "What does she want?" I asked.

Shahabuddin backed up. "She's in a good place," he said. "But she's been trying to give you something, and you won't take it. And she can't go any further until you take it. It has something to do with sweetness."

"She's in my dreams, every night," I said, "very real. She seems like she's really there."

"Yes," Shahabuddin said, "she *is* really there, because she is trying to contact you. She cannot go on until you take her gift." I just stared at him. "You'd better think of something," he said with a laugh. "I don't want her coming into my dreams."

"Okay," I said, stunned, but somehow also pleased that she had found her way to Shahabuddin, had contacted him, had seen him. He went on with my darshan, telling me I was going to go through a confusing time. He went on to explain that I would not *necessarily* have to go through the confusion, but it was the only way to get to my next stage of development. He named some people who were to be my guides, including Sufi Sam — that was comforting. He said I was going to write the gospel, of what he didn't know. Not another one of these enigmatic teachings to ponder!

Local mureeds occasionally joined the seminar, and right in the middle of our darshan one walked in and sat down. Shahabuddin shook his head no, and this seeker realized Shahabuddin was doing darshan and got up and left. However, in the next minute, Shahabuddin sent someone after him. After the mureed had rejoined the group Shahabuddin explained, "I was told (intuitively) not to send the person away who came in, and I forgot," and I believe he was also being kind. This student got to go to the front of the line and have darshan also.

One young person wrote down Shahabuddin's words for each person so we had that record to compare to what we remembered from our session. It was a very long, exhausting day by the time everyone's darshan was completed.

Back at the Calais Motel, I began pondering how to solve this Mother presence in my dream. The image of my mother's Christmas cookies came to me. She always made around a thousand cookies; my brother had her count them and record the number on our kitchen blackboard. She gave them away in tins to family and neighbors, beautiful, tiny, decorated, melt-in-the-mouth delicacies. I visualized myself taking and eating her Christmas cookies, accepting her sweetness, and she accepting my sweetness, both of us loving each other the way we were. I kept encouraging her to make her cookies right up until her last year of life. "Why?" she asked me. "You don't approve of white sugar." "That doesn't matter," I said. "It's your art. Your gift. What you offer so beautifully to the world. My opinion about sugar isn't important. You need to do this." So it was the perfect metaphor for us to let the love flow between us.

When I saw Shahabuddin the next day before he left for India, I reported that she wasn't in my dreams that night. She wasn't for many nights after that either. Then when I dreamed of her again, it was different. It wasn't her real presence so much as before.

After this month-long seminar with Shahabuddin, most of us attendees were wiped out, but he had to leave for an important meeting at the Hope Project (the Sufi School and charity at Murshid's tomb in India). As we shared our concluding meal he said, with tears in his eyes, that at the end of his life he was going to have to answer to Murshid about how well he had done on Earth spreading the Message. I wish I had hugged him, told him what a kind, deep, compassionate, funny, understanding teacher he was, and that Murshid would be most pleased with him. But I was too slow, and he was off in a flurry as usual, holding up a bottle of "No Tangles" hair conditioner as his goodbye message.

ISRAEL

The first night in Sarasota at dinner Shahabuddin said he was planning a trip to Israel to pray for peace, and he wanted Bob and me to go. He thought we would be very important members of the trip; our energy would be most essential. I said, "I don't know anything about Israel. I don't know what I could do." Bob said he didn't know anything about the turmoil in the Middle East either, and he didn't want to go. After dinner, Shahabuddin was getting a massage from one of his students in his living room, and we began to say our goodbyes. We thought he was nearly asleep, but before Bob and I could get to the door Shahabuddin sat up from the massage table like Lazarus rising from the dead. "Think about the Israel trip," he said, smiled, and lay back down.

Neither of us wanted to go, and we were sure we couldn't afford it. We had just retired from our teaching jobs and had recently taken a trip to San Francisco where I'd enrolled in an expensive fiction writing workshop. Bob had bought me a laptop computer so I could work on my novel, and now we were doing this month-long seminar with Shahabuddin and paying for a month of housing in Florida as well. He kept insisting all through the month, and we kept declining until we said finally, "No, we can't afford it, and we're not going!"

Almost immediately back at home, we received a check in the mail from my Aunt Gladys's estate. We had thought we had already gotten all of our inheritance, but unbeknownst to us there was still a substantial amount left to be distributed among her nieces and nephews. The afternoon after the check arrived, Shahabuddin called. He explained that his daughter was unable to go on the Israel trip; he had an extra ticket, and he wanted to ask us to go again for a reduced price. He quoted the price. It was the exact amount of the check that had arrived the day before. I was silent. He added that God would make it clear what we should do, and would we please call him back by morning.

"Yes," I said and hung up.

I looked at Bob. "What?" he asked.

"I guess we're going to Israel," I said, rolling my eyes.

Our son was worried. He didn't want us to go to Israel. My nephew said to my brother about my phone call, "Maybe it's a joke; it's April first." My brother, knowing me and my traveling with Shahabuddin, assured him it wasn't a joke, I was really going.

I wasn't worried about my safety until a day or two before when we were watching the evening news and saw the devastation from yet another suicide bombing. I got frightened that night but started to laugh in the middle of my wide-awake worry when I remembered Shahabuddin telling me during the last phone call about an oracle whom one of his mureeds had discovered. This oracle, after a great deal of persuading and, I think, some bribing(?), finally agreed to see Shahabuddin. The oracle told Shahabuddin the trip was going to turn out well; in fact Shahabuddin should take even more people. *And this is supposed to make me feel more reassured?* I half-smiled to myself in the dark. When I finally did go back to sleep, I dreamed that there were two ways to go to Damascus, and both were good. The dream was a reassurance on the first day in Jerusalem when our guide, Eliyahu instructed us to meet at Damascus Gate to go inside the old city.

The Tel Aviv Airport customs officials questioned us quite intensely. I was not very well informed about the itinerary or the sites to visit either. "What did I want to see in Israel?" "Oh, everything!" I babbled. "The Dome of the Rock, Mount of Olives ..." I sputtered and ran out. They looked skeptical. "I'm with David Less," I added, figuring Shahabuddin could explain it; surely he would know what to say to them, to tell them why we were there. He hadn't given us any instructions about what to say to get into the country. I hadn't thought about its being a problem.

"Stand over there," the officials said.

It looked as if about half of the group had been let in and half of us held back, including Shahabuddin. *Oh well*, I thought, *I'm in the half with Shahabuddin*, not really thinking what would happen if we weren't allowed into the country after we had flown all the way there. "Why now?" they asked Shahabuddin. "With all the bombings going on? Are you crazy?"

"I was just drawn," he said. "We came to pray for peace."

After about a forty-minute wait, they handed passports back, and we went through the customs station. The rest of our group stood with our bags they had gathered from the baggage carousel. Eliyahu was inside to hug us, bowing. "Welcome. Welcome," he said, almost crying.

"Welcome," I said back to him, bowing, feeling ridiculous. *Why did I say that?* I said to myself. Eliyahu was a dark-eyed young man with thick, dark curly hair, a beard, and tie-dyed t-shirt. He was our Israeli guide. Ibrahim was waiting by the bus. He was short, stocky, bald and in his fifties, our Palestinian guide. When he saw Shahabuddin, he began to weep; and he cried in the bus all the way to our hotel, the Dan Pearl, an elegant, nearly empty hotel located next to the western wall of the Old City. This location was chosen because its closeness to the wall was thought to be the most safe.

Wailing Wall, Dome of the Rock

Bob went out to buy water the next morning and came back with his eyes wide. "It's like the Old West out there," he reported, "people walking around with guns." We later found out that everyone in the army must carry his weapon even if he is off duty, and anyone who has served his/her time is still subject to being called up until age thirty-eight.

The first night we ate at an Israeli restaurant which used to have an outdoor patio that now was boarded and closed. The restaurant's front door was locked. The owners came, surveyed us standing there, unbolted the door, and let us through. The atmosphere was tense. In the corner was a young couple who appeared to be on a date. *What a weird date!* I thought, admiring these young people who forged on with their lives in spite of the terror and suffering. What used to be a beautiful restaurant with a terrace was now a bunker. After this, we ate at Palestinian restaurants; primarily, I believe, for our safety but also to contribute to the income of the poor Palestinians. The food was

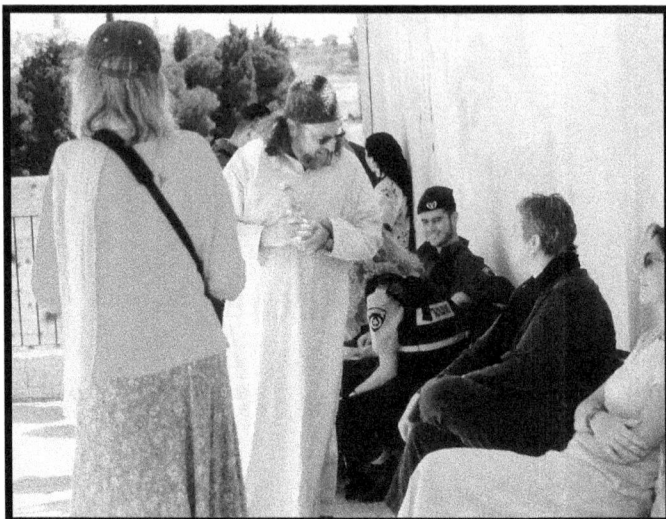

Shahabuddin at Peace Vigil

good, spaghetti sauce, hummus. I had a St. Peter fish. We didn't realize it then, but this was the food we would get at every restaurant. Bob ordered a dessert, chocolate cake. He was happy.

Back at the hotel in the night, we awoke to explosions. *Is it gunfire?* The explosions sounded close by. *Should we do something? Was there somewhere we were supposed to go for cover?* We laughed at breakfast when others asked if we had heard the fireworks last night.

We attended the Peace Vigil the first morning. It met every Friday above the Wailing Wall at 11:00 AM. We had come primarily to attend the circle sponsored by our hosts, spiritually-based peace workers: Israelis, Palestinians, and Christians who came week after week spreading blankets in the center with flowers, sacred books, and pictures, and then they circled to pray, sing, speak, chant, and meditate with the Dome of the Rock glittering in sunlight off to the right, Jews davening at the Wailing Wall below, and Jesus' Church of the Resurrection close by.

The Vigil was guarded by Israeli soldiers. The young woman soldier wore French fingernails and fashion sunglasses with her uniform and semi-automatic weapon. Some of the young Israelis in the circle wore gorgeous embroidered hippie clothes. Bob recited Black Elk's Prayer. "This is a prayer of oppressed people," he whispered to Ibrahim, our Palestinian guide.

"You're not supposed to say that!" Ibrahim giggled with his hand to his mouth.

After everyone in the circle had prayed, recited, or sung a song, we sat in silence for several minutes before leaving for lunch deep in the Palestinian part of the city.

Hannalise and Miriam, whom we invited to lunch, accompanied us back to our hotel. We wove our way through dark alleyways past multitudes of open-air market stalls heaped with produce, clothes, cooking utensils, and hundreds of other items we didn't stop to examine. Hannalise is an artist who paints huge paintings of the energy of Heaven funneling down to Jerusalem. Miriam's a singer and an actor. She lived in New York in the sixties and was on the stage with Satchidananda in the Woodstock movie.

We passed a street off to the right where Hannalise pointed. "That's where Jesus carried his cross." We stopped and stared but didn't go there. It was hard to believe the location of Christ's Passion was right in front of us. We passed more outside stalls with fabric, hats, and cooking merchandise, then ascended stairs toward the street and outside the walled gate. We were walking next to a busy Jerusalem street.

Hannalise had asked Bob to write Black Elk's Prayer for her. He began at lunch but didn't get it finished, so he paused to complete it, using a parking meter for a table, since the two women were about to leave. Suddenly Shahabuddin said, "We have to get going. This isn't a stroll!" He was hurrying. I didn't know why. And then the sirens started, and the ambulances raced by, many of them. We were stepping quickly, single file.

At the Hotel Dan Pearl our backpacks had to be checked, and our bodies were traced with a wand before we could enter the revolving glass door. One of our fellow travelers was there, standing in the doorway. With a stricken look on his face, he said, "There's been a suicide bombing." Shahabuddin told Hannalise and Miriam to come in, that he'd send them home by taxi. We should all come to his room in half an hour.

When we assembled, he told us he'd called home. His assistant in Florida would call our families to notify them we were safe. The newscast that evening reported six killed and seventy injured. Ibrahim was crying again. We didn't find out until we were back in America that the explosion had been two blocks away.

The first morning at seven-thirty, and then every morning we met in Shahabuddin's room to learn the Upside Down Heart meditation. We unplugged the veins and arteries from our hearts, turned them upside down and moved them over in our chests to let all its blessings spill forth on this troubled land, and we meditated. I was totally intrigued by this meditation.

The first morning at the sumptuous breakfast at the hotel, tables were piled high with cheeses, tomatoes, olives, cucumbers, apricots, figs, pastries, eggs of all sorts, cereal, coffee, tea. Shahabuddin pulled out the chair next to Bob and me, sat down with one piece of bread on his plate, grinned and asked, "Barbara, how did you like that Upside Down Heart meditation?"

I smiled back and said, "I loved it!"

"I did it especially for you," he said.

I did not quite know what to make of that remark except because I'm a poet he would know I liked visualizing and exercises rich with imagery.

We began a morning ritual of sitting together at breakfast throughout our stay in Jerusalem. One morning I was late to breakfast. "Oh," he said, when I arrived. "I thought—I can't eat breakfast without Barbara," and I was pleased that he looked forward to it also.

I didn't think the meditation was so great as the trip went on, and every morning no matter how tired we were or how grumpy we felt, we were supposed to show up at 7:30 to "sit." Shahabuddin did not *make* us come, he just expected us to. I always felt like I should be presentable, so I tried to bathe and fix my hair, although others sometimes came in stocking caps and coats thrown over pajamas. And we sat there, every morning together, with our hearts wide open in love and peace for this troubled war-torn, bleeding land, and then we went on with our trip.

Then I started to get intermittent stabbing pains in my heart—short, staccato, strong stabs of pain. They would stop for a few minutes, then come again. Then they became more regular. When the pains continued for a couple days, I went to Shahabuddin.

He nodded. "It's just your heart opening up," he said. "You're not having a heart attack. Don't worry about it. This happened to me too when I first did this meditation."

Our trip went on, and our morning meditations continued every day, praying together with our wide open, exposed hearts. Wanting and praying for peace, all together as hard as we could. In the mornings, in the dark, whether we felt like coming or not. Everyone was always there, even Bob who would hardly get out of bed early for anything.

Back home six months later, I awoke with the stabbing in my chest. When we turned on the news later that day, we discovered Israel was bombing Lebanon. As we watched the war planes on television, the stabbing intensified.

"Could you turn the news off?" I asked Bob.

"Sure," he answered, and in a while the stabbing stopped. The prayers go on.

Eliyahu's room was deep purple and stacked full of books from floor to ceiling. He lived in a house with several other young people. I was startled to discover that he was not Israeli but the son of Berkeley hippies. But he is Israel—immigrated there, learned the language, became a Hassidic Jew. He has worked tirelessly for peace, giving talks and workshops, being a part of demonstrations, going whenever and wherever anyone asks him, doing whatever he or anyone can dream up, for years now. He and Ibrahim, our Palestinian guide, are best friends.

He came to Hedva's Shabbat in his rabbi clothes, plus his tie-dyed vest, his hair styled in the required curls on the side. He asked us to come bless his room. Our entire group squeezed inside and prayed aloud in his room. Hedva, at whose house we celebrated

Shabbat, had a bottle of water. She giggled and sprinkled it over everything and over all of us. Hedva's attire always consisted of gauzy layers of white with swirly skirts, and, on the last day on the way to the airport, she punched out multicolored sticky stars pasting them on our foreheads and on our suitcases.

Before serving us the evening meal at her house on Shabbat, she had us one by one recite the traditional Shabbat prayers and blessings in her kitchen, pronouncing the strange Hebrew words that didn't quite fit in our mouths while she washed our hands and giggled. Shahabuddin commented quietly, "Higher than any drug trip, yes?"

Her table was so loaded with food I wondered who besides our group was coming to dinner. She said we couldn't go until we'd eaten it all. The women donned scarves and blessed the braided chala bread. Jacob, broad-shouldered, graying, poured the goblet of wine so full it almost overflowed, shivering in its chalice as he chanted the blessing. He told me he was at Lama Mountain in New Mexico in the seventies with my writing friend, Natalie Goldberg.

On Hedva's wall were framed pictures of gurus of every predilection. I recognized some: Swami Rama, Ramana Maharshi, Yogananda, Sri Baba. Other faces I knew but couldn't say their names. She had cut-out stenciled words, "Love, Serve, Remember," pinned to her drapes. After a while we were finishing heaped plates while Shahabuddin passed out fruit from a huge pyramid in the center of Hedva's bountiful table. He handed me a pink-cheeked pear. I was stuffed but I took it anyway and bit in. Suddenly I was home in Nebraska in my childhood yard eating a pear from my father's tree. It was the same fruit, familiar, grainy, and fragrant. I ate it all, savoring the juice, even though I was about to pop.

Soon we were stomping in a joyful snaky line dancing behind Eliyahu around Hedva's living room. With gusto we spun and loudly sang the words which felt like gibberish. Making the songs and prayers sound like nonsense, Eliyahu explained, was how Jews disguised their sacred words during persecution.

PART FOUR: ON THE PATH

Shahabuddin had disappeared. In a while he came from the back room with Hannalise announcing it was time to leave. After we dropped Hannalise and Miriam off, Shahabuddin revealed he loved meditating with Hannalise because she entered such a deep state. He added, laughing, "It's not easy to get her to come back!"

We moved every day or every other day. It was impossible to keep everything straight, and as always we had brought too much stuff. We had to pack and unpack at every stop. I left my bathing suit in a plastic bag in the lobby of the hotel at the Dead Sea. Realizing this, I reclaimed it before we left. I wouldn't have cared. Since getting older I haven't been able to find a suit I like anymore, and this one had a little skirt (real old lady suit, I thought!). I really had no intentions of doing any more water activities either. Then I left my black silky "traveler's jacket" in the motel closet in the YMCA of Tiberius along with my gauzy white scarf from India that worked for body covering and a head covering for mosques. I was pretty sure where it was but was confused about the name of the place, the hotel. We were moving so fast, and we weren't where our itinerary said we were supposed to be. I knew we could forget all that with Shahabuddin. If something looks more interesting or exciting on the way, that's where we'd go.

When I tried to tell Eliyahu, he said, "*Where* did you leave it?" I said I'd think about it. Then when I decided for sure where it was and told Shahabuddin, Eliyahu had taken off for someone's bris and Shahabuddin said we'd have to wait until we had a native speaker to call about it. By the time we got a speaker, made some calls, there was supposedly no jacket, no scarf.

I suffered and suffered. Wanting to call again. Perhaps it was in a different hotel? Perhaps we could call again. That black jacket went with all my clothes. Shahabuddin's son, Vadan, sympathized. I couldn't give it up. Until. Until I finally got the bigger picture. Where was I? In the Holy Land! All of these people had lost family! Homes! Homeland! Couldn't get them back. Everyone had lost someone, something precious. What was I doing moping over this miniscule loss?

Moses' Tomb

We drove through the desert where the Bedouins had houses (someone said given to them by the government to entice them to stay in one spot) and no jobs. They were barren and boxlike, with one or two bony animals standing nearby. We stopped at a mosque-like structure that seemed to appear out of nowhere. It was a tomb tended by a man in a flannel shirt, blue jeans, and a checkered headdress. He was smoking a cigarette and was accompanied by a small dark-eyed boy. Outside the tomb were two shepherds with their sheep. Inside this open-air adobe structure in a room on the second floor was an enormous casket enclosed in a wire encasement. The casket was covered with a shimmering green silken cloth fringed in gold.

Whose tomb is it? I wondered. We hadn't been told ahead of time. I asked a couple of people before someone said, "Moses."

Moses? No one knows where Moses is buried! But apparently someone believes they do. We did prayers as a group and silently. I felt a very high and wonderful energy, authenticity, and silence. We were told our group could come back for a three-day retreat. Bob got positively intoxicated there. This spiritual intoxication is akin to what the whirling dervishes experience during their

222

spinning and the highs we often got doing the Dances of Universal Peace or zikr.

Bob radiated as our bus rolled on toward the River Jordan with the dry desert atmosphere on one side and the misty Dead Sea pastels on the other. We were headed toward the desert commune where the young Israelis studied the Kabbalah, where we were slated to do Dances of Universal Peace and go to the cave of the Dead Sea scrolls.

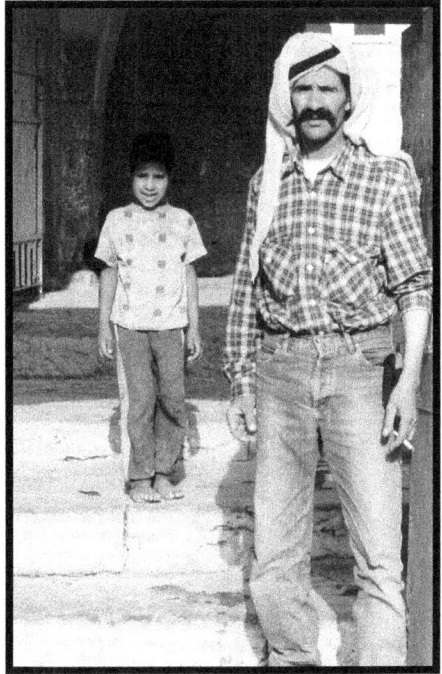

Keepers of Moses' Tomb

IN THE COMMUNE

In the commune on the desert, we dance in a boiling hot building. People who live here say we can't open the doors because of the mosquitoes. Shahabuddin quips we'll probably warm it up soon. He starts the dancing having us chant "Allah, Allah" — a room full of Israelis and Americans, winding us tightly into a spiral. People's tight faces melt with relief as they dance out months of suffering and pain. Midway, someone brings the water cooler and they decide to open the doors anyway. Toward the end, we meditate in the dark and a woman's voice talks to the mosquito biting her. Shahabuddin invites the mosquito his way.

An Israeli and Bob exchange gifts. Bob intends to give him a pen for his wife who let him come. He bows and hands Bob a knitted cap.

Bob's gone outside to smoke as I get ready for bed
in our small room. I go out in my pink and white
striped pajamas to find him. He's at a picnic
table in the dark with Miriam, her friend who's
slicing honeydew melon, Shahabuddin, Vadan
and Andy. We tell again the story of the
inheritance check arriving from Aunt Gladys,
Shahabuddin's trip offer the next day ... Bob
gets my journal with Gladys' picture at the head
nurse's desk at Veteran's Hospital taped to the front
and Shahabuddin says, "Let's pray for Aunt
Gladys." We put our fingertips on the table and
he begins ... "Keep on loving us. Keep on loving
us. Keep on loving us."

On the bus, leaving the commune, Shahabuddin called me to
the back of the bus and pressed something into my palm. I opened
my hand. It was a shell cartridge. "What's this?" I asked.

"I found it this morning on the desert. God told me to give it
to you."

I looked at this empty bullet casing in my palm. "What am I
supposed to do with it?"

"I don't know," he answered, shaking his head. "Maybe
write a poem about it."

I nodded and took it. I made my bumpy way back toward
my seat in the front of the bus steadying myself by holding onto
the backs of others' seats, clutching my "gift" from God tightly in
my hand.

God told Shahabuddin? He talks like this often. I'm not
exactly sure what it means, but, of course, it makes me feel special.
The brass cartridge sits on my windowsill altar at home.

Everyone wanted us to be on *his* side. We went to visit Miriam
and Hannalise's house in the countryside, and they took us for a
walk around their neighborhood, past a monster sculpture made
out of discarded junk by Hannalise, up a hillside with wildflowers

Cave of the Dead Sea Scrolls

where Miriam sang to us, and then to a synagogue built out of asbestos. Because it's a synagogue it cannot be torn down even though the asbestos has been recognized as dangerous. Inside, some Jewish rabbis and scholars immediately took Miriam aside asking her to translate, asking her to say they hoped we would support their position. Shahabuddin stood quietly, head tilted, his hands crossed on his thigh, and then asked Miriam to please tell them we came to pray for peace.

The afternoon of the suicide bombing one of sheiks working with the peace vigil came to the hotel to talk to us ("If you have two children, you cannot buy just one of them ice cream."). After this, we were scheduled to visit a Christian school where a scholar there would give us a talk. As we wove in a line through the streets toward the school, we stopped at the sheik's shop where he let the entire group help ourselves to chocolate out of his candy jars. Stepping back into the street, a young Palestinian man looked our group over and then shouted "Fuck you!" as we kept walking. Inside the school, the Christian scholar asked us each to introduce ourselves. Shahabuddin suggested we each tell a secret about ourselves. I realized shortly into this process that all the time would be consumed, and there would be no time for the scholar's lecture. I'm not sure why Shahabuddin directed the afternoon this way. Perhaps he realized the scholar and our group would benefit more from this intimate sharing than a prepared lecture. I was quite surprised that many people revealed quite personal secrets, and the scholar did not seem to mind at all that he had no time. He listened intently to what each person shared and then spent some time at the end urging us to attend a Peace Demonstration that evening to light candles at the site of a suicide bombing a year earlier. We didn't promise, but said we would consider doing so.

After dinner we decided to drive by the demonstration site in our taxis. We could see an angry-looking gathering of Palestinians on the opposite side of the street, holding placards, yelling and pointing at the Israelis. We disembarked from the taxis, had a brief meeting on the street, and decided that we would not go to the demonstration. We had come to pray for peace.

Back home my son was trying to explain to his college instructors what his parents were doing in Israel at such a time. "Well," he would say, "they didn't go for a vacation! They are praying for peace." I'm sure his teachers were wondering why we didn't pray at home. Eli too.

We called home from Miriam and Hannalise's one night on one of Ibrahim's three cell phones. It was a very peaceful starry night at their home outside the city. "I suppose you're seeing some weird shit!" Eli said with anxiety. "No," we said, "it's been quite beautiful."

And we danced in an old mosque in Acre on the Mediterranean. It was crumbling, shadowy, and dusty. Bird shit dotted the floor.

"Here's the practice," Shahabuddin said, "You have to think this wazifa, but not think it."

How do you do that? I thought; then I was gone into Oneness. I did it! I was there! What I was always trying to achieve. I didn't know I was there until the dance was concluding and we were coming out of the door into the afternoon sunlight, and I was back into my separateness, separate me, looking at my friends and teacher.

Suddenly there we all were walking down the street to David Friedman's art studio where he was going to talk about his symbolic paintings, Jungian psychology, and the Kabbalah. A young girl with a backpack stopped. "Are you tourists?" she asked. "Yes," we answered.

"Thank you for coming!" she exclaimed. We bowed. She bowed and went on down the empty Israeli street, our group the only tourists in sight.

Israel was the most far-out trip we'd ever taken with Shahabuddin; we went right into the middle of a war. One woman who joined us for a day to see the cave of the Dead Sea scrolls said she hardly ever went anywhere because of the danger, rarely left her house anymore. Another Israeli woman joined us when we went to Ibrahim's home on Mount Olive for dinner where Ibrahim had gathered at least thirty people, journalists, people of different religions, and clerics standing in exotic robes—all served by his wife, daughters, and daughters-in-law. His one hundred-year-old mother sat on the couch, holding a corn cob, watching television, shouting out "Allah" every once in a while. The Israeli woman was timid and afraid. She had never ventured into this Palestinian area of Jerusalem before even though she was in her mid-thirties.

The last time we went to the Peace Vigil we were interviewed by a news crew from Turkish television. They particularly wanted to know what this group from America, lead by an American sheik, was doing here and what Shahabuddin's opinion of the whole Middle Eastern crisis was. (Shahabuddin's opinion: "You don't need one more opinion.")

Elias Jabbour at the House of Hope calls himself a Palestinian Israeli Christian Arab; he has worked his whole life for peace, as did his father. He brought forth a huge lunch from his kitchen, but we had just eaten lunch! We looked at Shahabuddin for some guidance of what to do. He shrugged, said very quietly, "Do what you can do." I didn't see how I could manage putting food into my mouth but wanted to be a good grateful guest and respond to the kindness of our hosts. I watched Shahabuddin take a couple bites and then push the rest of the food around on his plates. I swallowed a few mouthfuls—chicken, spaghetti, hummus—and mixed it up good on my plate.

Elias told us about Sulha, a traditional tribal peacemaking system, where those in disagreement go slowly, one step at a time, accepting first a cup of coffee. If the disputants take the cup of coffee, they agree to agree about the first stage of disagreement. They work up to having a meal together.

This was the first trip where Shahabuddin kept reminding us it wasn't about us. We hadn't come there to grow or to work on ourselves. We had come to lend a little support to those who were working for Peace, to give them some comfort and love. It wasn't a vacation; yet it was the most intensely joyful and profound trip we'd taken with him. And, the realization was dawning that my spiritual journey had become much bigger than a search for my own enlightenment.

Even my worst day when I wouldn't try to float in the Dead Sea and finally smacked my head and split my lip on a tree, was a very high day for me once I remembered, that this trip wasn't about me.

PART FOUR: ON THE PATH

NOT REMEMBERING

They were all floating in the Dead Sea
    except me   La illaha ila allah
in a circle holding hands
  in the salty water
  so thick you could not sink
except me
who like Thomas had my doubts   La illaha ila allah
even of my beloved
who sat in the Dead Sea
and cradled his legs
saying, "See!"

They all floated and swan
    except me   La illaha ila allah
while I paced back and forth
    forth and back
  finger in my mouth
  on the bank
watching as they plastered themselves   La illaha ila allah
  with Dead Sea mud all over
      "So good for the skin"
"Are you going to do that?" I asked my guide
"Of course," he said," I don't want to miss anything   La illaha ila
  allah

Not me either but I was missing everything
Paralyzed on the shore
Afraid on the side to take off my hat
    too much sun on my face
    of sinking to the bottom
    what to do with all that mud
    what would become of my hair   La illaha ila allah

Forgetting why I'm here
Forgetting why I came
          La illaha ila allah
          Hu

229

PATH OF LIGHTNING

LEAVING JERUSALEM

We go to the Peace Vigil a last time.
11:30 on a terrace above the Wailing Wall.
Soldiers with machine guns.
Keeping silence, I hear John
and Yoko singing in my head.
Then *we* dance and sing
    Shalom Aleichem
    As-salaam Alaikum
    Peace be with you
looking deep into light blue,
dark brown, loving eyes.
The people from Turkish television
ask Shahabuddin his opinion.
"You don't need," he says, "one more opinion."
"It's not up to us. It's up to God."
When they shove the mike in front of me,
I say, "It's like John Lennon said,
We've got to give peace a chance."

Into the bus to the airport,
stand in line in security,
bags searched, x-rayed,
answer questions. "Who did
you see in Jerusalem?" I think
of sweet, dark Eliyahu, son of Berkeley hippies,
his small purple room full of books,
working all this time for peace;
Hedva, Jewish ancient one in sweeping,
sequined skirt, puts stars on our foreheads
on the bus; Hannalise who painted the energies
of the Heavens funneling down to Jerusalem;
Miriam who wrote us ecstatic love poems,
Ibrahim, who cried after the suicide bombings.

Bob and Subhan go to buy liquor,
Bob and Nizam go to the restroom,
make it to the shuttle bus as the doors are closing.
Goodbye ancient, white rock, crumbling city.
All the Prophets manifested here!
Goodbye pain, suffering, explosions, and joy.
Goodbye city of Herod's temple.

PART FOUR: ON THE PATH

Goodbye old walled city where Armenians, Jews,
Palestinians, Christians all live together,
only streets dividing them.
Goodbye Wailing Wall, Dome of the Rock,
Church of the Holy Sepulcher, Rabia's Tomb
Goodbye Hassids in black, tiny hats, curls.
Goodbye beautiful young Israelis in '70s
  embroidered hippie clothes
Goodbye, old city, Holy City, Jerusalem.

(From *The Upside Down Heart*)

I didn't write anything in Israel; I didn't have time. I hoped I could remember details but didn't know how I would ever keep straight all the names of people, events, places. I hadn't even taken any notes.

When we arrived home exhausted, Eli informed us the drain was backed up in the basement laundry room. Every time he took a shower the room started to fill with water and feces. The next morning while Bob started with Drano and wires trying to unclog pipes, I received the phone call that one of our friends had been found dead of a heart attack in his apartment. We began making other phone calls, gathering with shocked friends, attending memorial services and a funeral while having discovered the sewer was clogged somewhere between the house and street. We had to bring in a crew with sledge hammers to break up the basement floor to remove the old pipes before replacing them with new. I began to try to write down as much as I could remember of the trip before it started to fade.

The writing began to shape itself into one particularly long narrative poem, "We Came to Pray for Peace," and some shorter ones. I started to search for a venue to publish them as a chapbook. My Sandhills Press editor (who had published my first poetry book) said he would, of course, be interested, but he had no funds then to do it. There was a graduate student at Wayne State who had a press and was printing small books. "How about if Sandhills brings it out," I asked, "and I stand the expense?"

"Of course, no problem!" Mark Sanders was eager for such a deal, and Scott McIntosh (the Wayne graduate student) was happy to print the book. So, *The Upside Down Heart* (named for the meditation we did daily) came into being quite rapidly with a print of Hannalise's painting on the cover.

I sent several copies to Jerusalem to Miriam and Hannalise, asking them to distribute them there. I sent a batch to Shahabuddin and never heard anything from him. That didn't bother me much. Shahabuddin never replies to my letters and cards, and I didn't really expect a reply to these. However, the next time I saw him I thought he might say *something*. After all, I thought, one of the reasons he dragged me along to Israel, was so I might document the trip in writing.

Finally, I could stand it no longer. I said, "So, Shahabuddin, what did you think of my Israel book?"

"Oh," he said, "I hope you don't mind. I've been photocopying them like crazy and handing them out to people."

I laughed. "I have more copies!"

"Give me some!" he said, and when we came back from lunch he was reading poems out loud from this book to the group.

THE CARAVAN

Perhaps because of *The Upside Down Heart*, I was asked to teach writing at The Caravan of the Beautiful in Sarasota. It's a great gathering of yoga teachers, a thanka painter, a well-known Indian musician, dancers, musicians, peacemakers, and meditators at a beautiful resort site on the Manatee River. I accepted and went without Bob making plans to room with an old friend, Veronica. On the second day I woke up feeling tipsy and icky in my stomach. Nauseous. I was getting a migraine, which I tend to do sometimes in large crowds and at Sufi events. But sometimes more than that was happening. I felt extremely sick to my stomach, and something inside of me was pulling to the right side at the top of my skull, beating with large wings on the inside of my head like it wanted out, as if it were trying to exit through the top of my scalp.

Veronica and I got ready for breakfast. *I'll feel better when I eat*, I thought; and since we had a few minutes she wanted me to see the Manatee River. Our lodging was in individual cabins just a short walk from the Manatee. We walked through viny plants and lots of ground vegetation. I kept feeling like I was going to tip over and was very sick to my stomach as we walked out on the pier and talked to two other attendees. The man's sleeveless shirt showed off his tattooed arms, and he spoke with an Australian accent. The gorgeous woman leaning on her bicycle next to him had the most astonishing color of reddish-purplish hair and spoke with a French accent. Even though I was so sick, I remember thinking they were not the typical Sufi workshoppers. When we worried aloud about alligators and swimming, he said alligators weren't dangerous; people only got that idea from old Tarzan movies where they'd show them sliding into the river. They were trying to get *away* from people.

I got sicker on the way to breakfast and stopped to take a migraine pill. Veronica took my arm and said *she* thought I was going to tip over!

"I'm sick!" I said. Just then it occurred to me that I was going out of my body (or my spirit was *trying* to get out of my body). I don't know how I knew this; I just did.

Food didn't help. During meditation I seemed to go away, and afterward I was even sicker. I stood up, sort of swaying and bobbing in this main room where meditation was held and where Kothrenada was getting ready to teach her class. I knew I had to find Shahabuddin. I thought somehow he could fix this, whatever it was. I turned around. There he was.

"How do you feel?" he asked, peering at me.

"I'm so sick," I said. "I feel like I'm going out of my body!"

"Sit down," he said, bringing a chair up behind me.

"And I have a migraine."

"Your third eye is completely open," he said, "that's why you're so nauseous. I can't fix your migraine," he laughed. "I can work on the other."

233

Kothrenada, now a Doctor of Chinese Medicine, was writing notes on the board for her upcoming lecture. "Get her feet," he said to her. She bent to work on them.

Shahabuddin touched the top of my head, particularly on the right side toward which I felt I was fluttering, and worked around my temples. Kothrenada worked on the tops of my feet. All the while liquid streamed out of my eyes and down my cheeks, although I did not feel as though I was crying. Victoria, an attendee at the camp and mureed of Shahabuddin's, stood behind Kothrenada with a concerned look on her face while they both ministered to me for several minutes. I remembered I had been envious of the woman on retreat in Bali who was so sick when she was opening. Ha! What had I been thinking!

Shahabuddin said, "It's okay to be so open, but you must learn to take care of yourself when this happens." Suddenly I remembered having many strange dreams the night before and said so. "Yes," he said. "Others did too. This place is where they do alcoholic recovery. Maybe it's not so good for our retreats."

The intense nausea was starting to recede. Shahabuddin said I should beam my third eye out like a big spotlight when I felt it opening to keep from being so sick, and I should have Kothrenada do acupuncture on me later.

Later, he cornered me again. "And what are you doing with your psychic abilities?"

"Well, my poetry ..."

"Yes," he nodded.

"And I give a reading to anyone who asks."

"And?"

"What else should I be doing?"

"I have a feeling," he said, "that it should be global ... "

I looked at him puzzled, waiting, thinking ... *Oh, no, now I'll have to go back to Israel.*

"I'll get back to you," he said.

"All right," I said relieved. I wasn't ready for any huge commitment. I was just starting to feel a little better from the nausea.

PART FOUR: ON THE PATH

Later I remembered I had dreamed I was walking on the ceiling, how I used to experience being out of my body as a child. Maybe I had gone out of my body in my sleep and didn't quite get back in all the way.

I got migraines the next two days at the Caravan. When Kothrenada did acupuncture she said something about my picking up on things that others dumped. I noticed I would start to get a migraine going into the large meeting hall after yoga had been done there or after singing class with Mukesh, the Hindu musician; but it was nothing like the tipsy, icky first morning.

Did Shahabuddin fix me? I'm not sure, but I did feel better in a short while after he worked on me, and I felt his love and concern for my well being. He hasn't gotten back to me yet on what else he thinks I should be doing with these abilities.

PART FIVE

Chasing the White Goose

Shahabuddin often would mention that he wished Murshid Hazrat Inayat Khan, "hadn't said this thing but he had." What thing? That life was a struggle. So, Shahabuddin wanted to impress on his mureeds that just because we'd found "the path" didn't mean we weren't going to struggle anymore. (And too, he'd remind us, "the path" was supposed to end — it was only to lead us somewhere.) I had gotten the struggle idea through my head. I had experienced a very real Dark Night of the Soul, but somehow it hadn't occurred to me that there might be struggle as well in the teacher/student relationship.

When I started writing this memoir, Natalie Goldberg, my writing friend, cautioned, "Don't reach too soon for gratitude in this story." I didn't see why not. I was so grateful for Shahabuddin. At last I had my teacher, had found my path, was on my way after the years of confusion, looking here and there, wanting God so desperately, and I *was* truly grateful. I knew other people had disappointments in their teachers or even felt betrayed, but I felt like I could trust Shahabuddin completely.

But the last seminar we had in Florida with Shahabuddin was different. One of his old mureeds was having trouble. He had called us before we'd left with complaints about Shahabuddin concerning manipulation, dishonesty, and about how Shahabuddin showed favoritism to certain mureeds in their community.

Bob and I had missed all the trials of living in a community. We didn't have to raise funds, volunteer on projects, help maintain the grounds and meeting hall, or put up with others in the community. As in any spiritual community, in Shahabuddin's there are plenty of quirky personalities which have to relate to each other. The average, everyday person usually is not to be found there. Shahabuddin himself made a remark to Bob about not having to live there in Sarasota in the community so we didn't understand the pain.

239

When we'd come for a workshop, we were treated as the out-of-town guests. We'd try to contribute financially and with manpower to projects when we were in town, but mostly we'd get to enjoy the benefits without any of the hassles of slugging out the day-to-day details of maintaining a spiritual community financially, emotionally, and physically.

The mureed who had complained shared hardly any specific examples of his distress except for Shahabuddin's having favorites. There were some other complaints about the money he had given to the community and being taken for granted. His insistent upsetness, however, was enough to sow some doubt into my perception, and I kept studying Shahabuddin for most of the two weeks wondering about these things. Nothing much had changed, but now my critical judgment had been unleashed. Certain remarks Shahabuddin had made in the past would flash through my head ... Hmm: *How about that time he told Bob in darshan he was going to be wealthy? That hasn't happened yet.* ... Or ... *Bob broke his leg to slow down his spiritual development?* ... that seemed ridiculous! Now, little nagging questions I had so easily let evaporate came parading back and crowded into my head.

Bob and I talked about Shahabuddin's having favorites. We had always thought we were among his favorites and were pleased to be so. "Is that wrong?" I asked Bob in our bedroom in our rented house in Sarasota. A gecko screeched intermittently outside our bedroom window. "I don't know," Bob answered. "There are certain people you click with and get energy from. I guess you'd naturally want to spend more time with them. And you'd want to have *fun* some of the time. (In *A Rare and Precious Thing*, John Kain says, "Teacher Adyashanti says when students start to worship him too much he will invite them over to play poker. 'Then I take their money and they get a little different view of me.'") I remembered in the Intensives how Shahabuddin said he needed some friends.

I wanted to support my friend and let him complain, but I began having trouble being sympathetic to my friend and at the same time not becoming critical of Shahabuddin. When Bill Clinton screwed up I never expected him to be perfect because he was the President. I just shrugged and said, *He's human,* and let it go; but boy, if the spiritual teacher's integrity is in question, it's something else. We do expect them to be perfect. You start wondering if they are authentic teachers. Can they be trusted?

Still the seminar went wonderfully. Shahabuddin was back from a Sufi camp in the Alps and was open, tuned, deep, and very present. The theme was a surprise—it dealt totally with zikr—the practice of remembering (La illaha ila allah) and other wazifas. There was some instruction on how to prepare, but the time was mostly spent chanting, not thinking, just gone into the sound. Even I, with my "always thinking" mind, was into sound part of the time, and when I would open my eyes I would see Shahabuddin's glowing face and think, *Yes, it's he, my teacher.* (I reasoned he's got flaws and is a human being; I have to be a grown-up and be aware of his weaknesses, watch out for them; but he can still be my guide.)

The second day we came at 3:30 in the morning to do zikr until 6:00 AM. This was most wonderful for me because this was the time when my mind was finally still. We did practices in total darkness, listening to the sounds of all the voices around us. When people got tired, they lay down and slept. And the zikr went on.

The next night I dreamed I was chasing a white goose and awoke wondering if maybe my unconscious was presenting me with a metaphor of my dilemma with Shahabuddin (a wild goose chase?). I paid attention because studying my dreams had begun my spiritual journey.

We kept watching for evidence of manipulation. We didn't see anything like that going on except perhaps referring too many Intensive attendees and people on retreat in his house to Kothrenada for expensive acupuncture treatments. I wasn't so sure about this. Maybe it wasn't so ethical to be sending people signed up for *his* seminar to his wife for acupuncture work. With Bob and me I thought it was different; we'd known both of them a long time. She was our friend, and we chose to support her business.

After we'd had our treatments with Kothrenada, Shahabuddin gave us a tour of his fruit trees. He kept saying he was so happy to have us there. We grumbled later that *he* hadn't invited us over; we had to get there by having expensive treatments from Kothrenada. He picked us a star fruit and an avocado from his trees. Earlier in the week he had been talking about diet in class. Jumping in at break, I asked him what I should be eating, adding I'd been having trouble with my stomach and digestion since leaving home. There I went again, thinking he was going to fix what was wrong with my life. Shahabuddin gave me an answer because I had asked him what to do. He said, "No raw food. Soups. Cooked vegetables. Grains. Probably not fruit. Eat like this for six months. Everything's changing now."

"I've always eaten raw vegetables," I whined a little.

"But you're getting older now," he said.

So when he handed me the products of the trees in his yard, I looked at them in my hands and said, "Well, I can't eat these!"

"Oh, anything from here's okay." He smiled and went on around the corner of his house.

Now, that's an example, I thought, of where his credibility rubbed a little thin. Either I can eat raw fruits and vegetables or not. These are okay? They are blessed because they are from his yard? Sometimes the guy was a little loopy. I used to just let it go, but I guess that's the kind of thing my friend was talking about.

(The star fruit rotted before we had a chance to eat it. I ate the avocado with no ill effects.)

The last day of the seminar, no teaching took place. The entire time was consumed with an explanation of and an appeal for money for The Abrahamic Reunion, the Middle Eastern Peace Movement instigated by Shahabuddin, made up of various religious faiths and sects, males and females, who meet, pray, eat, and discuss issues in the Middle East. These meetings are an absolute first—men and women, with various and sometimes opposing religious positions, meeting and performing each others' prayers! I am tremendously proud of Shahabuddin for his devotion, time, and effort spent on working for peace in the

Middle East. However, I did want to have some conclusion to our seminar and didn't relish spending all the time on this appeal. Bob finally got up and went outside.

Then during break Shahabuddin appeared as a walking market stall. He had Rising Tide bags hung on his arm and a box of Rising Tide t-shirts in his arms and was calling out like a carnival barker, "Get them while they last. Special low price. Today only!" holding up the bags with the Rising Tide logo on them.

Bob wanted a t-shirt and couldn't find his size. Shahabuddin, bound and determined to sell him one, frantically dug through the box looking for an extra-large. Standing there I was appalled at this image of him scrounging so for money. (Bob says he thought he was also just trying to help him find a shirt.) "It's like the bazaar," I announced, thinking of the pesky salesmen at the Grand Bazaar in Turkey.

"You think I'm bizarre?" Shahabuddin asked, half-serious. I almost said, "Yes." Now looking back, my heart grows soft. After all, there was the rent to pay on the building, the community to support. He probably needed to hustle. And if you want to make a judgment, Shahabuddin will oblige by showing you himself in his imperfection as well.

We had asked for a blessing for our fortieth wedding anniversary. But back in our seats, the session was concluding, and time was up. I was pretty sure he had forgotten. I said, "Shahabuddin?" He looked up. "You ready?" He called Bob and me to the front, gathered all the participants in a close circle around us, and not only gave us a blessing but also spontaneously remarried us complete with vows, blessings, prayers, and wonderful wishes, all on the spur of the moment.

Thinking I had seen the last of him, I felt bad that I hadn't given him a hug; but somehow one of our friends had asked him for a recommendation for a restaurant that served good soup (Bob has trouble swallowing) where we might celebrate our anniversary, and Shahabuddin suggested *his* place. He greeted us at the door wearing his big straw hat and an equally big grin, quipped "HAPPY BIRTHDAY" and proceeded to choreograph for us a most delicious many-coursed anniversary dinner of fish, vegetables, salad, soup, noodles, and bread in his kitchen with heavenly music playing. When I asked about his cooking for retreats, he said he wasn't doing that anymore, but he would do it for me. As we all told stories, he sat quietly humming, happy to be serving us. This is the image of Shahabuddin I carried away from Florida tucked deeply into my heart.

My back was full of knots after arriving home from Florida. I decided to get a massage, and while the masseuse was working out the most painful, difficult knot deep in my shoulder blade, burning bile shot up my esophagus. The long-lasting burning hurt worse than the knot. At home Bob said, "Introjects ... stuff you've swallowed." Most of the knots seemed to have to do with this worry about Shahabuddin. Bob said he didn't want to say too much about it, knowing how much I care for Shahabuddin, how faithfully I did my practices every morning, how hard it must be for me now. I wiped away a tear and went to do the dishes.

Bob said to figure out what I've gotten from Shahabuddin besides my mind being more quiet. But peace of mind is huge because I was always tortured. Now lots of times my mind still churns and lots of times I still watch it, but it's more like I'm watching it from a distance. "Oh," I say, "that's just my mind," like "Oh, it's just that show that's on television." I'm not so identified with the turmoil. It doesn't torture me so much. I am not suffering like I used to. I have to say I am almost always happy, and the Dalai Lama says the purpose of life is for people to be happy. Once in a while something throws me, and I get off balance and lose the happiness. But even when Bob and I have a fight, and in the midst of problems and difficulties — even money problems, because money used to be the one thing that triggered me the most emotionally — I am still almost always happy. And I would have to say these conditions have come directly out of my Sufi practices given to me by Shahabuddin. I have said over and over I do not know for sure what enlightenment or realization is, only that I'm pretty sure I want it; but if this is all I obtain from my practice of Sufism, that is enough, and my life is so much better.

PART FIVE: CHASING THE WHITE GOOSE

I have become awake to the beauty that surrounds me; much more attuned to light, color, smell, sounds, birds, flowers, people's faces, the dance of life about me. It's as if everything metamorphosed to Technicolor from black and white or I got second sight. I feel as if I've become a kinder person. (I hope it's true.)

Lisa, my writing friend, says I've had a lot of "God experiences." I suppose I've had some *mystical experiences,* but some of the other things seem more important.

My heart has opened more and more.

My Sunday depression has left me.

And I was most unhappy about living in Norfolk, Nebraska. This tiny town where nothing happened. No restaurants, hardly any movies, no museums, no wide range of friends. We were considered the "oddballs." I absolutely couldn't bear to stay here. The town hasn't changed; nonetheless, I am content. I do have a couple good friends, but mostly it's my attitude. I find what I need within.

This week the Madison, Wisconsin Sufi newsletter arrived containing an essay from Shahabuddin. I read it immediately and was deeply affected. The "heart" of the teaching follows:

> I believe that we are divine instruments through which the creative force of the universe can experience itself. When we have awakened, we have thinned the wall of our individuated ego enough so that it will no longer have the same relationship with us as it does now. That which we call God can experience itself, can see itself, through the thinned lens of our limited ego, of our limitation. Now we have a very thick lens through which we see life. What's the thick lens? The accumulation of beliefs that we call "me." This is *my* house, this is *my* friend, this is *my* belief, this is *my* like, *my* dislike. Those beliefs are all thickening the ego. Instead of that which is the creating principle being able to see through the lens, it sees only the list. There is no movement of the very thing that's trying to experience itself through us.

We have come so far since birth, since coming to the planet and then stopped. We've stopped by becoming not just attached to our own point of view, but by becoming hypnotized by our own point of view, drugged by our own point of view. The idea that we could be other than we are is just an idea. We don't believe it; underneath it all. We think, "Oh yeah maybe someday somebody will hit me with a magic wand and I will experience this ecstatic condition. Someday if I do the right meditation and the right practices I will experience a state of awakening."

No, you and I cannot awaken. Only that which is eternal, that which is unattached can awaken. Not you, and not me. But there is something that is common to all of us that can awaken. How can it awaken? It will awaken when we create a vehicle for its awakening. If we don't create the vehicle for the awakening of the creator, the creator will not awaken in us. Our job is not to awaken. The very idea that there is a goal called awakening, that very idea thickens the nature of individual ego and firms up the belief that we are this limited being. And the circle continues.

Actions in which we focus on "other than self" make up the path which leads to a state of "thinning" — a state of non-attachment in Buddhist terms. In Sufi terms we would say that this is the state where the moth has finally flown into the flame. It seems so simple; and it is. As you focus on another, you're creating a spiritual path for yourself. As you focus on yourself, you are inhibiting yourself from experiencing spirit! Why? Because the lens gets thicker. "It" cannot see itself.

As you focus on another, you are sending a message to the creative principle inside you. What's the message? This is You! See Yourself! Recognize Yourself! The creative principle says, "Well I can't see myself." And then we say, "But I see you and you can see it by the way that I love you!" and something in eternity awakens in us individually. "Oh! this limited being loves me in my many forms. I remember who I am!"

246

PART FIVE: CHASING THE WHITE GOOSE

When you see someone who is suffering, and you
recognize not the suffering but the thatness both in
the person and in you, and you feel pain, the natural
response is "I'm so sorry." It's a very different "I'm so
sorry" than we're used to.

By serving others, by recognizing others, we begin to
thin the lens of our ego and see through a different lens,
a much thinner one, a much clearer one. It doesn't give
us much protection. It's not so comfortable with thin.
But it's not tragic by any means either. More pain, but
more joy.

(From *On Collective Awakening*)

Last Saturday we spent with our old neighbors. After they'd
gone, Bob went to play the piano, and I had what Lisa might call
one of my "God experiences." I tried to articulate it in a brief letter
to Shahabuddin.

> Dear Shahabuddin,
>
> It's late. Our former neighbors have gone home.
> They've spent much of the evening sharing their pain
> over problems with their adolescent daughter. Bob
> is playing the piano in the back room while I scrunch
> under a comforter on the loveseat in the living room. The
> haunting melody floods through my heart and pours
> out of my eyes. I know each note before he touches the
> keys. Unknowingly my body has memorized his music.
>
> Suddenly I *am* my neighbor, suffering her pain of her
> daughter's teenage years. Finally, after all these years, I
> *experience* your teaching ("See yourself. This *is* you!") in
> my body, heart, and soul. This has come about, I believe,
> because of a combination of the Intensive of zikr, my
> confusion about our teacher/student relationship, your
> teaching on Collective Awakening, and Bob's playing.
> For a few moments, I *am feeling* what my neighbor
> *feels*. The Beginning of Remembering? I cry silently in

247

gratitude, in ecstasy, love, thankfulness, and unity while
Bob plays on.

Your mureed,
Vajra

May all beings be well
May all beings be happy   Peace Peace Peace

In the meantime, one morning I opened the small cedar
cabinet in the downstairs bathroom. There's an envelope flap with
"Love" written on it. It vibes with Shahabuddin's sweet energy.
After I taught writing last April at The Caravan of the Beautiful,
it was decided to send the presenters a $500 honorarium besides
paying their expenses. It was an unexpected boon for us; but even
nicer was the "Love" in Shahabuddin's hand on the envelope. We
could feel it. The printed letters positively smiled.

I had forgotten about it. Bob slipped the back of the envelope
into the medicine cabinet shelf, which I rarely open, so this
morning reaching for a brush, I got a shot of Shahabuddin's
"love." And I remembered, that is why I wanted to be around
him, and that is why I chose to be with him. You know, the Beatles
had it, after all ... "All you need is love. ... Love is all you need."

I had to decide right away whether or not I was going to
teach at the next Caravan of the Beautiful. My heart had grown
lighter, and I decided, "yes!" Shahabuddin and I had no contact
really until I arrived in Florida for the Caravan, and I was excited
and happy to see him. He was gathering folks for grace in front
of the cafeteria, and we had not seen each other yet. "Oh, Vajra's
here!" he announced, looking up. And when the grace circle
broke, he greeted me with a hug and a kiss. My worry and doubt
about our relationship had dispersed like the storm clouds after
a thundershower. I had decided that another mureed's very real
crises with him was not mine. Shahabuddin had said we should
look at what's right in a relationship instead of what's wrong. I

had assumed he was only speaking about marriages. Now, I saw it applied to any intimate relationship (spiritual teachers and mureeds as well).

Shahabuddin's halo slipping a little made things better; I no longer expected him to be God. In *A Journey in Ladakh,* writer Andrew Harvey says his friend had fallen out of love with his guru, but still the friend said,

> I sometimes think that what I saw him as in the beginning was his true self, was his essential self, and that I have lost him in a little since, lost him in biographical and psychological trivia, as you might "lose" part of the moon behind rags of cloud.

I was no longer expecting Shahabuddin to be perfect. I knew we were deeply united by love, and that he was the teacher I was *choosing* for this zigzagging path. My friend Suzanne says Shahabuddin's always been willing to put one foot in front of the other one and pick up the whole mess of all of us and just keep trudging forward, pulling all of us along with him toward God. It's up to us whether we want to go along or not. This stuff would probably come up again. It was all part of the path. As Shahabuddin reminds us, we are only moving toward the One; we're not there yet. Finally, the mureed must love the teacher and love the path more than her notions of what the path or the teacher should be.

Although I felt I had succeeded in developing a more global consciousness, my little self was throwing tantrums again. As I evaluated my own spiritual progress, I seemed to be making none at all. Another zigzag! I appeared to be daydreaming during my practices, staring out the window; nothing seemed to be happening. I'd been at this for years now! Bob kept saying I was trying too hard and had too many concepts. I felt myself getting angry when I'd think about it.

I marched over to Shahabuddin's table in the cafeteria the second morning after breakfast before Mukesh's singing class and said I wanted to talk to him sometime about my practices. He cocked his head and asked, "Have you been crying more?"

"I'm going to cry now," I said, but I felt mad. "Am I supposed to be doing something when I'm sitting there?"

Shahabuddin spoke very softly. There were others still at the breakfast table. "You can have those experiences you've been wanting," he said, "but I'm afraid you will just leave."

"Leave?" I said, asking for clarification. "You mean die?"

"Yes," he nodded his head.

"I'm not ready to die!"

He said, "You should do a retreat … No, You should teach."

I asked puzzled, "What should I teach?"

"How to write. How to be psychic. What you don't know. What's in here?" He touched my heart. "You've always known what you've wanted."

An image of praying to die at the communion rail flashed before me. As I sat quietly, he asked, "Do you know how far Israel was from Egypt?"

"No?"

"Only about two hundred miles. Why do you think the Israelites were wandering in the desert for *forty* years?"

"I don't know."

He looked me in the eye and said, "It had something to do with self-pity. You don't need to get all wrapped up in your self-pity."

"Okay," I left the table, and he went to sing with Mukesh.

The next night my writing students read their funny, touching pieces, which brought laughter and tears. Shahabuddin approached me toward the end of the evening near the door. "Do you get it now?" he asked, peering into my face the way he does, his face close to mine. "Now, do you see? You couldn't teach them how to write that if you didn't have it? Do you get it now?"

"I guess so," I answered.

"Do you?" he asked again, looking deeply into my eyes with those deep penetrating Shahabuddin eyes.

PART FIVE: CHASING THE WHITE GOOSE

Before I left I was invited to come to Sarasota to teach writing and perhaps do a retreat.

Back home I'm listening to some CDs of a seminar we were not able to attend. Shahabuddin instructs clearly that our path is the development of the personality. It includes getting rid of the impressions we brought with us into incarnation and the ones we've picked since we've been here; that's what our ego is.

I'm finally getting it! It's a REAL relationship, like in Sufism God's a *living* God. The whole thing's real. I'm not an angel, neither is Shahabuddin. I have a body. The teacher has a body. Sufis live in the world. Shahabuddin says on the CD he's met some of the people who live in caves and sometimes it's hard to tell if they're enlightened or autistic; they have no personalities. Our path is to live with others, to learn to be a human being. Self-analysis is looking at the self in relation to one's family, peers, and friends.

I have to breathe, eat, shit, love, fight. And find illumination here. Within all this. My teacher's a human being like me. We have a real relationship. Things change. It's dynamic. Like marriage. Like kids. Ah so! Shahabuddin is not a cardboard cutout teacher! But, as my wise friend Suzanne says, we have to hold on to "what's unshakeable." "That," she says, "stays unshakeable." And I remember Shahabuddin teaching in one of our seminars "We are sitting on a pile of gold. Why do we want to pick up rocks?"

God Bless You, Dear Shahabuddin. I don't know if you remember … one time in a seminar we each had to pray for one other person, and I was supposed to pray for you. I didn't know you very well then. I just stood in front of you trembling inside for what I could possibly say that would be worthy of my great, wonderful teacher, who as I perceived you then, hardly even needed any prayer. Then it came to me. I thought of the Vulcan salute from Star Trek and held up my fingers in that double V, looked straight into your eyes and prayed: "Shahabuddin, Live long and prosper!"

BIBLIOGRAPHY

Garfield, Patricia. *Creative Dreaming*. New York: Ballantine Books, 1976.

Gilbert, Elizabeth. *Eat, Pray, Love: One Woman's Search for Everything Across Italy, India and Indonesia*. London: Penguin Books, 2006.

Ginsberg, Allen. *Collected Poems, 1947-1980*. New York: Harper and Row, 1984.

Harvey, Andrew. *A Journey in Ladakh*. Boston: Houghton Mifflin, 1983.

Kain, John. *A Rare and Precious Thing: The Possibilities and Pitfalls of Working with a Spiritual Teacher*. New York: Bell Tower, 2006.

Khan, Hazrat Inayat. *The Sufi Message of Hazrat Inayat Khan*. Geneva: International Headquarter Sufi Movement, 1982.

Less, Shahabuddin David. "On Collective Awakening." *Madison Sufis Newsletter*, August 2006.

Neihardt, John G. *A Cycle of the West*, Lincoln, NE: University of Nebraska Press, 1965.

Neihardt, John G. *Black Elk Speaks: Being the Life Story of a Holy Man of the Oglala Sioux*. Lincoln, NE: University of Nebraska Press, 1961.

Petri, Hilda Neihardt, ed. *The Giving Earth: A John G. Neihardt Reader*. Lincoln, NE: University of Nebraska Press, 1991.

Rúmí, Jalálu'ddin. *The Essential Rúmí*. Translated by Coleman Barks. San Francisco: HarperSanFrancisco, 1995.

Schmitz, Barbara. *How Much Our Dancing Has Improved*. Omaha, NE: The Backwater Press, 2005.

Schmitz, Barbara. *The Upside Down Heart*. Grand Island, NE: Sandhills Press, 2002.

St. John of the Cross. *Dark Night of the Soul*. Translated and Edited by E. Allison Peers. New York: Doubleday, 1959.

Underhill, Evelyn. *Mysticism: A Study in the Nature and Development of Man's Spiritual Consciousness*. New York: E. P. Dutton, 1972.

Yogananda, Paramahansa. Los Angeles: The Self-Realization Fellowship, 1972.

www.ingramcontent.com/pod-product-compliance
Lightning Source LLC
Chambersburg PA
CBHW071414090426

42737CB00011B/1463